Oracle9i
New Features

Robert G. Freeman

McGraw-Hill/Osborne

New York   Chicago   San Francisco
Lisbon   London   Madrid   Mexico City   Milan
New Delhi   San Juan   Seoul   Singapore   Sydney   Toronto

McGraw-Hill/Osborne
2600 Tenth Street
Berkeley, California 94710
U.S.A.

To arrange bulk purchase discounts for sales promotions, premiums, or fund-raisers, please contact **McGraw-Hill**/Osborne at the above address. For information on translations or book distributors outside the U.S.A., please see the International Contact Information page immediately following the index of this book.

Oracle9*i* New Features

   4567890 FGR FGR 0198765432
ISBN 0-07-222385-5

Publisher	**Proofreader**
Brandon A. Nordin	Linda Medoff
Vice President & Associate Publisher	**Indexer**
Scott Rogers	Jack Lewis
Acquisitions Editor	**Computer Designer**
Jeremy Judson	Jean Butterfield
Project Editor	**Illustrators**
Jennifer Malnick	Michael Mueller, Lyssa Wald, Michelle Galicia
Acquisitions Coordinator	**Series Design**
Athena Honore	Jani Beckwith
Technical Editor	**Cover Designer**
Scott Gossett	Damore Johann Design, Inc.
Copy Editor	
Laura Ryan	

This book was composed with Corel VENTURA™ Publisher.

As always, this book is dedicated
to the people who make it possible
for me to do what I like to do—my family.
To my parents, who raised me to never quit
and to pursue excellence; to my wife, Debbie,
who is ever patient with me and my late
nights of writing; and to my five kids, who are
always patient with their father and his
occasional lack of presence.

About the Author

Robert G. Freeman has worked with Oracle for more than ten years. He currently works for CSX Technology as a Senior Database Architect. He is the author of several books including *Oracle 7.3 to 8 Exam Cram*, *Oracle 8 to 8i Exam Cram*, and *Mastering Oracle8i*. When he's not busy working at CSX or writing books, Robert can be found speaking at user group meetings, spending time with his family, flying, or doing Karate.

Contents

Acknowledgments

As always, this book is dedicated to those who helped put it together. Thanks to Michael Chapiro and William Bathurst, who each contributed a chapter to this book. Thanks to the good folks at Oracle Press who gave me this opportunity: Jeremy Judson, Acquisitions Editor at McGraw-Hill; Athena Honore, who kept me somewhat on schedule early on; and to Jennifer Malnick, who kept me on schedule with that verbal whip of hers as the book progressed. Thanks also to Scott Gossett, a wizzo of a technical editor.

Thanks to Gary Chancellor, my Oracle mentor; to Jeff Kellum, who gave me my first opportunity to become a professional author; and to Mr. Alfaro and Ms. Skutnik, for keeping me on the black belt path. Thanks to Bob Just, who is a great GSAM, and thanks to all the troops in the Oracle DBA group at work—Nancy, Maritza, John, Yang, Charles, Don, Tim, Bill #1, Bill #2, Rich, Nirupaum, Gunjan, and Ronald—you are all tops!

Most important, thanks to my wife and kids, who put up with my occasional crankiness when I was behind schedule, and thanks to Clifford the cat for keeping my feet warm on a number of late nights…Purrrrrrrrr.

Introduction

In 2001 Oracle released its latest generation RDBMS, called Oracle9i. Oracle9i is feature-rich, providing the DBA with a number of new tools to ease administration, improve performance, and improve availability and recoverability. This book was written to help get the Oracle8i DBA and/or developer up to speed quickly with Oracle9i's new features. You will find it rich with examples to help you get started. We hope our effort helps to smooth your transition to Oracle9i and use its new features pays off.

In an effort to get this book out in a timely manner, we made some choices as to which of the numerous Oracle9i new features we would give coverage to, and in how much depth. Our choices were led by the desire to give the biggest bang for their buck. Thus, you will find within the pages of this book that there are topics we have given a great deal of coverage to, topics that we have treated in passing, and even topics that we do not cover at all. You have to make these choices when you are limited to just so many pages and just so much time. I hope you will find that the choices we made are worthy, and that you find this book a worthwhile introduction to Oracle9i.

As was true with Oracle before, Oracle9i is still evolving. This book was written using the first release of Oracle9i. No doubt that, as new releases of 9i appear, functionality will change and you might find that some topics in this book are no longer all that accurate. It is our hope that you will find this book helpful and that it may continue to lead the way and herald each new arrival of Oracle's RDBMS product. In my estimation, you can never have too many good Oracle books!

As with any book, errors will be found and questions will arise. You can contact me at dbaoracle@aol.com to report corrections or make a (nice) comment. If you have questions, surf over to www.revealnet.com, where I hang out as one of the SYSOPs of the Quest Revealnet Labs DBA Pipeline. There you can ask questions and get answers from a number of DBAs and developers. Finally, if you like this book, please remember that I wrote it. If you don't like this book, then remember that Mike Ault wrote it.

CHAPTER

1

Oracle9i Database Administration and Management Features

- The compatibility parameter
- Oracle-managed datafiles
- Oracle9i shared memory areas
- The default temporary tablespace
- UNDO tablespaces in Oracle9i
- Resumable space management
- Persistent initialization parameters
- Supported platforms for Oracle9i

elcome to the first chapter of *Oracle9i New Features*. This chapter is the beginning of your journey into Oracle9i's new and enhanced features. Of course, DBAs want features and enhancements to make the management of their Oracle databases easier, quicker, and with as little impact on their users as possible. Oracle9i responds to this need with many new management features, and it is these features that we will address here.

The Compatibility Parameter

As we begin to review many of the new, changed, and enhanced features of Oracle9i, a word about the *compatibility* parameter: this parameter, which is located in the database parameter file (init.ora), controls which database features you can, and cannot, use. It might well be a good idea when migrating to Oracle9i to leave *compatibility* set to the version of the database you are migrating from until you are comfortable with Oracle9i. This is because you will not be able to use the new features of Oracle9i with the compatibility parameter set to a value that is greater than 9.0.0.0. This makes it easier if you find you need to roll back your database upgrade or migration, since you will not have taken advantage of some Oracle9i feature that will have to be backed out before you can roll the database back to the previous version.

Also, certain database default actions (such as creating a tablespace) are different depending on the value of *compatibility*. Once you have migrated or upgraded to Oracle9i and you are comfortable with the new database, set the *compatible* parameter to 9.0.0.0, and you can start using some of the new Oracle9i features that you will find inside this book.

Migration/Upgrade Notes

Generally, all operating systems support a direct migration from Oracle 7.2 or later to Oracle9i using the **mig** utility or the database migration assistant. Many platforms even support migration from Oracle 7.1. If you are running Oracle8i, then you will need to upgrade the database following your platform-specific instructions. This generally involves starting the 8i database under the 9i RDBMS software and running an upgrade script. Please refer to your platform-specific documentation for exact instructions on migrating or upgrading to Oracle9i from your current Oracle version.

Oracle-Managed Datafiles (OMFs)

The first new Oracle9i feature you are going to learn about in this chapter are *Oracle-Managed Datafiles* (OMFs). OMFs give Oracle the ability to manage Oracle database files for you. OMFs are part of the Oracle9i move to make the Oracle database easier to manage. Previous to Oracle9i, when you dropped a tablespace, you would also have to remove the physical datafile associated with that tablespace. With Oracle9i, you can leave physical file management to the database itself, using OMFs. In this section, you will learn about the types of datafiles that are managed by this feature, and some of the benefits and restrictions of OMFs. Then you will learn how to configure your database to take advantage of OMFs, and you will find some examples of using OMFs.

OMF Uses, Rules, and Restrictions

In this section, you will learn about the uses, rules, and restrictions involved in using OMFs. First, we'll look at the concept of using OMFs, when they should be used, and when they should not. Then we'll move on to OMF management issues.

Introducing OMF

You can use OMF when creating database datafiles, tempfiles, online redo logfiles, and database control files. To use OMF, you must first configure the database to use OMF (see the "Configuring the Database to Use OMF" section). Once the database is configured for OMF, Oracle will create the datafiles required during the execution of a DDL statement such as **create tablespace**—if you do not specifically define the datafiles associated with that statement. OMF can be associated with tablespaces, temporary tablespace, redo logs, and control files in Oracle9i. Let's look at some specifics of OMF with regards to the creation of tablespaces, redo logs, and control files.

Tablespace OMF   You can create any tablespace using OMF, even the SYSTEM tablespace. To configure Oracle for this operation, you need to set the *db_create_file_dest* parameter in the database parameter file (see "Configuring the Database to Use OMF," later in the chapter, for more on configuring OMF). For example, when you create a tablespace by issuing the **create tablespace** or **create temporary tablespace** commands without any datafile names, Oracle will create the needed datafile for that tablespace. Also, if you issue the **create database** command and do not provide a datafile name for the SYSTEM tablespace, then an OMF datafile will be created. Also, if you define a DEFAULT tablespace or an UNDO tablespace in the **create database** command, then an OMF will be created for each of those tablespace types. The default size for any OMF is 100M, and the datafile(s) are set to **autoextend** with an unlimited maximum extent.

If you wish to define a file size other than 100M for a datafile, include the **datafile** keyword, and then include the **size** parameter (without a filename), and the datafile will be created at the requested size. You can also include **autoextend off** to disable the setting of **autoextend** on the OMF when it is created. An example of this is shown here:

```
CREATE TABLESPACE new_tbs DATAFILE SIZE 500M AUTOEXTEND OFF;
```

This next example is of the creation of a tablespace using two OMFs:

```
CREATE TABLESPACE new_tbs DATAFILE SIZE 500M, SIZE 500M AUTOEXTEND OFF;
```

You can change the datafile size (via the **alter database datafile resize** command) or change the datafile **autoextend** parameters without affecting the ability of the Oracle database to manage the datafile.

As datafiles associated with tablespaces fill, they will extend—as long as the ability to **autoextend** has not been changed by the DBA. If desired, rather than extending the existing OMF, the DBA can opt to create an additional datafile for the tablespace by issuing an **alter tablespace add datafile** command. If the DBA does not include the datafile name, then the new datafile added will be an OMF. You can mix and match OMF and non-OMF datafiles in the same tablespace if you desire. Oracle will not remove any non-OMF datafiles unless you use the new **including contents and datafiles** keyword of the **drop tablespace** command.

When you drop a tablespace that contains OMF, Oracle will remove the OMFs associated with that tablespace from the operating system. For example, issuing a **drop tablespace** command will cause Oracle to remove the datafiles associated with that tablespace—as long as they are Oracle managed. Of course, if you have defined the names and locations of the datafiles, then Oracle will not remove those datafiles. You will be responsible for that administrative activity yourself.

Another interesting bit of functionality is that you can mix and match OMF with manually defined ones. For example, the following command is perfectly legal:

```
CREATE TABLESPACE new_tbs DATAFILE SIZE 500M,
'd:\oracle\oradata\mydb\mydb_new_tbs_02.dbf' SIZE 500M AUTOEXTEND OFF;
```

In this event, Oracle will create both the OMF and the manually defined datafile. If you drop the tablespace, the default action will be that Oracle will remove only the OMF, and the DBA will need to manually remove all datafiles that are not Oracle managed. This feature can be extended to existing tablespaces that use manually created datafiles. For examples, adding additional OMFs to an existing tablespace can expand space allocated to the tablespace created originally in Oracle8i with manually created datafiles. You will find several examples of Oracle-managed file operations on redo logfiles later in this section.

Redo Log OMF   If you decide to use Oracle-managed redo logfiles, you can create as many redo log groups as you need, bounded of course by the **maxlogfiles** clause setting you used in the **create database** command. You can multiplex each of those groups with up to five additional OMF members (again bounded by the **maxlogmembers** setting when the database is created). The different redo log group members are created in different locations, as defined by multiple parameters such as *db_create_online_log_dest_n* (see "Configuring the Database to Use OMF," later in the chapter, for a list of these parameters).

You can initially create a database with the **create database** statement, using OMF redo logs. Simply omit the name of the database datafiles, as you can see in the example in "Creating a Database Using OMF," later in the chapter.

Depending on the operating system, if none of the *db_create_online_log_dest_n* parameters are set, then one member for each redo log group will get created in the location pointed to by the *db_create_file_dest* parameter. If neither parameter is set, then Oracle will return an error when you issue the **create database** statement.

If you issue either the **alter database drop logfile group** or **alter database drop logfile member**, Oracle will remove the associated logfile group or member—if they were created as OMFs. By default, Oracle-managed redo logs are 100M in size. You will find several examples of Oracle-managed file operations on redo logfiles later in this section.

Control File OMF   If the CONTROL_FILES parameter is not listed in the database parameter file when you create the database, and if the database parameter *db_create_online_log_dest_n* is configured, Oracle will create the control files for you as OMF in the directories defined. As with the redo logfiles, you can configure the database so up to five copies of the control files will be created (see the upcoming "Configuring the Database to Use OMF" section). If the *db_create_file_dest* parameter is set, but the *db_create_online_log_dest_n* is not, then a single control file is created in the *db_create_file_dest*. If the *db_create_online_log_dest_n* parameters are set, then the control files will be written there.

Depending on the operating system, if neither the *control_files*, *db_create_online_log_dest_n* nor the *db_create_file_dest* parameters are set, Oracle might choose to do a couple of things. In some cases, Oracle might create an OMF control file in a default directory that is OS specific. In this case, the control files will not be Oracle-managed control files. If you wish the control files to be Oracle managed, you will need to make sure that the OMF parameters (either *db_create_file_dest* or *db_create_online_log_dest_n*) are correctly set. On some platforms, Oracle will simply signal an error if the location of the control file is not defined by the presence of the *control_files* parameter.

When to Use, and Not to Use, OMF

Oracle OMF is useful in different situations. First, it is quite useful in low-use smaller databases to reduce the administrative overhead associated with such a database. This feature reduces the overall administrative overhead required for such databases and also helps to ensure that old, unused datafiles do not reduce the overall availability of disk space. Configuring the database to use this feature does not imply that the alternative ability to define datafile names and locations is not available. In fact, you can use both features of the database if you choose.

The OMF feature can be particularly useful for development and test databases. With this feature, you can allow the developers some latitude to create and remove their own tablespaces (though there is no support at this time for forcing the use of OMF).

Another use of OMF is to simplify management of a standby database. Previously, when you added a tablespace or datafile to the primary database, human intervention was required on the standby database to perform the same operation. Now, with OMF, this is no longer the case. If the standby database is configured to use OMF, then the creation of a tablespace or addition of a datafile to the primary database will result in the automated creation of that tablespace or datafile on the standby server. No other administrative activity is required.

NOTE
If datafiles are removed from the primary database, Oracle will not automatically remove the related datafiles on the standby database.

Also, if you have a large database environment that is using large disk arrays, you might find OMF of use to you as well. In these environments, typically a small number of large file systems are created that are striped across a number of disks. The main idea is to stripe across as many disks as you can. This can cause significant performance gains.

OMF is not an appropriate choice for use with a high-volume or mission-critical database that is not using high-end striped disk arrays. For example, OMF would not be recommended on systems with many smaller file systems, or systems running RAID-5. This is because the nature of managed datafiles is such that such DBA tasks as IO distribution are not really supportive of this feature (and kind of defeat the whole purpose, in a way). Also, the managed datafile feature does not support the use of raw disk devices.

Administering OMF

When Oracle creates managed database datafiles, it follows a naming convention for these datafiles. You cannot create a new datafile using the OMF naming convention. Any attempt to do so will result in an error. The naming conventions of the database datafiles are shown in the following table. (Note that these might be different for various operating system ports. Check your operating system documentation for the file-naming convention used.)

File Type	Naming Convention	Example
Datafile	ora_{tablespace_name}_{unique character string}.dbf	ORA_NEW_TBS_ZV3NZF00.DBF
Tempfile	ora_{tablespace_name}_{unique character string}.tmp	ORA_TEMP_TBS_ZV3NZF01.TMP
Redo logfile	ora_{online redo log group number}_{unique character string}.log	ORA_4_ZV307100.LOG
Control file	ora_{unique character string}.ctl	ORAZV307100.CTL

NOTE
Up to eight characters of the tablespace name
are used. This is why the second part of the name,
the unique character string, is important, as two
tablespaces might have unique names, but the
first eight characters of the tablespace might be
the same.

As a DBA, you can use the names of OMF in SQL statements, just as you would normal datafiles. For example, you can use the **alter database rename file** or **alter tablespace rename datafile** commands to rename an Oracle database-managed datafile, you can drop a specific Oracle-managed redo logfile with the **alter database drop logfile** command, and so on.

To rename an OMF datafile, you will first need to offline the tablespace that the OMF datafile is associated with (or offline the OMF datafile). Then, physically rename the datafile at the OS level. Once you have renamed the OMF file, you can issue the **rename** command from within the database (using the **alter database** or **alter tablespace** command) to rename the OMF within the database. Finally, online the tablespace or datafile.

If you rename the OMF datafile using a file-naming convention that does not follow the OMF naming convention, that file will no longer be an OMF. Finally, you cannot rename any existing non-OMF Oracle datafile to a filename that has "ORA_" at the beginning. This will cause an error, as ORA_ prefixes are reserved for OMF.

Here is an example of renaming an existing OMF datafile:

```
alter session set db_create_file_dest = '/home1/teach3';
create tablespace sdgtest4 datafile size 2m;
select file_name,tablespace_name
from dba_data_files where tablespace_name = 'SDGTEST4';
FILE_NAME                                       TABLESPACE_NAME
----------------------------------------------  --------------------
/home1/teach3/ora_sdgtest4_xx5vcmqf.dbf         SDGTEST4

ALTER TABLESPACE sdgtest4 OFFLINE;

HOST ls
ora_sdgtest4_xx5vcmqf.dbf
host mv ora_sdgtest4_xx5vcmqf.dbf ora_sdgtest4_xx5vsdg4.dbf
alter tablespace sdgtest4 rename datafile
 '/home1/teach3/ora_sdgtest4_xx5vcmqf.dbf' to
 '/home1/teach3/ora_sdgtest4_xx5vsdg4.dbf';

ALTER TABLESPACE sdgtest4 ONLINE;
```

The backup and recovery procedures for Oracle-managed database datafiles are no different than those for DBA managed datafiles. Also, the use of the Oracle

imp and **exp** utilities are not affected by the presence of OMF. The procedure for recovering from the loss of a control file when using backup control files or re-creating the control file using the results of an **alter database backup control file to trace** has not changed either.

Configuring the Database to Use OMF

To use OMF, you first must configure certain database parameters. These parameters define the locations that the different OMF should be created in. The parameters associated with OMF are seen in Table 1-1 (you can find examples in the "Examples of Using OMF" section, next).

Note that each of the parameters described in Table 1-1 can be dynamically altered via the **alter system** or the **alter session** command, such as

```
ALTER SYSTEM SET DB_CREATE_FILE_DEST='d:\oracle\data\my_datafiles';
```

Parameter Name	Default	Purpose
db_create_file_dest	None	This defines the file system where OMF and tempfiles are to be located. This location is also used for Oracle-managed control files and redo logs if the DB_CREATE_ONLINE _LOG_DEST_*n* parameter is not configured.
db_create_online_log_dest_n	None	This parameter defines the file system location where Oracle-managed online redo logs are to be created. The *n* value is replaced by a number, 1–5. This allows for up to 5 multiplexed copies of each redo log group member, and up to 5 copies of the control files to be created.

TABLE 1-1. *Database Parameters*

Changing the location to create files does not affect Oracle's ability to manage datafiles already created in other directories.

NOTE
Even if you have not configured db_create_file_dest
or db_create_online_log_dest_n, *you can still*
configure them dynamically and take advantage
of OMF without having to shut down and restart
the database.

Examples of Using OMF

In this section, you will learn about the various database operations that can use OMF. First, you will configure a parameter file so you can use OMF. You will then learn about creating a database using OMF for the SYSTEM tablespace, UNDO tablespace, default tablespace, redo logs, and control files. We will then move on to examine the impacts of several different types of operations involving OMF. This includes dropping tablespaces and adding and removing online redo logs to the database. In this example, we will be using my Oracle9i database, called mydb.

NOTE
These examples are not intended to be a "how-to"
on the overall process of the creation of a database.
There are several steps that occur before and after
the steps being demonstrated. It is assumed that you
are already familiar with the procedure to create
a database.

Configuring the Database to Use OMF

The first step in using OMF is to configure the init.ora database parameter file to support the use of this feature. Here is an example of the init.ora for the mydb (we have left out many of the settings that don't pertain to configuration of OMF).

```
db_name=mydb
undo_management=auto
undo_ts
DB_CREATE_FILE_DEST=c:\oracle\admin\mydb\data
DB_CREATE_ONLINE_LOG_DEST_1=c:\oracle\admin\mydb\redo
DB_CREATE_ONLINE_LOG_DEST_2=d:\oracle\admin\mydb\redo
```

In this example, the mydb database has been set up to use automated undo management. An UNDO tablespace called MYUNDOTBS has been defined as the *undo_tablespace* parameter, which serves to enable the Oracle-managed datafile feature. In this case, when Oracle creates a datafile, it puts it in the c:\oracle\ admin\mydb\data directory.

Next, two different directory locations for redo logs and control files to be created in have been defined using the *db_create_online_log_dest_1* and *db_ create_online_log_dest_2* parameters. Notice that the directories are using two different drives to protect the redo logs and control files from accidental erasure and for some IO balancing.

Creating a Database Using OMF

Now let's create our database! If we wanted to just let Oracle do all the work for us, we could actually just issue the command **create database**. In this case, if the OMFs are configured in the init.ora, Oracle will create everything for you. To exert a bit more control over our database creation process, however, let's use the following **create database** command to create the **mydb** database:

```
CREATE DATABASE mydb
DATAFILE SIZE 200M
LOGFILE GROUP 1 SIZE 20M, GROUP 2 SIZE 20M
DEFAULT TEMPORARY TABLESPACE dflt_ts TEMPFILE SIZE 50M
UNDO TABLESPACE myundotbs DATAFILE SIZE 50M
MAXLOGFILES 5
MAXLOGMEMBERS 5
MAXDATAFILES 200
NOARCHIVELOG;
```

So, in our example, the database mydb will be created with a SYSTEM tablespace that is 200M in size. Based on the parameters we set in the previous section, the datafile for the SYSTEM tablespace will reside in the directory c:\oracle\ admin\mydb\data. Next, we have defined a default temporary tablespace called dflt_ts. This tablespace is 50M in size and will also be created in c:\oracle\ admin\mydb\data. We have also created an UNDO tablespace called undo_ts that is 50M in size. Again, this tablespace's datafile will be in c:\oracle\admin\mydb\ data. When this database is created, the redo logfiles will be created in two locations. The first member of each group will be in the directory c:\oracle\admin\mydb\redo, and the second will be in the d:\oracle\admin\mydb\redo directory.

Management of OMF

Now that our database is created, let's look at some examples of administrative functions involving OMF. This includes adding and dropping tablespaces. Other administrative items you will learn about are the changing of the default locations for datafile creations and the process of adding and dropping redo logs from a database that is using OMF.

Adding a Tablespace   Adding a tablespace is a simple operation when using OMF. Simply issue the **create tablespace** command with only the name of the tablespace, and Oracle will create the tablespace using the 100M default datafile size, as shown in this example:

```
CREATE TABLESPACE auto_created_tbs;
```

If we wanted a larger tablespace created, we could include the DATAFILE clause and indicate what the size of the datafile should be. Also, in this next case, the datafile's ability to extend will be disabled by including the NOEXTEND clause in the statement. The resulting statement is seen in this example:

```
CREATE TABLESPACE bigger_tbs DATAFILE SIZE 200M NOEXTEND;
```

The previous statement creates a 200M datafile, and disables the AUTOEXTEND functionality of the datafile. You can also use OMF when creating temporary tablespaces, as shown in this example:

```
CREATE TEMPORARY TABLESPACE temp_obj_tbs DATAFILE SIZE 200M NOEXTEND;
```

Dropping a Tablespace   Now that we have created tablespaces, there will be a need to drop them from time to time. In this example, let's drop the bigger_tbs we created earlier in this section. Simply use the **drop tablespace** command, and Oracle will handle the rest, as shown in the following example:

```
DROP TABLESPACE bigger_tbs;
```

The datafile for the bigger_tbs tablespace will be dropped by Oracle automatically during the execution of the statement.

NOTE
Even if the db_create_file_dest parameter has been changed, Oracle will remove any OMF—as long as it remains in its original directory.

NOTE
*The **including contents** clause of the **drop tablespace** statement has had a new clause added to it, **and datafiles**. When this clause is included in the **drop tablespace** command, the tablespace will be dropped and all associated datafiles will be dropped as well. This is a new feature in Oracle9i!*

Changing the Location of Datafile Creation   The **alter system** and **alter session** commands can be used to alter all the parameters associated with OMF. Thus, we can change the location that database datafiles, as well as redo logs, are created in. Here is an example of changing the location of the parameter *db_create_file_dest*, and then creating a datafile after that operation:

```
ALTER SYSTEM SET DB_CREATE_FILE_DEST='d:\oracle\admin\mydb\data';
CREATE TABLESPACE new_tbs DATAFILE SIZE 150m NOEXTEND;
```

In this case, any newly created datafile will be created in the d:\oracle\admin\mydb\data directory. If we dropped any tablespace that had datafiles in the old directory, those datafiles would be removed by Oracle, just as Oracle would remove the datafiles for the new_tbs tablespace just created.

Adding a Redo Log Group   When we created our database, two redo log groups of 200M each were defined for our database. Let's create a third logfile group. To do this, simply issue the following command:

```
ALTER DATABASE ADD LOGFILE;
```

Alternatively, you can issue the following command:

```
ALTER DATABASE ADD LOGFILE GROUP 3 SIZE 300M;
```

Note that in this example we have indicated that the redo log group will be 300M, as opposed to the 100M default size.

Dropping a Redo Log Group   Perhaps you have discovered that your existing redo log members are not large enough and you wish to re-create them so they are larger. In this case, first you need to remove one of the existing redo log groups, and then re-create it. This is a simple operation, performed with the **alter database** command:

```
ALTER DATABASE DROP LOGFILE GROUP 1;
```

Something to keep in mind is that it's not possible to add an additional log group member that is an OMF (that is, **alter database add logfile member to group 2**). You can drop an OMF redo log member, however, with the **alter database drop logfile member**. In this event, Oracle will remove the dropped redo log member.

NOTE
As a DBA, you should already be aware that if you are going to drop a logfile group, it cannot be the current logfile group.

Managing Oracle9i Shared Memory Areas

Oracle9i has made several changes to the management of shared memory areas contained with the SGA. This includes database parameter changes, the ability to dynamically change shared memory allocations, and the ability to support multiple database block sizes within the Oracle9i database. Let's look at each of these features, and how they relate to Oracle9i memory areas, in a bit more detail.

Multiple Database Block Size Support

Oracle now supports multiple database block sizes. This was done, in part, to allow transportable tablespaces to be plugged in from databases with differing database block sizes. Each Oracle9i database has a *standard block size* assigned, which is defined by the *db_block_size* parameter and is assigned to the database when it is created. This block size must be used for the SYSTEM, TEMPORARY, and ROLLBACK tablespaces and is the default block size used for other tablespaces. As with previous versions of Oracle, once you determine the standard block size, it is set in stone unless you re-create the database. When you upgrade from Oracle8i to Oracle9i, the standard block size for your database will be whatever the block size of the Oracle8i database was when it was created.

When creating a tablespace, you can use the *blocksize* parameter of the **create tablespace** command to create that tablespace using a *nonstandard block size*. Oracle9i can support up to four nonstandard block sizes that can range anywhere from 2K to 32K in size, depending on operating-system restrictions.

```
CREATE TABLESPACE my_16k_tbs
BLOCKSIZE 16k
DATAFILE 'd:\oradata\mydb\data\my_8k_tbs.dbf' size 100m;
```

The DBA_TABLESPACES and V$DATAFILE views have had a block-size column added to them that defines the assigned block sizes for each tablespace, as shown in this example:

```
SQL> select tablespace_name, block_size
  2  FROM dba_tablespaces
  3  where tablespace_name = 'MY_16K_TBS';
TABLESPACE_NAME                 BLOCK_SIZE
------------------------------- ----------
MY_16K_TBS                           16384
```

NOTE
To use nonstandard block sizes, you must set up some subcaches in shared memory. This will be discussed in the following section.

New Oracle9i Memory Database Initialization Parameters

Oracle9i has introduced several new database initialization parameters that have impacts on memory allocations in the database. In this section, you will learn about the new db_cache_size parameter and the memory subcache configuration parameters introduced to support the new multiple database block size features of Oracle9i.

The *db_cache_size* Parameter

Oracle9i has deprecated the *db_block_buffers* parameter, which controls the size of the database buffer cache component of the SGA, in favor of a new parameter, *db_cache_size*. This parameter is defined in bytes (*K* and *M* can be used to indicate kilobytes and megabytes) and allocates memory in blocks based on the standard block size of the Oracle9i database (just as *db_block_buffers* does). Note that the *db_block_buffers* parameter is backward compatible. The new features of Oracle9i (such as being able to dynamically change the size of the database buffer cache, or the use of multiple database block sizes) are not available when using the *db_block_buffers* parameter, and you cannot define both parameters at the same time. If you try, an ORA-00381 error will be raised.

NOTE
When you migrate or upgrade your 7.x, 8.x, or 8i Oracle database to Oracle9i, you will probably want to replace the db_block_buffers *parameter with the* db_cache_size *parameter. Do this so you can take advantage of the new Oracle9i features such as dynamically changeable SGA memory configurations.*

The *db_keep_cache_size* and *db_recycle_cache_size* Parameters

As with the *db_block_buffers* parameter, the *buffer_pool_keep* and *buffer_pool_recycle* parameters have been deprecated in favor of new parameters in Oracle9i. The new parameter *db_keep_cache_size* replaces the *buffer_pool_keep* parameter. The new *db_recycle_cache_size* parameter replaces the *buffer_pool_recycle* parameter. Both old parameters are still available for backward compatibility, but the old parameters are not dynamically alterable as the new parameters are. Also, you cannot use both the old and new parameters at the same time.

NOTE
In Oracle9i, the db_keep_cache_size *and*
db_recycle_cache_size *memory areas are separate
memory areas and are not allocated out of the
default buffer pool, as was the case in Oracle8i
and the* buffer_pool_keep *and* buffer_pool_recycle
parameters.

Configuring Memory Subcaches

To take advantage of Oracle9i support for multiple block sizes, you will need to
allocate shared memory subcaches. Five new parameters are introduced in Oracle9i
to support the subcaching feature: *db_2k_cache, db_4k_cache, db_8k_cache,
db_16k_cache*, and *db_32k_cache*. These parameters are defined in bytes, and
Oracle allows the use of *K* to denote kilobytes and *M* to indicate megabytes. Note
that these allocations require additional memory, and are not taken from the
memory allocated by the *db_cache_size* parameter. Additionally, you cannot use
the subcache parameter that is the same for the block size of your database. Thus,
if your *db_block_size* is 4K, you cannot use the *db_4k_cache* parameter. An example
of setting these parameters would look like this:

```
DB_2K_CACHE_SIZE=8364032
DB_8K_CACHE_SIZE=8000K
DB_16K_CACHE_SIZE=10M
```

In this example, three different memory caches have been allocated. First, the 2K
cache is allocated about 8 megabytes, defining the cache size in bytes. Second, the
8K cache is allocated with about 8 megabytes by defining the cache size in kilobytes
using the *K* indicator. Finally, we allocate 10 megabytes to the 16K cache by using
the *M* identifier. Note that each memory cache is considered part of the overall size
of the SGA. Also note that, in each case, Oracle would choose to round the allocations
to the nearest granule size. For example, in our last case, Oracle would round the
10M to 12M, which would be the nearest granule multiple. A *granule* is a unit of
contiguous memory whose size depends on the estimated total size of the SGA. A
granule is either 4 megabytes (in the case where the estimated SGA total size will be
less than 128 megabytes); or if the database is to be larger than 128 megabytes, then
the granule will be 16 megabytes. All growth and shrinkage of SGA structures is
done based on granule boundaries.

Data Dictionary Views and Memory Subcaches

When you create a memory subcache, the individual subcaches do not appear in
V$SGA. The total combined memory allocated to all the subcaches and the default

cache will appear in V$SGASTAT under the line for the setting of *db_block_buffers*. If you want to see the individual pools, you will need to use the *v$buffer_pool* view, as shown in this example:

```
SQL> select id, name, block_size, current_size, buffers
  2  from v$buffer_pool;
        ID NAME             BLOCK_SIZE CURRENT_SIZE    BUFFERS
---------- ------------------- ---------- ------------ ----------
         1 KEEP                     8192            0          0
         2 RECYCLE                  8192            0          0
         3 DEFAULT                  8192            4        501
         4 DEFAULT                  2048           12       5676
         5 DEFAULT                  4096            0          0
         6 DEFAULT                  8192            0          0
         7 DEFAULT                 16384           12        759
         8 DEFAULT                 32768            0          0
```

In this case, we see that three buffer pools are currently defined. The name column contains the type of buffer pool. In the case of subcaches and the default buffer pool, the name is always default. The BLOCK_SIZE column is what really tells us what is going on. In this case, there is the default buffer pool for our block size, which is 8K. Also there are the 2K and 16K buffers established, as can be seen from the output. The CURRENT_SIZE column gives the current size of the individual buffer cache in megabytes. Note that this size might actually be larger than the size that was defined for it because Oracle will round the subcache size up to the nearest granule (see the next section for more on granules). The buffers column indicates how many BUFFERS are currently allocated to the cache.

Dynamically Changeable Shared Memory

Often, when performance-tuning a system, you will find you need to change the size of the database buffer cache or the shared pool. Previous to Oracle9i, this would require a shutdown of the database system. For 24/7 environments, shutting down a system, even for a short time, can mean lost productivity, lost business, even lost customers.

Oracle9i solves this problem by allowing the DBA to dynamically alter the size of the shared memory areas. This includes the principle areas of the SGA:

- The default database buffer cache

- The memory subcaches

- The shared pool

NOTE
The redo log buffer, large pool, and java pools cannot currently be dynamically resized.

All Oracle shared memory areas are dynamically settable via the **alter system** command. Some examples of setting these areas are shown here:

```
ALTER SYSTEM SET SHARED_POOL=50000000;
ALTER SYSTEM SET DB_CACHE_SIZE =50000000;
ALTER SYSTEM SET DB_16K_CACHE_SIZE=10M;
```

A new parameter, *sga_max_size*, is used in Oracle9i to indicate the maximum overall size of the SGA. Thus, you can dynamically expand the SGA by altering the size of any of the buffers, but you cannot alter them such that the total amount of memory allocated is greater than that set by the *sga_max_size*. The default value of *sga_max_size* is the total size of the configured SGA at instance startup. If you set *sga_max_size* to a value smaller than the amount of memory initially allocated at instance startup, then *sga_max_size* will default to the total amount of memory initially allocated. You cannot dynamically change this parameter, so take care to make sure it is set correctly if there is some chance that you will want to increase overall SGA memory use. Note that, contrary to some documentation, this parameter will cause Oracle to reserve memory of an amount of *sga_max_size* on most operating systems (Solaris 8 was the exception at the time this book was written), so be careful when setting it to avoid causing swapping or paging.

Automated PGA Memory Management

The PGA in Oracle consists of two different memory types: not tunable and tunable. Several database parameters can be used to configure the tunable area. These parameters include *sort_area_size*, *hash_area_size*, *bitmap_merge_area_size*, and *create_bitmap_area_size*. In Oracle8i, these parameters were able to be set dynamically; however, it was difficult to really tune them well. Often, however, more memory was allocated to a given session than was really needed. As a result, memory was wasted.

Now Oracle9i offers the option of automated PGA space management. Two new parameters have been introduced to allow the DBA to have the PGA dynamically configured by the RDBMS software, removing this responsibility from the DBA. The first parameter is *pga_aggregate_target*, which allows you to set a target aggregate amount of memory that becomes the target amount of PGA memory available to be allocated. This memory can be allocated in bytes, kilobytes, megabytes, or gigabytes (using the *K, M,* and *G* symbols to denote the allocation type). This parameter can be set only at the system level, but it is dynamic in its nature.

A second parameter, *workarea_size_policy*, which can be set at the system or session level, establishes whether a given session's PGA size should be sized automatically or via the database init.ora parameters. There are two valid values for this parameter. When set to AUTO, the database will size the tunable PGA memory, and the total aggregate allocated amount of PGA memory will be bounded by *pga_aggregate_ target*. When set to MANUAL, the size of the PGA memory allocation is based on the various database parameter settings. If the *pga_aggregate_target* is set, then the *workarea_size_policy* will default to AUTO.

In the V$SYSSTAT and V$SESSTAT views, three new statistics have been added that relate to automated PGA memory. These are

- **Work Area Executions: Optimal Size**   Represents the number of work areas that had an optimal size, and no writes to disk were required.

- **Work Area Executions: One Pass Size**   Represents the number of work areas that had to write to disk, but required only one pass to disk.

- **Work Area Executions: Multipasses Size**   Represents the number of work areas that had to write to disk using multiple passes. High numbers of this statistic might indicate a poorly tuned PGA.

In addition, new columns have been added to V$PROCESS to help tune the PGA.

- **PGA_USED_MEM**   This reports how much PGA memory the process uses.

- **PGA_ALLOCATED_MEM**   This is the amount of PGA memory allocated to the process.

- **PGA_MAX_MEM**   This is the maximum amount of PGA memory allocated by the process.

Also, three new views are available to help the DBA extract information about the PGA:

- **V$SQL_WORKAREA**   Provides information about SQL work areas.

- **V$SQL_WORKAREA_ACTIVE**   Provides information on current SQL work area allocations.

- **V$SQL_MEMORY_USAGE**   This displays current memory-use statistics.

Oracle9*i* Default Temporary Tablespace

Oracle9*i* has introduced a new feature called the *default temporary tablespace*. In the past, whenever you created a user, the user would be given the SYSTEM tablespace as its default temporary tablespace. Left unchanged, this could lead to serious fragmentation and IO issues with the SYSTEM tablespace, because many users would be creating and removing temporary segments.

To deal with this problem, Oracle9i introduces the default temporary tablespace. The default temporary tablespace is either set at database creation with the **default temporary tablespace** clause of the **create database** command, or it can be set or changed after database creation with the **alter database default temporary tablespace** command. When the default temporary tablespace is changed with the **alter database default temporary tablespace** command, all users assigned to the previous default temporary tablespace will be reassigned to the newly defined temporary tablespace. Users assigned to a temporary tablespace that was not the default temporary tablespace will remain unchanged. Note that the tablespace selected to be the new default temporary tablespace must be of the same block size as the standard block size of the database. Also, any default temporary tablespace must be of type TEMPORARY.

If you wish to know what tablespace is current assigned as the default tablespace, you can use the new DATABASE_PROPERTIES view. Look in the PROPERTY_NAME column for the value DEFAULT_TEMP_TABLESPACE, and you will find the tablespace name in the associated PROPERTY_VALUE column. Here is an example of such a query:

```
SQL> column property_value format a16
SQL> select property_name, property_value from database_properties
  2  where property_name = 'DEFAULT_TEMP_TABLESPACE';
PROPERTY_NAME                      PROPERTY_VALUE
------------------------------ ----------------

DEFAULT_TEMP_TABLESPACE           NEW_TEMP
```

Finally, note that Oracle will no longer allow you to assign a permanent locally managed tablespace as a user's temporary tablespace. This was allowed in Oracle8i, but the users session would get an error when it tried to create a temporary segment in the tablespace.

Automated **UNDO** Management in Oracle9i

One of the more maintenance-intensive architectural components of a pre-Oracle9i database was the management of rollback segments. It was often time-consuming to first decide how many rollback segments to create, how big to make them, and how many extents to make them. Then you had to monitor the use of the rollback segments to ensure that you were getting optimal use of the rollback segment configuration that you had created.

Oracle9i introduces automated UNDO management to alleviate the need to manage rollback segments. To use the Oracle9i automated UNDO management features, you must first create an UNDO tablespace. Then you must configure the Oracle9i instance to use the Oracle9i automated UNDO management feature.

NOTE
In Oracle9i, according to Oracle documentation, Oracle has actually deprecated the use of rollback segments for undo space management. This implies that Oracle intends to do away with rollback segments all together at some point. While this is not likely to occur for some time, it is probably a good idea to start learning about and using UNDO tablespaces.

Creating the UNDO Tablespace

There are two different ways of creating an UNDO tablespace. The first method is by the use of the new UNDO clause of the **create tablespace** command. The second method is through the use of the **create database** command. Let's look at each of these methods in more detail.

Using the CREATE UNDO TABLESPACE Command

In Oracle9i, you can create an UNDO tablespace with the new UNDO clause of the **create tablespace** command, as shown in the following example:

```
CREATE UNDO TABLESPACE undo_tbs
DATAFILE '/ora100/oracle/mydb/data/mydb_undo_tbs_01.dbf' SIZE 100m
AUTOEXTEND ON;
```

In this case, we have created an UNDO tablespace called UNDO_TBS. As you can see, the **create undo tablespace** command syntax is much like the **create tablespace** command, including the **datafile** and **size** clauses. Note that when creating an UNDO tablespace, you can use only the **datafile** clause and a restricted form of the extent_management clause of the **create tablespace** command. Thus, you cannot define any default storage characteristics for an UNDO tablespace. Also note that Oracle creates an UNDO tablespace as locally managed tablespace, and that there is no option to create it as a dictionary-managed tablespace.

Once an UNDO tablespace is created, it will be brought online, along with the undo segments within it, each time the database is started. This can be seen in the messages that will appear in the alert log each time that you start the database.

NOTE
At the very least, you will still need to have the SYSTEM rollback segment.

Creating an UNDO Tablespace with the CREATE DATABASE Command

You can opt to create an UNDO tablespace when you initially create a database. Oracle has modified the **create database** command to support the definition of UNDO tablespaces during the database creation process through the use of the **undo tablespace** clause, as shown in the following example:

```
CREATE DATABASE mydb
CONTROLFILE REUSE
LOGFILE GROUP 1 ('d:\oradata\mydb\redo\mydb_redo_01a.log',
                 ' e:\oradata\mydb\redo\mydb_redo_01b.log ')  SIZE 50K,
        GROUP 2 ('d:\oradata\mydb\redo\mydb_redo_02a.log',
                 ' e:\oradata\mydb\redo\mydb_redo_02b.log ')  SIZE 50K
MAXINSTANCES 1 MAXLOGFILES 5  MAXLOGHISTORY 100 MAXDATAFILES 100
ARCHIVELOG
DATAFILE  'e:\oradata\mydb\mydb_system_01.dbf'
SIZE 100M AUTOEXTEND ON NEXT 20M MAXSIZE UNLIMITED,
DEFAULT TEMPORARY TABLESPACE temp_ts
TEMPFILE  'e:\oradata\mydb\mydb_temp_ts_01.dbf' SIZE 20m
UNDO TABLESPACE undo_ts DATAFILE  'e:\oradata\mydb\mydb_undo_ts_01.dbf'
SIZE 50M AUTOEXTEND OFF;
```

Note that we have used the **undo tablespace** clause of the **create database** command to create an UNDO tablespace called undo_ts. Further, we used the **datafile** clause to define the name and location of the datafile associated with the UNDO tablespace, and we also included the **size** and **autoextend** clauses.

When issuing a **create database** command, there are several rules that you should consider that relate to UNDO tablespaces. The rules will differ depending on how the database is configured (see the next section, "Configuring the Instance for Automated UNDO Management"). If the database instance is not configured for automated UNDO management, and you omit the UNDO TABLESPACE clause, then the **create database** statement will work as it always has, with no UNDO tablespace being created.

If the instance is configured for automated UNDO management, however, then the default behavior of the **create database** statement changes. If you do not include the **undo tablespace** clause, then Oracle will create an UNDO tablespace for you by default. This tablespace will be called SYS_UNDOTBS. This tablespace will be created using a default size of 100M for the database datafile.

Dropping an UNDO Tablespace

To drop an UNDO tablespace, simply issue a **drop tablespace** command. Oracle will drop the tablespace. If that UNDO tablespace is the active UNDO tablespace, then Oracle will generate an error.

Configuring the Instance for Automated UNDO Management

To take advantage of Oracle9i automated UNDO management features, you must configure the database. Configuration of the database for automated UNDO management is done through changes to the databases parameter file (init.ora). The parameters in Table 1-2 have been added to Oracle9i to support automated UNDO management.

Let's look at a couple of notable aspects of these parameters. Some SQL commands such as **set transaction use rollback segment** will, by default, return an ORA-30019 error to the session issuing the SQL statement. This is because these commands are not compatible with automated UNDO management. Because such an error might cause problems with existing scripts, you can set the *undo_suppress_errors* parameter to avoid getting the ORA-30019 error message.

If you have managed Oracle databases before, no doubt you are familiar with the "snapshot to old" error messages. These messages appear for several reasons, but principally they appear because a read-consistent image of the data that a given session needs is no longer in the rollback segments of the database. The *undo_retention* parameter is used with automated UNDO management to provide a guide to Oracle on how long it should retain UNDO after the transaction that has generated it has committed. By default, *undo_retention* is set to 900 seconds. This means that Oracle will try not to reuse generated UNDO space for 900 seconds after the transaction committing it has been committed.

The keyword here is try, because if Oracle runs out of available UNDO space, it will begin to use space that was otherwise protected by the *undo_retention* parameter. The *undo_retention* parameter can be modified dynamically with the **alter system** command. This is handy if you are finding that long-running transactions are getting "snapshot to old" errors from Oracle, though you might also need to add space to the UNDO tablespace. The *undo_retention* parameter also has some significant impact on another new Oracle9i feature, flashback queries, which we will cover in Chapter 3.

Finally, note that the *undo_tablespace* parameter is dynamic. This implies that you can have multiple UNDO tablespaces, however, you can have only one active UNDO tablespace in use at any given time.

Parameter Name	Default Value	Valid Values	Dynamic?	Description
undo_ Management	MANUAL	AUTO, MANUAL	No	Determines whether automated UNDO management is enabled in the database. AUTO enables automated UNDO management and MANUAL disables the feature.
undo_ tablespace	The first available UNDO tablespace, SYS_ UNDOTBS, uses the SYSTEM rollback segment if no UNDO tablespace is available	Valid UNDO tablespace name. Multiple UNDO tablespaces are not supported, though Oracle does not generate an error.	Immediate for system	Defines one or more UNDO tablespaces that should be used by Oracle for automated UNDO management. If this parameter is set, and *undo_management* is set to AUTO when issuing a **create database** command, then you must include all tablespaces listed in this parameter in the **create database** statement or the statement will fail. You can list multiple tablespaces here but only the last one listed will be used since Oracle allows only one.
undo_ suppress_ errors	TRUE	TRUE, FALSE	Immediate for system, session allowed	Allows you to control the displaying of error messages that result from certain SQL commands when the database is in automated UNDO management mode.

TABLE 1-2.   *Oracle9i UNDO Management Parameters*

CAUTION
There is a bug in Oracle9i versions 9.0.1.0, 9.0.1.1, and 9.0.1.2 that you need to be aware of. If you are using automated UNDO, this bug can cause your database to become unopenable. A patch is available for this bug from Oracle.

Parameter Name	Default Value	Valid Values	Dynamic?	Description
undo_retention	900 Seconds	0 to the maximum value allowed by 32 bits	Immediate for system	This parameter defines the minimum amount of time that Oracle will retain UNDO after it has been generated and after the generating transaction has been completed. This parameter can be modified dynamically using the **alter system** command. Note that Oracle will make a best effort to retain UNDO for the requested amount of time, but there is no guarantee.

TABLE 1-2. *Oracle9i UNDO Management Parameters* (continued)

The Data Dictionary and Automated UNDO Management

New data dictionary views, V$UNDOSTAT and DBA_UNDO_EXTENTS, have been created that are associated with automated UNDO management. Also, the V$ROLLSTAT and V$ROLLNAME views can be used to monitor overall performance of UNDO tablespaces. Just as with Oracle8i, though, there is really little you can do to tune UNDO tablespaces. Let's take a look at the V$UNDOSTAT and DBA_UNDO_EXTENTS views in a bit more detail.

V$UNDOSTAT

The V$UNDOSTAT data-dictionary view provides system-generated statistics, collected every 10 minutes for the last 24 hours. This view can be used to monitor and tune UNDO space. Use this view to determine whether you have allocated sufficient space to the UNDO tablespaces for the current workload. In particular, the UNDOBLKS column is useful in determining if the tablespace is large enough. This column indicates the total number of undo blocks that were used during the statistics collection period. Thus, if the number of undo blocks consumed during the collection period is significantly larger than the size of the UNDO tablespace, you might well consider increasing the size of the UNDO tablespace for performance reasons.

Also watch the UNXPSTEALCNT column, as high numbers in this column indicate that unexpired blocks (as determined by the *undo_retention* parameter) are being expired prematurely and the space is being taken for use by transactions because available UNDO space was not available for those transactions. This is particularly important for new databases as more and more people begin to use the system, generating more undo, which can lead to "snapshot to old" error messages. Finally, the SSOLDERRCNT and NOSPACEERRCNT columns keep track of the number of Oracle errors generated during the snapshot. If these columns are non-zero, consider increasing the size of your UNDO tablespace.

DBA_UNDO_EXTENTS

This view provides information on each extent in the UNDO tablespaces, including the commit time for each transaction. It is also with this view that you can determine which tablespaces are defined as UNDO tablespaces.

Resumable Space Management

Ever run a large data load, just to have the database run out of space on you and roll back the entire thing? Perhaps you ran a large **select** statement that ran for six hours before it ran out of temporary tablespace space during its final large sort. With Oracle9*i*, rather than fling the box out of the window in anger, you can take advantage of the new Oracle9*i* resumable space management feature. In this section, first we'll look at when resumable space management can be used, and then how to enable and disable this feature. Finally, we'll review some of the various administration issues around resumable space management and provide some examples of resumable space management in action.

Resumable Space Management Features and Limitations

Resumable space management can be used to manage the impacts a space failure of a long-running transaction may have on a session. Some of the space failures include:

- **Running out of tablespace space**   This includes errors such as ORA-1650 (Unable to extend rollback segment), ORA-1653 (Unable to extend table), and ORA-1654 (Unable to extent index), in which Oracle is not able to allocate another extent due to lack of available space. Adding space to the given tablespace generally solves this error condition (though coalescing space might be an alternative). If this error involves a temporary tablespace, other user sessions can result in the release of temporary segments in the tablespace, thus freeing space for the suspended session.

■ **Maximum number of extents reached**   This includes errors such as ORA-1628 (Max # of extents reached for rollback segment), and ORA-1631 ORA-1654 (Max # of extents reached in Table or Index). In this case, the object has a MAX_EXTENTS value assigned to it, which has been reached. The solution to this problem is to increase the MAX_EXTENTS setting for the object in question.

■ **Attempt to exceed a tablespace quota**   This includes error ORA-1536 (space quota exceeded for tablespace). The solution to correcting this problem is to increase the user quota for the tablespace in question.

When one of these conditions is reached, and if resumable space management has been enabled for the session, then the resumable statement will be suspended. At the time the statement is suspended, an error will be raised in the alert log. In addition, the user session running the query will become suspended, until either the time-out period passes, or the error condition is resolved. Also, Oracle has provided an **after suspend** system trigger event that can be used to automate a response to a SUSPEND condition.

Once a statement is suspended, it will wait for a defined period of time (two hours is the default). After that period of time elapses, the error will be raised, and the statement rolled back. During the period of the statement suspension, if the condition that caused the statement to be suspended is corrected, then the statement will automatically resume execution. Thus, for example, if space in the temporary tablespace were released by another user session, the query that was suspended because it ran out of temporary tablespace space would resume automatically without user intervention.

Suspended operations can be monitored through the use of the DBA_RESUMABLE and USER_RESUMABLE views (see "Data Dictionary Views Associated with Resumable Space Management," later in the chapter). Also, Oracle provides a package called DBMS_RESUMABLE that allows you to manage the Resumable Space Management features of the database, which we will discuss later in this section.

Candidate Database Operations for Resumable Space Management

There are many different kinds of operations that can take advantage of resumable space management. The following table lists these operations:

Operation Type	Comment
SELECT queries	If the query runs out of temporary sort space, then it can be suspended and resumed.
INSERT, UPDATE, DELETE operations	These operations can be suspended if they raise an out-of-space exception.

Operation Type	Comment
INSERT AS ... SELECT operation	This operation can be suspended if it runs into an out-of-space condition.
Import/export operations	Resumable space management is supported by the IMP and EXP facilities of Oracle.
SQL*Loader	Supports resumable space management operations
CREATE TABLE ... AS SELECT	Supports resumable space management
CREATE INDEX	Supports resumable space management
ALTER INDEX ... REBUILD	Supports resumable space management
ALTER TABLE ... MOVE PARTITION	Supports resumable space management
ALTER TABLE ... SPLIT PARTITION	Supports resumable space management
ALTER INDEX ... REBUILD PARTITION	Supports resumable space management
ALTER INDEX ... SPLIT PARTITION	Supports resumable space management
CREATE MATERIALIZED VIEW	Supports resumable space management
CREATE MATERIALIZED VIEW LOG	Supports resumable space management

Resumable Space Management Administration

In this section, you will learn about several administrative issues in regard to Oracle resumable space management features. First on the hit parade is the DBMS_RESUMABLE package, followed by a look at some restrictions that exist for this feature in regard to dictionary-managed tablespaces. Following that will be a look at some of the data dictionary views associated with resumable space management.

Controlling Resumable Space Management Features

Resumable space management is controlled on a session-by-session level, and is disabled by default. Any user who wants to enable resumable space management must first be granted the *resumable* system privilege. Having been granted that privilege, the user will enable resumable space management features by issuing the command **alter session enable resumable**. Likewise, to disable resumable space management, issue the command **alter session disable resumable**. If you wish to cause specific users to enable resumable space management, then create a login trigger to alter the users' sessions when they log in to the database.

Any session that is suspended during a resumable space operation is suspended for a specific period of time, after which it will error out and abort completely. By default, when you enable resumable space management, this time-out is 7,200 seconds, or two hours. You can modify this default value by including the *timeout* parameter to the **alter session enable resumable** command, as shown in the following example:

```
ALTER SESSION ENABLE RESUMABLE TIMEOUT 14400;
```

In this example, our time-out is set to 14,400 seconds, or four hours. Keep in mind that the longer you make the time-out interval, the more likely that suspended sessions will occur and pile up. This can cause resource contentions on your database to appear, as suspended sessions do consume a certain amount of overhead. If you should wish to change the time-out, simply issue another **alter session enable resumable** command with a different time-out value. Alternatively, you can use the **dbms_resumable.set_timeout** procedure (we will discuss this package in the next section).

With each execution of **alter session enable resumable**, you can also specify a name to be associated with the set of resumable sessions. This makes it easier to identify sessions in the data dictionary views for resumable space management such as DBA_RESUMABLE. An example of enabling resumable space management and defining a name for the sessions is shown here:

```
ALTER SESSION ENABLE RESUMABLE TIMEOUT 14400 NAME 'ROBERT';
```

Note that if you do not define a name, a system default name will be used.

The DBMS_RESUMABLE Package

The principle method of managing the Oracle resumable space management features is the use of the DBMS_RESUMABLE package. This package contains five procedures that can be used in concert with resumable space management. These subprograms are **abort**, **get_session_timeout**, **set_session_timeout**, **get_timeout**, and **set_timeout**. We will look at each of the subprograms in a bit more detail in the following sections.

DBMS_RESUMABLE.ABORT   The purpose of the **abort** procedure is to cancel all suspended statements for a given session. When calling **abort**, for the command to succeed, you must be the owner of the session, have **alter system**

privilege, or have DBA privileges. Here is the syntax for the **dbms_resumable.abort** procedure:

```
PROCEDURE DBMS_RESUMABLE.ABORT
(session_id IN NUMBER);
```

DBMS_RESUMABLE.GET_SESSION_TIMEOUT   The purpose of the **get_session_timeout** function is to return the current value of a given session's resumable space management time-out setting in seconds in the form of a NUMBER type. If the session is not present, a –1 error is returned. The syntax for the **get_session_timeout** function is shown here:

```
FUNCTION DBMS_RESUMABLE.GET_SESSION_TIMEOUT
(session_id  IN NUMBER)
RETURN NUMBER;
```

DBMS_RESUMABLE.SET_SESSION_TIMEOUT   The purpose of the **set_session_timeout** procedure is to set the current value of a given session's resumable space management time-out setting in seconds. This change is immediate in its effect, and no error is returned if the session does not exist. The syntax for the **set_session_timeout** function is shown here:

```
PROCEDURE DBMS_RESUMABLE.SET_SESSION_TIMEOUT
(session_id IN NUMBER,
timeout IN NUMBER);
```

DBMS_RESUMABLE.GET_TIMEOUT   The purpose of the **get_ timeout** function is to return the current value of the current session's resumable space management time-out setting in seconds. There are no parameters to this procedure. This function returns a NUMBER type.

DBMS_RESUMABLE.SET_TIMEOUT   The purpose of the **set_ timeout** procedure is to set the value of the current session's resumable space management time-out setting in seconds. This change is immediate in its effect. The syntax for the **set_ timeout** function is shown here:

```
PROCEDURE DBMS_RESUMABLE.SET_TIMEOUT
(timeout IN NUMBER);
```

DBMS_RESUMABLE.SPACE_ERROR_INFO   The purpose of the **space_ error_info** function is to return space-related errors. It is generally called by an after-suspend trigger (see the "After-Suspend Trigger" section). This function returns a great deal of information about the cause of a given statement failure in the form of its OUT parameters. This allows you to customize the system's response to a given failure condition. Thus, you can choose to suspend statements for certain failure conditions (say, out of temporary tablespace space), and just abort the statement in the case of other conditions (such as running out of rollback segment space). This function returns TRUE if a suspended statement was discovered, and FALSE if it was not. The syntax for the **space_error_info** function is shown here:

```
FUNCTION DBMS_RESUMABLE.SPACE_ERROR_INFO
( error_type          OUT VARCHAR2,
  object_type         OUT VARCHAR2,
  object_owner        OUT VARCHAR2,
  table_space_name    OUT VARCHAR2,
  object_name         OUT VARCHAR2,
  sub_object_name     OUT VARCHAR2)
RETURN BOOLEAN;
```

Resumable Space Management Restrictions

Oracle9i resumable space management comes with certain limitations when used with dictionary-managed tablespaces. If the creation of an object (that is, table or index) fails and the DDL includes an explicit *maxextents* clause that caused the failure, then that failure will cause an error to be generated and the object creation will not be resumable. The solution to this problem is to set *maxextents* to UNLIMITED while creating the object and then **alter** the object to reset *maxextents*, if that is what you wish to do. This applies only to DDL that is actually creating the object, not subsequent DML operations (**select**, **insert**, **update**, or **delete**) on that same object. Also, this does not apply to locally managed tablespaces.

Another limitation with regard to dictionary-managed tablespaces has to do with space management for rollback segments. If a rollback-segment space allocation fails, and the associated rollback segment is in a dictionary-managed tablespace, then the operation will fail. This restriction does not apply if you are using Oracle's new UNDO tablespaces, or if the tablespace that the rollback segments belong to is locally managed.

Note that statements that involve remote operations (such as DML statements using database links) do not support resumable space management. In regard to parallel execution, any parallel process that runs into a space management error will be suspended, and will restart when the problem is corrected. The remaining parallel processes will continue until they run into an error and are suspended or they complete. Note that this might cause multiple calls of the after-suspend trigger (see the next section for more on the after-suspend trigger). Note that if the parallel execution server process receives any nonrecoverable error, then the entire statement will fail and any suspended process will be aborted.

After-Suspend Trigger

Each time a SQL statement is suspended because of a space management failure, Oracle will call an after-suspend event trigger, if one exists. This trigger can be used for a number of reasons, including controlling which type of space allocation failures you wish to suspend, and which you wish to allow to fail. You can also use the trigger for notification purposes, such as sending e-mail to notify the DBA or a monitoring group that the process had failed. The Oracle documentation provides a good example of an after-suspend trigger. Check it out!

Data Dictionary Views Associated with Resumable Space Management

The main views associated with resumable space management are the DBA_RESUMABLE and USER_RESUMABLE views. These views contain information on each statement that is currently suspended. Here is an example of a query against the DBA_RESUMABLE view:

```
SQL> select user_id, session_id, error_msg from dba_resumable;
   USER_ID SESSION_ID        ERROR_MSG
---------- ---------------   -------------------------------------------------------------
        26          7        ORA-30036: unable to extend segment by 128 in undo tablespace

                             'SECOND_UNDO'
```

In this example, session 7 has a suspended session. It is apparently stalled, waiting for UNDO space in the UNDO tablespace called SECOND_UNDO. At this point, a DBA would have a few options to resume this statement. The DBA could add space to the UNDO tablespace or enable **autoextend**. The DBA could also choose to just wait for UNDO segments to be released by other transactions so they could be used. Of course, once Oracle has resolved the problem, it will automatically restart the suspended session.

Another view that has some use with relation to resumable space management is the V$SESSION_WAIT view. In this view, there will be an event for each statement that is suspended. The name of the event is "Suspended on space error." Here is a query that displays this event:

```
SQL> select sid, event, seconds_in_wait from v$session_wait WHERE sid = 7;
       SID EVENT                                              SECONDS_IN_WAIT
---------- -------------------------------------------------- ----------------
         7 statement suspended, wait error to be cleared                  517
```

Also, the V$SYSTEM_EVENT and V$SESSION_EVENT views provide wait information on suspension events. Here are some example queries from those tables of a session waiting on a suspended session:

```
SQL> select event, total_waits, time_waited from v$system_event where
  2  event like '%suspend%';
EVENT                                                TOTAL_WAITS TIME_WAITED
-------------------------------------------------- ----------- -----------
statement suspended, wait error to be cleared              186       37204

SQL> select sid, event, total_waits, time_waited from
  2  v$session_event where event like '%suspend%';
       SID EVENT                                                TOTAL_WAITS TIME_WAITED
---------- -------------------------------------------------- ----------- -----------
         7 statement suspended, wait error to be cleared              193       38605
```

Resumable Space Management and Oracle Utilities

In this section, you will learn about the use of reusable space management in concert with Oracle utility programs. First, we'll look at how this feature works with Oracle's IMP and EXP facilities. Then you will learn about resumable space management and SQL*Loader.

Using imp and exp with Resumable Space Management

To facilitate the use of resumable space management in Oracle9i with Oracle's **imp** and **exp** utilities, new parameters have been added to the **imp** command. The new parameters include

- *resumable*
- *resumable_name*
- *resumable_timeout*

These parameters enable resumable space management when using the **imp** utility. As with an Oracle user session, if the **imp** session is suspended, then the **imp** process will freeze until the suspension time-out passes (in which case, the process will fail). Of course, if the space failure is fixed during the suspension, then the **imp** process will simply continue to process the work until it's finished or it's suspended again. The default is to not have resumable space features enabled with the **imp** facility.

Using SQL*Loader with Resumable Space Management

Oracle's SQL*Loader product has had the following command-line parameters added:

- *resumable*
- *resumable_name*
- *resumable_timeout*

These parameters enable resumable space management features when loading data using SQL*Loader. The default is to not have resumable space features enabled.

Persistent Initialization Parameters

In this section, you will learn to set up the new server parameter file (spfile), which allows parameter settings to be persistent. We will then look at how to change parameters and ensure that the change is persistent. Finally, we will look at some management issues related to spfiles.

Oracle has long offered the ability to change a certain number of database parameters dynamically using the **alter system** or **alter session** command. One problem with this was that the dynamic changes that were made were valid only until the instance was shut down. For those changes to persist through future database shutdown-startup cycles, you needed to change the database parameter file manually. If these changes were not made, then the database settings would revert to those in the database parameter file during the next database shutdown-startup cycle, which could lead to a variety of problems.

Creating the Server Parameter File

The **spfile** is a binary version of the old init.ora text database parameter file. The **spfile** is created using a new Oracle command, **create spfile**. To be used to start the database, the **spfile** must reside on the server (as opposed to a regular text parameter file, which can reside remotely). Oracle will start the database using either a **spfile** or a normal database parameter file, following these rules: When you start the database, Oracle first checks for a system parameter file called spfile<instance_name>.ora, then a system parameter file called spfile.ora in the $ORACLE_HOME/dbs directory on a UNIX system. If neither exists, then it looks for the traditional init.ora file. You can still use the **pfile** parameter to point to a nondefault database parameter file, but this must be a normal, text-based parameter file and cannot be a **spfile**.

1. Create the server parameter file using the **create spfile** command as shown here:

   ```
   CREATE spfile='c:\oracle\admin\mydb\pfile\spfiletmydb.ora'
   FROM PFILE='c:\oracle\admin\mydb\pfile\initmydb.ora';
   ```

2. Shut down the database and restart it using the following commands:

   ```
   SHUTDOWN IMMEDIATE
   STARTUP PFILE= c:\oracle\admin\mydb\pfile\spfilemydb.ora
   ```

NOTE
The only comments that will survive a conversion to a spfile are those contained in the same line of a parameter. Stand-alone and header comments are not preserved.

A few rules to note about the **create spfile** command: first, if you do not define the name of the server file to be created, then Oracle will create an spfile in the default location of the Oracle parameter files (that is, %ORACLE_HOME\database in NT or $ORACLE_HOME/dbs in UNIX). The spfile will take on the default name spfile{oracle_sid}.ora. Further, if you do not define the name of the source pfile, then the default pfile for the database will be used.

When creating an spfile with the **create spfile** command, Oracle will overwrite the old spfile, so be careful. If you try to overwrite an spfile that you started the database with, then Oracle will generate an error.

Also, you cannot point to an spfile from a normal parameter file by using the **ifile** command. Instead, include an **spfile** command in the normal parameter file to point to an spfile.

Setting Persistent Parameters

In Oracle9i, you will still use the **alter system set** command to change a parameter and ensure that change is persistent across database shutdowns. A new clause to the **alter system** called **scope** has been introduced to allow the DBA to indicate how Oracle should interpret the desired persistence of the change. There are three options to the **scope** clause:

■ *spfile*   The parameter being changed will be changed in the spfile, but will not take effect until the next time the instance is cycled. This is the only way that static parameters can be modified in the spfile. Attempting to use any other **scope** for static parameters will result in an error.

■ *memory*   The parameter being changed will be changed only for the instance that is currently active. The parameter in the spfile will not be updated, and thus the parameter is not persistent. You cannot use this parameter for static parameters.

■ *both*   The parameter being changed will be changed in the current instance and will be updated in the spfile for the database. Thus, the change will persist through future cycles of the database instance.

Also, a new **comment** clause has been added to the **alter system** command. This clause allows you to associate comments with the parameter being set. This allows you to document the change being made (which is a really good idea!). Here are a couple of examples of using the **alter system** command to change parameters in an spfile:

```
ALTER SYSTEM
SET query_rewrite_enabled=TRUE COMMENT='Change on 9/30' SCOPE=BOTH
```

This example sets the *query_rewrite_enabled* parameter to a value of TRUE. We have also associated this parameter change with a comment that indicates the date we made the change. Finally, we indicate the **scope** of the change is BOTH, so that the change will take place immediately and will also be reflected in the spfile of the database. Here is another example:

```
ALTER SYSTEM
SET shared_pool_size=100m COMMENT='Change on 9/30' SCOPE=BOTH,
aq_tm_processes=5 COMMENT='Change on 9/30' SCOPE=BOTH
```

In this case, we are changing two parameters at the same time. If you wish to remove a parameter that is set, you would simply issue an **alter system** command with the parameter set to 0 (or " if it is a string parameter), as shown in this example:

```
ALTER SYSTEM SET db_16k_cache_size=0;
```

Also, you can use the *deferred* parameter to cause the change to take effect only for future sessions that connect to the database, as in this example:

```
ALTER SYSTEM
SET query_rewrite_enabled=TRUE COMMENT='Change on 9/30' SCOPE=MEMORY
DEFERRED;
```

If you are running real application clusters in Oracle9*i*, you can define the *sid* that the change is associated with by using the *sid* parameter. If you wish the change to take effect for all instances, you can use an asterisk (*) in the *sid* parameter to indicate this. The default for *sid* is * if the database was started with an spfile; otherwise, the default is the current instance. Here is an example of the use of the *sid* parameter:

```
ALTER SYSTEM
SET query_rewrite_enabled=TRUE COMMENT='Change on 9/30' SCOPE=MEMORY
DEFERRED SID=mysid2;
```

Finally, if you are using real application clusters, you might want to remove a previously set spfile setting for one of the instances of the cluster. To do this, you can use the **alter system** command with the **reset** clause, as shown here:

```
ALTER SYSTEM
RESET query_rewrite_enabled SCOPE=MEMORY DEFERRED SID=mysid2;
```

Managing the spfile

Let's look at a few of the management issues relating to spfiles. First, we will look at how to create a text parameter file from an existing spfile. Then we will look at some of the data dictionary views that can be used in Oracle9*i* that relate to spfiles.

Creating a Text Parameter File from an spfile

There might be times that you will want to convert an existing spfile into a standard text database parameter file. You might want to do this for documentation purposes, backup and recovery purposes, or if you just want a parameter file to work with when creating a new database. Oracle provides the ability to convert an spfile into a text parameter file through the use of the new **create pfile** command, which works like the **create spfile** command, but in reverse. Here is an example of the operation of this command:

```
CREATE PFILE='c:\oracle\admin\mydb\pfile\initmydb_pfile.ora'
    FROM spfile='c:\oracle\admin\mydb\pfile\spfilemydb.ora';
```

Note, in this case, that we have defined the location of the pfile to be created. If we did not define the pfile name and location, Oracle would default to putting the file in the default pfile location (that is, %ORACLE_HOME\database in NT or $ORACLE_HOME/dbs in UNIX). The default name of the file will be the default parameter filename for the database. If you do not include a filename for an spfile, then the default database spfile name will be used. Of course, if you choose to use the defaults and the source file does not exist, then the statement will fail.

Data Dictionary Views and spfiles

The data dictionary provides some useful views that allow you to display not only the current value of database parameters, but also how the parameters will be set in the future (again, assuming we have set them using DEFERRED or SCOPE=spfile). There are three principle views that we can use to display database parameters. Let's take a moment to look at these.

V$PARAMETER   This view remains generally unchanged from Oracle8i. It provides the current settings that are in effect for the instance for a given parameter. One thing that is new is that comments that are associated with the parameter are listed in this view.

V$PARAMETER2   This view is new for Oracle9i. This view lists the parameters that are current for a given database session. Its format is generally the same as V$PARAMETER except for the inclusion of an ORDINAL column. The ORDINAL column shows you the actual order of the parameters, which is handy for parameters that have included a list of strings.

V$SPPARAMETER   This view is new for Oracle9i. Its purpose is to allow you to view the settings of parameters in the instance spfile.

Oracle Supports Fewer Platforms in 9i

Here is a list of platforms that Oracle has announced it will support for Oracle9i:

- Sun Sparc Solaris
- HP 9000 Series HP-UX (64-bit)
- Compaq Tru64 UNIX
- AIX-based systems (64-bit)
- Sun Sparc Solaris (64-bit)
- Linux Intel
- IBM OS/390
- IBM DYNIX/ptx
- Alpha OpenVMS
- Microsoft Windows NT
- Microsoft Windows 2000

CHAPTER
2

Oracle9i Architecture Changes

- Index-organized table changes
- Skip scanning of indexes
- Extraction of object metadata
- Online object operations
- Persistent initialization parameters
- Automatic segment space management
- Bitmap join indexes
- Identifying unused indexes
- Cursor sharing
- Shared server improvements
- Create tablespace default changes
- Quiescing the database

racle9i introduces new architectural changes that you will want to know about-from administration and management changes to, in this chapter, architecture changes. From database objects to internal ways of dealing with space management inside an object, lots has changed since 8i. Chapter 2 will look at many of these topics, and get you up to speed on some of the nice new features you can put to work in 9i.

Index-Organized Table Changes

Oracle9i has strengthened the capabilities of index-organized tables (IOTs). In this section, you will learn about new options that Oracle9i introduces, including new indexing options for IOTs, online rebuilds of secondary IOT indexes, and parallel DML.

Index-Organized Table-Indexing Options

Oracle8i introduced support for secondary indexes on index-organized tables. In Oracle8i, secondary indexes on IOTs had to be B-tree indexes. In Oracle9i, you can create bitmap indexes on IOTs. The addition of bitmap indexes offers more flexibility through the following features:

- A bitmap index tends to be much smaller than a B-tree index.

- The optimizer has more access path options when choosing the correct execution plan for a given query.

- Bitmaps allow for bitwise operations, which are very fast. Bitwise operations are available when two or more bitmap indexes are available and a query involves an AND or OR operation.

To create a bitmap index on an IOT, you must create a mapping table. A mapping table contains the logical ROWID in the IOT that is associated with each bit in the bitmap index. Thus, the mapping table translates the bit in the bitmap index to an associated logical ROWID in the IOT. To create the mapping table and allow for the creation of bitmap indexes on your IOT, you must add the **mapping table** clause to the **create table** command when creating your IOT. Here is an example of the creation of an IOT with a mapping table, and the creation of a bitmap index that is associated with the IOT:

```
CREATE  TABLE state
( state_code          VARCHAR2(2) PRIMARY KEY,
  state_name          VARCHAR2(30),
  state_zip_prefix    VARCHAR2(2) )
ORGANIZATION INDEX
MAPPING TABLE TABLESPACE users;

CREATE BITMAP INDEX bx_state_01 ON state (state_zip_prefix);
```

In the previous listing, we created an IOT called STATE. Using the **mapping table** clause, we have defined a mapping tablespace for this IOT that will cause Oracle to create a mapping of logical to physical ROWIDs that will be stored in a heap-organized table. This is required for us to create the bitmap index as seen in the **create bitmap index** statement following the creation of the state IOT. Note that the mapping table will be created in the users tablespace.

You will also note that Oracle doesn't give you an opportunity to name the mapping table. In this case, if you look in the DBA_TABLES data-dictionary view, you will find that the mapping table was created with the name SYS_IOT_MAP_<sequence number>. The sequence number is generated automatically by Oracle, of course. Here is an example of a query showing a mapping table:

```
SELECT owner, table_name, iot_type
FROM dba_tables
WHERE table_name LIKE '%SYS_IOT%';

OWNER                   TABLE_NAME            IOT_TYPE
--------------------    --------------------  ----------------
SCOTT                   SYS_IOT_MAP_5293      IOT_MAPPING
```

NOTE
There is some performance overhead associated with mapping tables. Create them only if you really need them.

IOTs, Parallel DML, and Overflow Segments

Oracle9i allows parallel DML to occur with partitioned IOTs. This can lead to faster access to IOTs by queries. Oracle9i also allows you to use the **alter table move** command to move an IOT with an overflow segment to a different tablespace, an operation that was restricted in Oracle8i. Note that this operation can be done online as well.

Rebuilding B-Tree Secondary Indexes on IOTs

In Oracle9i, secondary indexes on index-organized tables can be rebuilt online. This allows these indexes to be rebuilt while DML activity continues. This online secondary-index rebuild also allows all row guesses to be rebuilt online. Note that parallel DML will be restricted on index-organized tables during any online rebuild operation. You cannot rebuild a bitmap index or a cluster index in Oracle9i.

NOTE
*You can now also validate the structure of indexes and tables online with the **analyze validate** command!*

Skip Scanning of Indexes

Have you ever executed a query and discovered it didn't use any indexes because the columns in the query were not in the leading edge of the query, but deeper within the structure of the index? Say, for example, that I have a table called CHILD, and in it are three columns, PARENT_ID, CHILD_ID, and comment. Also assume that I have created a composite primary key index on this table using the PARENT_ID and CHILD_ID columns, with PARENT_ID being the leading column in the index (see Figure 2-1).

If I issue a query such as this one;

```
SELECT COUNT(*) FROM child WHERE parent_id=1;
```

then Oracle will be able to use the concatenated primary key index that is associated with the primary key of the table because PARENT_ID is the first column in the index, or on the leading edge of the index. In Oracle8*i*, if I wanted to issue this query;

```
SELECT COUNT(*) FROM child WHERE child_id=1;
```

I would end up being forced to do a full table scan instead of being able to use the index because I didn't use the columns of the index starting with the leading edge. Versions of Oracle before Oracle9*i* would use an index only if you used columns from the leading edge inward.

Oracle9*i* has addressed this problem by introducing *skip scanning* of indexes. With skip scanning, you do not need to use the leading column of an index, and you can use any column or columns that the index is built on, regardless of the order they were created in the index.

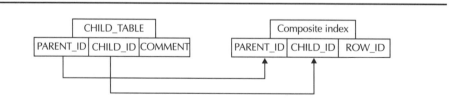

FIGURE 2-1. *A table and its composite primary key index*

Thus, if I issued the preceding query in Oracle9i, I could use the composite index, even though PARENT_ID was the leading column. Oracle will scan each branch block entry of the B-tree to determine whether the values in the leaf block associated with that branch block might contain values that satisfy the **where** clause criteria. For example, take the following query:

```
SELECT COUNT(*) FROM child WHERE child_id=30;
```

As with the previous query, Oracle is instructed to find all rows where CHILD_ID is equivalent to 50. Oracle will scan through the branch blocks of the index, finding those branch blocks where the value of 50 might be found for CHILD_ID, and moving down to the leaf blocks. Branch blocks that cannot contain a value of 50 for the CHILD_ID column are pruned during the scan, saving valuable input-output (I/O) time. Figure 2-2 gives an example of such an operation.

As you can see in Figure 2-2, we have eliminated the I/O to fully one-third of the index blocks by using Oracle9i's new skip-scanning features. The skip-scanning method of accessing indexes

- Reduces the overall number of indexes needed for a given table, cutting the overhead associated with the maintenance of those indexes

- Decreases the problems caused by not being able to clearly determine which column of an index should be the leading column

- Is much faster than a full table scan and faster than even some unbounded range scans

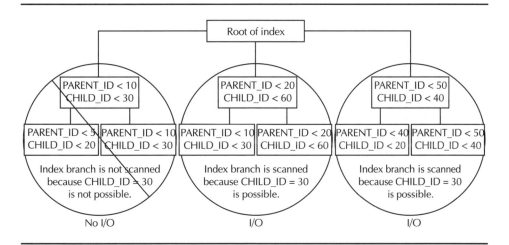

FIGURE 2-2. *Searching for the CHILD_ID value*

Skip scanning does have some overhead associated with it. This is because Oracle has to scan the index for each distinct value in the prefix column of the index. After the initial probe, Oracle then searches the inner columns for the appropriate values. This can be very costly in terms of performance, but often is still much faster than a full table scan. In addition to standard B-tree indexes, the optimizer can use skip scans for processing cluster indexes, descending scans, or statements with **connect by** clauses.

NOTE
Reverse key indexes and bitmap indexes cannot take advantage of skip scanning.

Extraction of Object Metadata

One of the biggest, and sometimes most painful, chores of DBAs is the extraction of data definition language (DDL) for objects that are already contained in the database. Oracle9i has sought to make this easier with the introduction of the *Oracle9i metadata* application programming interface (API). The data dictionary can be particularly tasking for junior DBAs, and this API eliminates the need to query the data-dictionary views to extract the object information required to re-create the object.

The Oracle9i Metadata API provides an alternative interface that allows you to extract Oracle DDL from the data dictionary. This functionality is supported through the new Oracle9i package **dbms_metadata**. You can extract the object information as either SQL DDL or XML for later transformation, and there are programmatic interfaces into **dbms_metadata** as well.

The **dbms_metadata** package allows several functions. Principal ones for nonprogrammatic use are **get_ddl** and **get_xml**. The **get_ddl** function returns the object information as SQL-runnable DDL, whereas the **get_xml** returns the data as object metadata in XML format. An associated XSL style sheet is available in $ORACLE_HOME/rdbms/xml/xsl. The two functions take the following format:

```
FUNCTION get_xml
(   object_type  IN VARCHAR2,
    name         IN VARCHAR2,
    schema       IN VARCHAR2 DEFAULT NULL,
    version      IN VARCHAR2 DEFAULT 'COMPATIBLE',
    model        IN VARCHAR2 DEFAULT 'ORACLE',
    transform    IN VARCHAR2 DEFAULT NULL)
    RETURN CLOB;
FUNCTION get_ddl
(   object_type  IN VARCHAR2,
    name         IN VARCHAR2,
```

```
schema      IN VARCHAR2 DEFAULT NULL,
version     IN VARCHAR2 DEFAULT 'COMPATIBLE',
model       IN VARCHAR2 DEFAULT 'ORACLE',
transform   IN VARCHAR2 DEFAULT 'DDL')
RETURN CLOB;
```

The GET_DDL procedure provides a good example of the use of the
dbms_metadata package. In this example, we will extract the DDL for the
table DEPT in the SCOTT schema:

```
SELECT DBMS_METADATA.GET_DDL
   ('TABLE','DEPT','SCOTT')
     FROM DUAL;

DBMS_METADATA.GET_DDL('TABLE','DEPT','SCOTT')
--------------------------------------------------
   CREATE TABLE "SCOTT"."DEPT"
   (    "DEPTNO" NUMBER(2,0),
        "DNAME" VARCHAR2(14),
        "LOC" VARCHAR2(13)
   ) PCTFREE 10 PCTUSED 40 INITRANS 1 MAXTRANS 255
     LOGGING STORAGE(INITIAL 65536 NEXT 1048576
     MINEXTENTS 1 MAXEXTENTS 2147483645
   PCTINCREASE 0 FREELISTS 1 FREELIST GROUPS 1
   BUFFER_POOL DEFAULT) TABLESPACE "USERS"
```

Note in this example that the first parameter is the type of object we wish to
extract. All the valid object type names are documented in the *Oracle9i Supplied
PL/SQL Packages and Types Manual*. Next, we supply the object name to extract, as
well as the schema name it belongs to. Note that the output includes all the various
parts of the **create table** statement that are needed to correctly reconstruct this table,
and that the output does *not* end in a semicolon or slash.

In this second example, we will extract the DDL from the **my_function** function,
which is in the SCOTT schema:

```
SELECT DBMS_METADATA.GET_DDL
   ('FUNCTION','MY_FUNCTION','SCOTT')
     FROM DUAL;

DBMS_METADATA.GET_DDL('FUNCTION','MY_FUNCTION','SCOTT')
----------------------------------------------------------------------
   CREATE OR REPLACE FUNCTION "SCOTT"."MY_FUNCTION" return number as
begin
dbms_output.put_line('This is a test');
return 0;
end;
```

Here again, we define that object type (FUNCTION) that we wish to extract. We also define the name and owner of the object. Note, in this case, that Oracle creates the entire DDL for us, including the **create function** keyword.

Oracle provides a programmatic interface to the **dbms_metadata** package for PL/SQL use as well. Examples of the use of this feature can be found in $ORACLE_HOME/rdbms/demo/mddemo.sql and $ORACLE_HOME/rdbms/demo/mddemo2.sql.

Online Object Operations

Oracle9i offers several new features regarding online management of schema objects. This includes enhancements to online operations on indexes, the ability to move the overflow segment of an IOT on line, and the ability to redefine and reorganize tables online.

Online Operations on Indexes

Several new features have been introduced in Oracle9i that add flexibility to rebuilding indexes online. The following index types can now be rebuilt and moved online:

- Reverse key indexes facilitating updates of stale logical ROWIDs

- Function indexes

- Key-compressed indexes on index-organized and hash tables

- Secondary indexes of IOTs

Oracle has introduced a few new commands to support online rebuild operations. The **alter table coalesce** command is used to coalesce the primary B-tree index of an IOT. The **alter index...update block references** command has been added to allow for online updates of logical ROWIDs for indexes on IOTs. The use of the **update block references** command will cause the rebuild to occur online, so you don't need to include the **online** keyword.

Moving an Overflow Segment of an IOT Online

You can now move the overflow segment of an IOT online using the **alter table** command, including the **overflow tablespace** command, as seen here:

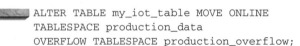

```
ALTER TABLE my_iot_table MOVE ONLINE
TABLESPACE production_data
OVERFLOW TABLESPACE production_overflow;
```

Reorganizing and Redefining Tables Online

Oracle9i offers the ability to reorganize and redefine tables and the associated indexes online with a minimum of outage required on the objects being rebuilt. This allows you to rebuild a table (for example, with a **create table as select** statement) without affecting online operations. Thus, you can remove data from it, lowering the high-water mark; reduce the number of extents on the table; or fix problems with inefficient database block usage due to incorrectly set database parameters. Also, you can change a hash table into an IOT, or change an IOT into a hash table. Perhaps you wish to partition the table, or change the partitioning method. All these operations are supported by online table rebuild and redefinition operations. Let's look at this new feature in a bit more detail.

Performing the Reorganization

Previously, to reorganize a table in Oracle, you would have to restrict DML access to that table during the period of the reorganization. In fact, because of the associated index rebuilds, **select** query performance could be degraded during reorganization such that it was just better to take a complete outage of the applications using that table rather than suffer the poor performance that might result.

Oracle9i offers a new process that allows you to do online rebuilds and redefinitions of tables and their associated indexes with a minimum outage requirement. This new process centers on the new Oracle package, **dbms_redefinition**. The procedure to actually perform a table rebuild is a bit complicated, so let's look at it a step at a time.

NOTE
*You will see many references to **dbms_redefinition** procedures. We will cover these in detail later in this section.*

1. Use the **dbms_redefinition.can_redef_table()** procedure to verify that the table that we wish to rebuild online *can* be rebuilt. There are a number of restrictions that apply to online rebuilding of tables, which are covered in "Rules and Restrictions for Online Rebuilding," later in the chapter. Here is an example of the use of the **can_redef_table** procedure:

```
EXEC DBMS_REDEFINITION.CAN_REDEF_TABLE('SCOTT', 'EMP');
```

Here is an example in which a table fails the examination of its ability to be redefined.

```
BEGIN dbms_redefinition.can_redef_table('SCOTT','EMP'); END;
*
ERROR at line 1:
ORA-12089: cannot online redefine table "SCOTT"."EMP" with no primary key
ORA-06512: at "SYS.DBMS_REDEFINITION", line 8
ORA-06512: at "SYS.DBMS_REDEFINITION", line 236
ORA-06512: at line 1
```

Note that in the previous listing, Oracle tells us that the problem is a missing primary key on the table to be redefined. After a primary key was added to the table, the subsequent check was successful, as seen here:

```
SQL> exec dbms_redefinition.can_redef_table('SCOTT','EMP');
PL/SQL procedure successfully completed.
```

No errors are returned by this run of the **can_redef_table** procedure, so we can continue.

NOTE
When you created your database, you may or may not have created the scott/tiger schema that contains the EMP table we use in this example. If you did create the scott/tiger schema, your EMP table may or may not have been created with a primary key, depending on which script you used to create it. If your EMP table does have a primary key, you will not see the error message highlighted in step one.

2. Now, we create an empty, interim table that represents the table as we wish it to look. Note that we need to create this interim table in the same schema as the table we wish to reorganize. The **create table as select** command is good for this type of operation. Also, we will need to make sure we have the primary key defined for this interim table, as this is a requirement for being able to do online moves of the table. Here is an example:

```
connect scott/tiger
CREATE TABLE new_emp
PCTFREE 10 PCTUSED 60
STORAGE (INITIAL 100k NEXT 100k)
PARTITION BY RANGE(empno)
              (PARTITION emp_id_50000
                    VALUES LESS THAN (3000) TABLESPACE emp_tbs_3000,
              PARTITION emp_id_100000
                    VALUES LESS THAN (6000) TABLESPACE emp_tbs_6000,
              PARTITION emp_id_all_others
                    VALUES LESS THAN (MAXVALUE) TABLESPACE emp_tbs_maxvalue)
AS SELECT * FROM EMP WHERE 1 = 2;
ALTER TABLE new_emp ADD PRIMARY KEY (empno);
```

Note that at this time, we could choose to redefine the table if we wanted. Also note that we didn't actually copy any records to the table at this time. We could add, drop, or modify the definition of a given column. All these actions are supported by the online rebuild process. We have decided, in this case, to partition the table, since it was previously unpartitioned.

3. Having built the interim table, we need to indicate to Oracle that we are starting an online rebuild of the SCOTT.EMP table. We do this by using the

dbms_redefinition procedure **start_redef_table()**. This procedure takes three parameters. The first is the table that is being redefined or reorganized, the second is the name of the interim table, and the third is an optional column mapping. If the column mapping is not supplied, Oracle assumes that the structure of the original table and the interim table is to be the same. If column mapping is used, then only the columns listed in the column mapping will be able to be moved to the interim table, and only those columns will be tracked by Oracle as they are modified. Here is an example of the execution of the **dbms_redefinition.start_redef_table()** for our example:

```
EXEC DBMS_REDEFINITION.START_REDEF_TABLE( UNAME=>'SCOTT',
ORIG_TABLE=>'EMP',INT_TABLE=>'NEW_EMP');
```

When the previous example is executed, Oracle will populate the NEW_EMP table with the current records in the EMP table. Oracle will also start tracking change deltas on the EMP table, but will not apply those deltas.

Note that in the previous example, we did not need a column definition because we are using the same columns. If we had decided to change a column definition, we would have needed to include a column definition in the procedure call. For example, we have the following column names in EMP:

```
EMPNO, ENAME, JOB, MGR, HIREDATE, SAL, COMM, DEPTNO
```

Say we want everyone to get the same commission percentage, 10 percent. Also, let's assume that we wanted to rename the ENAME column to EMP_NAME. In this case, our call to **dbms_redefinition.start_redef_table** would look like this:

```
DBMS_REDEFINITION.START_REDEF_TABLE('SCOTT','EMP','NEW_EMP',
'empno empno, ename emp_name, job job, mgr mgr, hiredate hiredate, sal sal,
10 comm, deptno deptno');
```

Note that we have included all the columns in both tables. Note also that with the ENAME column, we have the new column name, EMP_NAME, next to it. This indicates a mapping of ENAME to the new EMP_NAME column. We have also defined that the value 10, rather than any other value, should be placed in the new COMM column.

4. We now need to create any triggers, indexes, and constraints that are needed on the NEW_EMP table. In general, these will be the same objects that are on the EMP table, except the names will need to be different. Make sure that you create all referential constraints as disabled. Also, create any grants on the new table that will be needed. In the following example, we create the primary key constraint, a referential integrity constraint between the NEW_EMP table and the DEPT table, and a secondary index on the

DEPT column of the NEW_EMP table. All these objects will replace the objects defined on the source EMP table at the end of this process.

```
ALTER TABLE new_emp ADD CONSTRAINT fkredef_dept_emp FOREIGN KEY(deptno)
REFERENCES dept DISABLE;
```

5. Now, complete the redefinition process by using the **dbms_redefinition** subprogram **finish_redef_table**. This step will cause a short outage as Oracle locks the data dictionary to finalize the table rebuild. Oracle will also resynchronize the new table and all its associated indexes with the old table before dropping the old table. Here an example of using this procedure:

```
EXEC DBMS_REDEFINITION.FINISH_REDEF_TABLE('SCOTT', 'EMP', 'NEW_EMP');
```

6. Once the previous step has been completed successfully, you can drop the interim table, as it will no longer be required, as seen in this next code example:

```
DROP TABLE new_emp CASCADE CONSTRAINTS;
```

Manually Resynchronizing Tables

You might wish to resynchronize the interim table with the source table during the redefinition process. You can run the procedure **dbms_redefinition.sync_interim_table**. This can help reduce the time for the call to **exec dbms_redefinition.finish_redef_table** at the end of the redefinition process. Here is an example of a call to the **sync_interim_table** procedure:

```
EXEC DBMS_REDEFINITION.SYNC_INTERIM_TABLE('SCOTT','DEPT','NEW_DEPT');
```

If an Error Occurs

If an error occurs and it is determined that the redefinition process should be halted for the time being, you should run the **dbms_redefinition.abort_redef_table** procedure. This will stop all synchronization operations between the source and interim table so that you can drop the interim table without error. Oracle will allow you to run this procedure even if you have already dropped the interim table.

Rules and Restrictions for Online Rebuilding

There are a number of rules and restrictions that must be followed when rebuilding or redefining a table online. If any of these cannot be met, then the table cannot be rebuilt online. Both the source table and the interim table of the redefinition must have primary keys, and those primary keys must be built on the same primary-key columns. Tables owned by SYS or SYSTEM are also ineligible. Also, you cannot move a table to another schema, and new columns cannot be declared as NOT NULL until after you have finished the rebuild process.

You cannot rebuild tables that are part of a materialized view. Also, tables with materialized view logs cannot be rebuilt online. Clustered tables are also not eligible for online redefinition. The materialized-view container tables and advanced queuing tables cannot be rebuilt either.

Temporary and clustered tables cannot be redefined online. Tables that belong to SYS and SYSTEM cannot be redefined online. New columns to be added as part of the redefinition can be declared NOT NULL only when the redefinition is complete. Finally, no referential constraints between the table being redefined and the interim table can be defined.

Tables with the following column types are not candidates for online redefinition:

- Objects
- REFs
- Nested tables
- VARRAYs
- Typed tables
- FILE
- LONG (LOB columns are redefinable).

Privileges Required for Online Rebuilding

To perform an online redefinition of a table, you must have the following privileges:

- **alter any table**
- **create any table**
- **drop any table**
- **execute** on the **dbms_redefinition** package (the **execute_catalog_role** is granted this privilege)
- **lock any table**
- **select any table**

dbms_redefinition Package Procedures

The **dbms_redefinition** is used in coordination with table redefinition efforts to keep the interim table synchronized with the table being redefined during the process. The package contains five subprograms:

- **can_redef_table**
- **start_redef_table**

- **finish_redef_table**
- **sync_interim_table**
- **abort_redef_table**

Let's look at each of these procedures in a bit more detail next.

can_redef_table Procedure This procedure is used to determine whether a given table is a candidate for online redefinition. The syntax for this command is as follows:

```
Procedure DBMS_REDEFINITION.CAN_REDEF_TABLE
( uname            IN VARCHAR2,         -- User name
  tname            IN VARCHAR2 );       -- Name of the table to be checked
```

An example of the use of this procedure can be found earlier in the "Performing the Reorganization" section.

start_redef_table Procedure This procedure is used to indicate that Oracle should start moving data between the source and interim table, beginning the redefinition process. When this statement is executed, Oracle will begin to track each change made in the source table to replicate that change to the interim table at some future point. All logged changes are moved to the interim table when either the **finish_redef_table** or the **sync_interim_table** procedure is executed. The syntax for this command is as follows:

```
Procedure DBMS_REDINITION.start_redef_table
  ( uname            IN VARCHAR2,            -- User name
    orig_table       IN VARCHAR2,            -- Original (source) table
    int_table        IN VARCHAR2,            -- Interim table
    col_mapping  IN VARCHAR2 := NULL );      -- Column Mapping
```

An example of the use of this procedure can be found earlier in the "Performing the Reorganization" section.

finish_redef_table Procedure This procedure is used to indicate to the Oracle server that the redefinition process has completed, and that the DBA is ready for the interim table to be synchronized with the source table. Once this is done, the interim table and all indexes, triggers, grants, and constraints created on the interim table will be redefined, replacing the source table and its related objects. During this processing, there is a short period when the data dictionary is locked, requiring a short outage. The syntax for this command is as follows:

```
Procedure DBMS_REDFINITION.finish_redef_table
  ( uname            IN VARCHAR2,          -- User name
    orig_table       IN VARCHAR2,          -- Original (source) table
    int_table        IN VARCHAR2 );        -- Interim table
```

An example of the use of this procedure can be found earlier in the "Performing the Reorganization" section.

sync_interim_table Procedure　　This procedure causes Oracle to synchronize the interim table with the source Oracle table. The syntax for this command is as follows:

```
DBMS_REDFINITION.sync_interim_table
  ( uname            IN VARCHAR2,          -- User name
    orig_table       IN VARCHAR2,          -- Original (source) table
    int_table        IN VARCHAR2 );        -- Interim table
```

More information on the use of this procedure can be found earlier in the "Manually Resynchronizing Tables" section.

abort_redef_table Procedure　　This procedure causes all redefinition processes to be aborted. All logging of activity on the source table is halted, and the logs are removed. Once this procedure is run, you can remove the interim table. The syntax for this command is as follows:

```
DBMS_REDEFINITION.abort_redef_table
  ( uname            IN VARCHAR2,          -- User name
    orig_table       IN VARCHAR2,          -- Original (source) table
    int_table        IN VARCHAR2 );        -- Interim table
```

More information on the use of this procedure can be found earlier in the "If an Error Occurs" section.

Automated Segment-Space Management

Oracle9i introduces two ways to manage free space within a segment. The old method of using free lists is still supported, and a new method, *automated segment-space management,* is now available. With the old method (and still the default method), Oracle uses a structure called a *free list* to keep track of free blocks within a segment.

In Oracle9*i*, you can create a tablespace that is defined to use automated space management rather than free lists. When a segment is created in a tablespace that uses automated space management, Oracle creates a bitmap within blocks in the segment called *BMBs*. Normally BMBs take up the first three blocks in the segment, and the fourth block is the segment header.

The bitmap describes the status of the blocks within the segment, indicating how much space is available within the blocks to insert rows. As the block changes, the bitmap will change as well. Use of a bitmap is simpler and more efficient than using a free list. It allows for better space use, and eliminates the need to specify **pctused**, **freelists**, and **freelists groups** when defining objects within the tablespace. Automatic segment-space management is available only with locally managed tablespace.

Oracle has made this feature very easy to use. Simply include the **segment space management auto** clause when you issue the **create tablespace** command to create a tablespace. Automatic segment-space management will apply to all segments created within a tablespace created using the **segment space management clause**. Here is an example of a **create tablespace** statement that creates a tablespace that uses automated segment-space management

```
CREATE TABLESPACE my_auto_tbs
DATAFILE 'c:\oradata\mydb\mydb_my_auto_tbs_01.dbf' SIZE 100m
EXTENT MANAGEMENT LOCAL
SEGMENT SPACE MANGEMENT AUTO;
```

Automatic space management is much more efficient than a free list when used with tablespaces that will contain tables with varying row sizes. In fact, planned enhancements to the Oracle RDBMS will *require* the use of automatic segment-space management.

There are some restrictions to be aware of when using automated segment-space management. First, this feature is available only with permanent and locally managed tablespaces. Also, LOB columns cannot be created in a tablespace that is designated for automatic segment-space management. Finally, a tablespace created using automated segment space management cannot be altered to use freelist space management.

Bitmap Join Indexes

Bitmap indexes were introduced back in the Oracle8 days. Now, with Oracle9*i*, we can create *bitmap join indexes*. Bitmap join indexes represent the join of columns in two or more tables. With a bitmap join index, the value of a column in one table (generally a dimension table) is stored with the associated ROWIDs of the like value in the other tables that the index is defined on. This provides fast join access between the tables—if that query uses the columns of the bitmap join index. In Figure 2-3, we see a bitmap join index created between two different tables, a fact table and a dimension table.

In a data-warehouse environment, a bitmap join index might be a more efficient way of accessing data than a materialized-view join. When using a bitmap join index in a warehouse or EIS environment, you would create the join using an equi-inner join between the primary key column(s) of the dimension tables and the foreign key column(s) of the fact table.

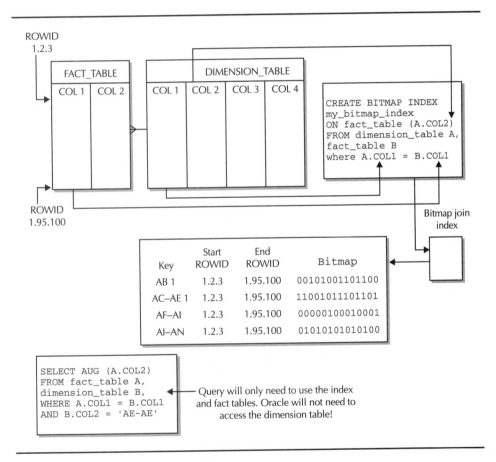

FIGURE 2-3. *A bitmap join index*

You create a bitmap join index using the **create bitmap index** command. Here is an example of the creation of a bitmap index:

```
CREATE BITMAP INDEX my_bitmap_index
ON fact_table(dimension_table.col2)
FROM dimension_table, fact_table
WHERE dimension_table.col1=fact_table.col1;
```

There are a few restrictions on bitmap join indexes that you should be aware of. These include the following:

- The bitmap join index is built on a single table. In the previous example, the bitmap join index is built on the FACT_TABLE table.

- Oracle will allow only one of the tables of a bitmap join index to be updated, inserted, or deleted from at a time.

- You cannot join the same table to itself, that is, no table can appear twice in the **from** clause.

- A bitmap join index cannot be created on an index-organized table or a temporary table.

- Every column in the bitmap join index must be present in one of the associated dimension tables. The joins in the bitmap index must form either a star or snowflake schema.

- Either primary key columns or unique constraints must be created on the columns that will be join columns in the bitmap join index.

- All the primary key columns of the dimension table must be part of the join criteria of the bitmap join index.

- All restrictions on normal bitmap indexes apply to bitmap join indexes.

- You cannot create a bitmap join index on an IOT.

Identifying Unused Indexes

Oracle8i introduced table-usage monitoring to help streamline the process of statistics collection. With Oracle9i, you can now also monitor the use of indexes within the database. Unused indexes are, of course, a waste of space, and also can cause performance problems, as Oracle is required to maintain the index each time the table associated with the index is involved in a DML operation.

To begin monitoring an index, you use the **alter index** command using the **monitoring usage** clause, as follows:

```
ALTER INDEX index_name MONITORING USAGE;
```

To stop monitoring an index, issue the **alter index** command again, this time using the **nomonitoring usage** clause, as follows:

```
ALTER INDEX index_name NOMONITORING USAGE;
```

While the index is in monitoring mode, you can use the V$OBJECT_USAGE view to determine whether the index has been used. Note that the view will show usage information only when queried by the index owner. The V$OBJECT_USAGE column USED can be queried. If the columns value is NO, then the index has not been used. If the columns value is YES, then the index has been used. This view also includes the columns START_MONITORING and END_MONITORING to indicate the time that monitoring was started and stopped on that index. The index name and its associated table name are provided by the INDEX_NAME and TABLE_NAME columns. Finally, the MONITORING column is provided to indicate if the index is currently being monitored. Any time the **alter table monitoring usage** command is issued, the V$OBJECT_USAGE row for that index will be reset. Here is an example of a query against this table:

```
SQL> select * from v$object_usage;
INDEX_NAME                          TABLE_NAME                        MON USE
------------------------------  -----------------------------   --- ---
START_MONITORING     END_MONITORING
------------------   ------------------
MY_BITMAP_INDEX                      TEST_DIM                     NO  NO
10/20/2001 00:01:42 10/20/2001 00:04:56
SYS_C002155                          EMP                          YES YES
10/20/2001 00:05:20
```

In this example, we see that there are two indexes. First, there is the MY_BITMAP_INDEX index, which was built on the TEST_DIM table. Because it is in the V$OBJECT_USAGE view, we know it was being monitored at one time. An index will not appear in V$OBJECT_USAGE unless it had been monitored at some point. We see, however, that MY_BITMAP_INDEX is not currently being monitored, and also that the USE column says NO, which indicates that the index was not used while it was being monitored.

Second, the SYS_C002155 index is listed. We see that it is currently being monitored from the YES in the MONITORING column. The YES in the USED column tells us that it has been used.

Cursor Sharing

Oracle9i offers several improvements involving *cursor sharing*. Cursor sharing allows an existing cursor to be reused by other sessions, reducing the overall time required for Oracle to parse the SQL statement. Several new features have been made in Oracle9*i* to make cursor sharing even more robust. The first involves the way that the cost-based optimizer (CBO) interacts with statements that contain bind variables.

In Oracle9*i*, when a statement contains a bind variable, the CBO will look at the values associated with those bind variables the first time the statement is executed. The optimizer will then use the value of the bind variables to determine the more efficient execution path. Oracle will use the same execution path for any subsequent execution of that SQL statement, regardless of the value of the bind variable in that statement. As a result, the operation might result in *safe* or *unsafe cursor sharing*.

If the literal in the **where** clause is such that changing it will not affect the execution plan of the query, then this is known as safe cursor sharing. An example would be if you had a list of patient names, with a unique identifier assigned to each patient. In that case, a statement such as this one

```
SELECT patient_name FROM patient WHERE patient_id=12345;
```

would be considered a safe cursor because the substitution of the 12345 for any other value would not result in a change to the execution plan. Oracle can determine whether a cursor is a safe cursor when it parses the cursor. It will look at the statistics gathered on the objects being accessed, as well as histograms to determine whether the cursor is safe.

An unsafe cursor is one in which the nature of the literal might cause a change to the execution plan if that literal's value should change. For example, say we query the PATIENT table again, this time looking for the last name Freeman:

```
SELECT patient_name FROM patient WHERE last_name='FREEMAN';
```

Assuming we have an index on the PATIENT table built on the LAST_NAME column, Oracle might or might not choose to use the index for this query. The problem is that, given that we execute the following query next,

```
SELECT patient_name FROM patient WHERE last_name='SMITH';
```

Oracle will use the same execution plan from the first query for this query. If it chose to use the index to resolve the first query, that index scan might be a bad idea in the second query. This is because there are likely to be few Freemans, but a number of Smiths. (Although, since I have five kids, there might well be a bunch of Freemans in there!)

Oracle9*i* allows you to instruct the optimizer to share only safe cursors through the use of the new **similar** value for the *cursor_sharing* parameter. The value **similar** will restrict cursor sharing to only those cursors that are deemed safe cursors. Thus, using **similar** will reduce the possible instability that can be introduced by setting *cursor_sharing* to **force**.

In association with the new *similar* parameter is the SQL hint **cursor_sharing_exact**, which will turn off cursor sharing, forcing the SQL statement to match a statement in the shared pool exactly for it to be reused. Also, you can use the **alter session** and **alter system** commands to alter the *cursor_sharing* parameters value.

Shared Server Improvements

Oracle9i has renamed the multi-threaded server (MTS) to *shared server*. The shared-server architecture increases the scalability of applications and the number of clients that can be simultaneously connected to the database. The shared server architecture also enables existing applications to scale up without making any changes to the application itself.

Several parameter names have been added and changed regarding the shared server. Oracle suggests that you use the new parameters in place of the deprecated ones. The new parameters and the old parameters they replace are as follows:

Old Parameter	New Parameter
mts_dispatchers	dispatchers
mts_max_dispatchers	max_dispatchers
mts_servers	shared_servers
mts_max_servers	max_shared_servers
mts_circuits	circuits
mts_sessions	shared_server_sessions

Also, Oracle has introduced a new view that you can use to monitor the shared server. This view is called V$SHARED_SERVER_MONITOR. The purpose of this view is to provide information to assist you in tuning the Oracle shared server. This view provides the following columns of information:

Column	Description
MAXIMUM_CONNECTIONS	The number in this column returns the largest number of virtual circuits that have been in use at one time since the instance started. You might need to increase the *circuits* parameter as this number approaches the value set for the *circuits*.

Column	Description
MAXIMUM_SESSIONS	The number in this column returns the largest number of shared server sessions that have been in use at one time since the instance started. You might need to increase the *shared_server_sessions* parameter as this number approaches the value set for the *shared_server_sessions*.
SERVERS_STARTED	The number in this column returns the total number of shared servers started since the instance started.
SERVERS_TERMINATED	The number in this column returns the total number of shared servers stopped by Oracle since the instance started.
SERVERS_HIGHWATER	The number in this column returns the largest number of shared server sessions that have been in use at one time since the instance started. You might need to increase the *max_shared_servers* parameter as this number approaches the value set for the *max_shared_servers*.

Additionally, Oracle has redesigned the connection protocols between the client process, the Oracle listener, and the dispatcher process, simplifying the process. This new *direct handoff* connection reduces network overhead and reduces the overall amount of network traffic required to create a connection between the client and the dispatcher process.

The dispatcher process has been improved, and network and database events are now handled using a common internal event model. This new event model reduces the overall CPU requirement of the dispatcher process and facilitates much more efficient networking.

Finally, you can use Oracle9i's OEM performance manager, part of OEM's performance pack, to monitor shared-server dispatchers, shared servers, and listeners. This product simplifies the management of shared servers through its GUI.

 NOTE
*Oracle9i databases running shared servers can support the **dbms_ldap** package. This was not the case in Oracle8i.*

Create Tablespace Default Changes

In Oracle9i, the **create tablespace** command defaults have been changed. First, when you create a tablespace in Oracle9i, it will be created as a locally managed tablespace, using the SYSTEM extent allocation method by default if the compatibility parameter is set to 9.0.0.0 or later.

Quiescing the Database

If you have ever tried to replace a PL/SQL package in a very busy database, then you know the frustration that you can experience because transactions have the package locked, keeping the DBA from changing the package. Other operations can suffer from locking problems, such as **alter table** or **alter index** commands or reorganizing or redefining a table. Of course, one solution is to shut down the database and restart it in restricted session. Unfortunately, this results in some undesirable effects:

- The memory caches are flushed.

- Users are booted off the system.

- Existing transactions might need to be killed.

- Startup and shutdown times might be long due to instance recovery.

Oracle9i offers a solution to these problems in the form of *a database-quiesced state*. When the database is put into quiesced state, all ongoing statements are allowed to complete, at which time the database is frozen. Also, when in quiesced state, all new non-DBA connections to the database are suspended, and the connection is not allowed to complete until the database is taken out of quiesce state.

To put the database in a quiesced state, issue this command:

```
ALTER SYSTEM QUIESCE RESTRICTED;
```

Once the SQL prompt returns, the database has been quiesced. Once you have completed your activities, you can take the database out of quiesced mode by issuing the following command:

```
ALTER SYSTEM UNQUIESCE;
```

To be able to use the databased-quiesced functionality, you must have resource manager enabled, and it must have been enabled since the last system startup. If you stop and start the resource manager between database cycles, you will not be able to quiesce the database until you have shut down the database and restarted it with the resource manager running. If this requirement is not met, any attempt to quiesce the database will result in an Oracle error.

Finally, if you perform a backup while the database is in a quiesced state, then that backup is considered to be an inconsistent backup. Thus, backing up an open database in a quiesce state still requires hot backups, and this mode cannot be used to suspend the database to break disk mirrors for backup purposes.

CHAPTER
3

New Oracle9i Availability and Recoverability Features

- Oracle9i flashback query feature
- Oracle9i LogMiner enhancements
- New instance failure recovery features
- New RMAN 9i features
- Oracle9i data guard

ne of the Oracle database hallmarks has been recoverability. Also, Oracle has long touted features that improve the availability of the Oracle RDBMS. In Oracle9i many of the recoverability and availability features have been improved, as well as new features introduced that further solidify Oracle's lead in recoverability and availability functionality. In this chapter we will look at these new features so you can learn how to create a bullet-proof Oracle9i database installation.

Oracle9i Flashback Query

In this section, we will look at a new feature introduced in Oracle9i—flashback query. We will first discuss what it is, and then we will look at setting up the database so you can use this feature, and we will cover how to actually use it. Following that, we will detail some of the restrictions and requirements associated with flashback queries.

What Is Oracle9i Flashback Query?

How many times have you wanted to see what a table looked like yesterday at noon? Perhaps you want to run some reports based on how data in the database looked yesterday at 6:00 A.M. Maybe an application error has caused sensitive data to be deleted and you need to get that data back. Until now, if you wanted to do any of these things, about the only hope you had was to recover a backup from a point before the time you were interested in. You could then roll forward the database to the point you were interested in. Alternatively, you could use LogMiner to extract the missing data if possible. For this very reason, some companies have reporting systems that are designed to be a day or two behind. Wouldn't it be nice if you could just log into the database and tell the database that you want to see the data as it looked yesterday at noon?

With Oracle9i's flashback query, you can, within certain constraints, query data as it looked at a specific date and time or SCN. Flashback query takes advantage of Oracle's multi-version read-consistency model to allow you to determine the time and date or SCN number for the data you wish to view. Having done this, any SQL query that is subsequently issued will return results that reflect that point. The applications of this feature are numerous, from reporting to recovering lost data, data analysis, modeling, and a number of other applications.

Sounds pretty cool, doesn't it? Let's look at how we use this feature!

Setting Up the Database to Use Oracle9i's Flashback Query

Before users can take advantage of flashback queries, some system setup is required. First, the database is using automated UNDO management. The *undo_retention* parameter must be set and the UNDO tablespace must be large enough so that undo generated during the period we want to query will not be overwritten. Of course, the size requirement of the UNDO tablespace is directly related to the number and size of transactions that occur on the database. If rollback segments, rather than an UNDO tablespace, are in use, then the rollback segments must be large enough so they will contain the undo required to reconstruct the view of the object at the time you establish for the flashback query.

Having set up the automated UNDO requirements or the rollback segments, you must grant the **execute** privilege on the **dbms_flashback** package to those users and roles that will need to have the ability to use the flashback query feature, as seen in this example:

```
GRANT EXECUTE ON dbms_flashback TO robert;
```

Using Oracle9i's Flashback Query Feature

Having set up the database to use flashback query, we will look at how to use the feature. First, we will look at the **dbms_flashback** package, followed by examples of using the flashback query feature in Oracle9i.

dbms_flashback Package

The principle around the feature is the use of the **dbms_flashback** package that is new in Oracle9i. This package contains several subprograms, including the following (we will provide examples shortly):

- **dbms_flashback.enable_at_time**   This subprogram allows you to define the time that you want to see the query output represent. Thus, if I wanted to query the EMP table as it looked at 11 A.M., I would use this subprogram.

- **dbms_flashback.enable_at_system_change_number**   This subprogram allows you to define the SCN that you want to see the query output represent. Thus, if I wanted a query against the EMP table to be consistent with SCN 12345, I would use this subprogram to enable flashback query, defining 12345 as the SCN.

- **dbms_flashback.disable**   This subprogram disables the flashback query feature.

- **dbms_flashback.get_system_change_number**   This subprogram allows you to get the current system change number. The SCN is returned as a NUMBER.

Doing Flashback Queries

Query flashback is used on a session basis, as opposed to database-wide. The general order of operations when using flashback query is to enable flashback query for a given session using either the **dbms_flashback.enable_at_time** or the **dbms_flashback.enable_at_system_change_number** subprogram. Having executed one of these subprograms, all queries will return rows as they looked at the defined time. Once you have completed the queries that you want to run, you issue the **dbms_flashback.disable** subprogram to disable flashback query for your session.

Here is an example of issuing a flashback query. In this case, we just finished giving our employees across-the-board raises, and we want to know what the old average salary was before. To get this information, we would issue the following query:

```
EXEC DBMS_FLASHBACK.ENABLE_AT_TIME( TIMESTAMP '2001-09-23 23:52:25');
SELECT avg(sal) FROM emp;
EXEC DBMS_FLASHBACK.DISABLE;
```

In this example, notice that we cast the time/date in the exec dbms_flashback. **enable_at_time** procedure with the **timestamp** constructor. We could also have used the **to_timestamp** function, like this:

```
EXEC DBMS_FLASHBACK.ENABLE_AT_TIME( TO_TIMESTAMP( '2001-09-23
  23:52:25','YYYY-MM-DD HH24:MI:SS');
```

Also, you should know that using the SCN is a more accurate way of defining the flashback point than time is. Here is an example of the use of flashback queries that involves the use of the system SCN. We include an example of using the time to define the flashback query period, as well:

```
-- First we drop and recreate the table my_table

SQL> DROP TABLE my_table;
Table dropped.

SQL> CREATE TABLE my_table (id  NUMBER, time_entered  DATE,
scn_number NUMBER);
Table created.

-- To avoid certain problems with this example, wait about 2 minutes between creating the
-- table and adding records to it.
-- Now, create some records to test with
SQL> INSERT INTO my_table VALUES (1, SYSDATE,
DBMS_FLASHBACK.GET_SYSTEM_CHANGE_NUMBER);
1 row created.
```

```
SQL> INSERT INTO my_table VALUES (2, SYSDATE,
DBMS_FLASHBACK.GET_SYSTEM_CHANGE_NUMBER);
1 row created.

SQL> INSERT INTO my_table VALUES (3, SYSDATE,
DBMS_FLASHBACK.GET_SYSTEM_CHANGE_NUMBER);
1 row created.

SQL> INSERT INTO my_table VALUES (4, SYSDATE,
DBMS_FLASHBACK.GET_SYSTEM_CHANGE_NUMBER);
1 row created.

-- commit the insert
SQL> COMMIT;
Commit complete.

-- Select all records from the table
SQL> SELECT id, TO_CHAR(time_entered,'mm/dd/yyyy hh24:mi:ss'),
scn_number FROM my_table;

        ID TO_CHAR(TIME_ENTERE SCN_NUMBER
---------- ------------------- ----------
         1 09/23/2001 23:52:00     850037
         2 09/23/2001 23:52:10     850038
         3 09/23/2001 23:52:20     850039
         4 09/23/2001 23:52:30     850040

SQL> INSERT INTO my_table VALUES (5, SYSDATE,
DBMS_FLASHBACK.GET_SYSTEM_CHANGE_NUMBER);
1 row created.

SQL> commit;
Commit complete.

-- let's see the SCN of the new record.
SQL> SELECT id, TO_CHAR(time_entered,'mm/dd/yyyy hh24:mi:ss'),scn_number
FROM my_table;

        ID TO_CHAR(TIME_ENTERE SCN_NUMBER
---------- ------------------- ----------
         1 09/23/2001 23:52:00     850037
         2 09/23/2001 23:52:10     850038
         3 09/23/2001 23:52:20     850039
         4 09/23/2001 23:52:30     850040
         5 09/23/2001 23:52:45     850047

-- Now, we will tell Oracle that we want to see only records from
-- SCN 850047 and before.
-- This would exclude the last record we entered in this case.
SQL> EXEC DBMS_FLASHBACK.ENABLE_AT_SYSTEM_CHANGE_NUMBER(850047);
PL/SQL procedure successfully completed.
```

```
-- Query my_table and we find the last record is not displayed,
-- as we would expect.
SQL> SELECT id, TO_CHAR(time_entered,'mm/dd/yyyy hh24:mi:ss'),
scn_number FROM my_table;
        ID TO_CHAR(TIME_ENTERE SCN_NUMBER
---------- ------------------- ----------
         1 09/23/2001 23:52:00     850037
         2 09/23/2001 23:52:10     850038
         3 09/23/2001 23:52:20     850039
         4 09/23/2001 23:52:30     850040

SQL> EXEC DBMS_FLASHBACK.DISABLE;

SQL>EXEC DBMS_FLASHBACK.ENABLE_AT_TIME( TIMESTAMP '2001-09-23 23:52:45');

SQL> SELECT id, TO_CHAR(time_entered,'mm/dd/yyyy hh24:mi:ss'),
scn_number FROM my_table;
        ID TO_CHAR(TIME_ENTERE SCN_NUMBER
---------- ------------------- ----------
         1 09/23/2001 23:52:10     850037
         2 09/23/2001 23:52:20     850038
         3 09/23/2001 23:52:30     850039
         4 09/23/2001 23:52:40     850040
```

Using Flashback with the Export Utility

Oracle has added two parameters to the EXP utility to allow you to do your export using the new flashback query options. These new parameters are *flashback_scn* and *flashback_time*. Simply set one of these command-line parameters to cause the EXP utility to export the database as it looked at the flashback point. If Oracle is unable to generate an export consistent with the flashback request, then the export will fail. Here is an example of exporting a database using the flashback query option:

```
exp system/manager full=y file=yesterday.dmp flashback_time='01-SEP-2001'
```

Oracle9i LogMiner Enhancements

Several new features have been introduced for LogMiner in Oracle9i. The following bulleted list contains a summary. Note that some of the features are backward compatible to redo logs generated by Oracle8 and later. LogMiner is not compatible with Oracle7 redo logs. Here is a list of the Oracle9i enhancements:

- The ability to translate DML statements that are associated with clusters
- Support for database DDL statements

- Extracting the dictionary to the redo logs or using the online data dictionary

- The ability to detect a stale dictionary

- The ability to skip redo log corruption that might occur in the redo logs

- The ability to display only committed transactions

In this section, we will look at each of these new features and see how they can benefit you. We will also look at some of the continuing restrictions for LogMiner in Oracle9i.

Translate DML Statements That Are Associated with Clusters

Oracle9i LogMiner now supports all DML operations that operate against Clusters. This allows you to reconstruct DML redo and undo that has occurred on index clusters.

Support for Database DDL Statements

Previously, Oracle LogMiner did not provide any usable output associated with DDL statements, rather, it was represented in the form of recursive SQL that occurred as a result of the DDL operation. Now, in Oracle9i, LogMiner will provide both the DDL statement and the user who issued the DDL statement.

When a DDL operation is mined from a redo log, the V$LOGMNR_CONTENTS column OPERATION will contain the value DDL, and the SQL_REDO column will contain the actual DDL statement that was executed. Note that no undo will be displayed for DDL statements. Here is an example of the output from V$LOGMNR_ CONTENTS for a **create table** statement that was executed.

```
SELECT username, operation, sql_redo
FROM v$logmnr_contents
WHERE operation='DDL';

USERNAME    OPERATION SQL_REDO
----------  --------- ----------------------------------------
SYSTEM      DDL         create table test_table (id number);
```

Extracting the Dictionary to the Redo Logs, or Using the Online Data Dictionary

Previously with LogMiner, you had to create a dictionary file. The dictionary file was used to translate the object IDs that were stored in the redo logs into real object names. This made the results of a log-mining session much easier to read because the actual name of the user and the object would appear in the LogMiner results, as opposed to object and user IDs, which would appear if you did not use a dictionary.

There are certain limitations with regard to the use of the dictionary. Primary is that the dictionary could quickly become stale as objects and users are added or removed from the database. Thus, there is a maintenance requirement that has to be considered when using dictionary files.

Now, in Oracle9i, LogMiner can store data-dictionary information in the redo logs. Alternatively, you can choose to mine the redo logs using the online data dictionary. Let's look at each of these options a little closer.

Extracting Database Information to the Redo Logs

To store the database information in the redo logs, rather than to a dictionary file, the database must first be in ARCHIVELOG mode. The process of storing the database dictionary information to the redo logs can be database intensive. The initial process will generate a significant amount of redo when it is first enabled. You can expect that, at a minimum, some 12M of redo will be generated when the option is first enabled, and probably more. As a result, depending on the size of your online redo logs, you might experience a large number of redo log switches initially, and LGWR will be busier than usual. All this additional processing will settle down after the initial writing of the required redo to the redo logs has completed.

To begin the process of writing dictionary information to the redo logs, you use the **dbms_logmnr_d.build** procedure, just as you would if you were going to build a dictionary file. When calling the package, you will use the option **dbms_logmnr_ d.store_in_redo_logs** to begin the build-out process to the redo logs. Here is an example of this call:

```
EXEC DBMS_LOGMNR_D.BUILD(options=>DBMS_LOGMNR_D.STORE_IN_REDO_LOGS);
```

When you are ready to mine logs, you will need to use the **dict_from_redo_logs** option of the **dbms_logmnr.start_logmnr** procedure, as seen here:

```
EXEC DBMS_LOGMNR.START_LOGMNR(OPTIONS=>DBMS_LOGMNR.DICT_FROM_REDO_LOGS);
```

Using the Online Data Dictionary When Mining Redo Logs

Rather than use a dictionary file or the redo logs, Oracle9i offers the ability to use the existing online dictionary to interpret redo log contents. This is handy if you want to quickly review the contents of a recent redo log. When you are ready to mine redo logs, you will need to use the option **dict_from_online_catalog** in the **dbms_logmnr.start_logmnr** procedure, as seen here:

```
EXEC DBMS_LOGMNR.START_LOGMNR(OPTIONS=>DBMS_LOGMNR.DICT_FROM_ONLINE_CATALOG);
```

There is no need to use the **dbms_logmnr_d** procedure if you are going to use
the data dictionary as the source for your LogMiner dictionary source.

Automated Dictionary Updates and Staleness Tracking

Oracle9i's LogMiner now provides the ability to do automated dictionary updates.
This allows you to keep the dictionary current after DDL is executed on the database.
Also, Oracle9i provides the ability to determine whether the dictionary is stale. Let's
look at these two options.

Automated Dictionary Updates

One of the problems with LogMiner before Oracle9i was that the dictionary file was
static. That is, it represented the state of the database data dictionary at a specific
time, and was not updated to reflect changes in the database data dictionary unless
it was manually rebuilt. Oracle9i eliminates this problem with the dictionary file by
introducing the ability for Oracle to keep the dictionary file updated when DDL
statements occur.

To take advantage of this feature, use the **dbms_logmnr.ddl_dict_track** option of
the **dbms_logmnr.start_logmnr** package. You can also use the **no_dict_reset_onselect**
option of the **dbms_logmnr.start_logminer** procedure to prevent the dictionary from
being reloaded at the beginning of every **select** operation on the V$LOGMNR_CONTENTS
view. This reduces the overhead associated with the refresh operation that would
otherwise occur.

Selecting Multiple Options   Now that we have introduced you to the
no_dict_reset_onselect and **dbms_logmnr.ddl_dict_track** options, you might be
wondering how you can call multiple options from the **dbms_logmnr.start_logmnr**
package at the same time. To do so, simply use the + character between each
option. Here is an example of this, using **no_dict_reset_onselect** and **no_dict_reset_
onselect**, and of using the redo logs as the dictionary source.

```
EXEC DBMS_LOGMNR.START_LOGMNR(OPTIONS=>DBMS_LOGMNR.DICT_FROM_REDO_LOGS+
NO_DICT_RESET_ONSELECT+ NO_DICT_RESET_ONSELECT);
```

Detecting Data-Dictionary Staleness

Previous to Oracle9i, LogMiner could not detect whether the dictionary file was
stale. In Oracle9i, redo records now include a value for the object version

number. This number changes any time the object itself changes. Thus, it's a simple affair for Oracle to compare the two version numbers and detect whether the dictionary information is current or not.

Skipping Redo Log Corruption

LogMiner will stop mining a log if it reaches some point of corruption in the redo log data stream. LogMiner in Oracle9i provides the ability to skip redo log corruption through the use of the **skip_corruption** option of the **start_logmnr** procedure. If corruption is encountered, it is noted in the V$LOGMNR_CONTENTS view. The column INFO will contain a message indicating that corruption had been encountered. Additional information is also presented indicating how many redo blocks were skipped.

Ability to Display Only Committed Transactions

Often, if we are using LogMiner to recover specific transactions, we really want only those transactions that were committed to be displayed. In other words, we don't want to see the DML for those transactions that were rolled back or incomplete. This makes it easier to find the actual transactions to recover, and can eliminate the presence of unneeded, uncommitted DML. To set up LogMiner to return only committed transactions, use the option **committed_data_only** when calling the procedure **dbms_logmnr.start_logmnr**, as shown here:

```
EXEC DBMS_LOGMNR.START_LOGMNR(OPTIONS=>DBMS_LOGMNR.COMMITTED_DATA_ONLY);
```

Use of this option will cause the rows returned in the V$LOGMNR_CONTENTS view to be grouped by transaction identifier, and only those rows with committed transactions will be returned. Also, the rows being returned will be returned in SCN commit order.

Oracle9i LogMiner Restrictions

In Oralce9i, some restrictions still remain when using LogMiner. The following are not supported:

- LONG and LOB data types
- Oracle object features (collections, types, or REFs)
- Index-organized table operations
- Operations involving encrypted data

New Instance Failure Recovery Features

"The system is down." No four words make a DBA cringe more. Unplanned systems outages are a big problem for systems that demand constant uptime. The enterprise depends on your system, still, failures will occur. To help the DBA deal with this eventuality, Oracle9i has added some new features to try to lessen the impact of unscheduled outages to your enterprise. These new features include methods of reducing crash and instance recovery times and fast-start time-based recovery (FSTBR). Let's look at each of these new features next.

Reducing Crash and Instance Recovery Times

If you are unfortunate enough to have an unscheduled systems crash, hopefully you will be fortunate enough that it's a crash that doesn't require any media recovery. In this case, crash or instance recovery will be all that is required, and Oracle has added a few new features to try to speed this up for you.

Now, when performing crash or instance recovery, Oracle will make two passes through the online redo logs. During the first pass, Oracle will quickly scan the redo log blocks, and determine which of those blocks will need to be recovered and which will not. This first pass is very fast because only the redo logs are read from during this pass. The database datafiles are not read at this point. Since this is sequential access, this is a very fast operation, and eliminating the initial read of the datafiles eliminates costly random IOs.

As the redo logs are read, those redo blocks that need to be recovered will be marked for recovery. Once Oracle has processed the first sweep through the redo log, it will then sweep through the redo log again, this time processing only the redo that needs to be applied to the Oracle data blocks to bring them to a consistent state. Once this process is complete, the checkpoint SCN is incremented and the recovery is complete.

Fast Start Time–Based Recovery

If you have a service level agreement (SLA) that specifies a mean time to recover (MTTR) the database associated with that SLA, then there needs to be some way of trying to limit the time required to recover the database during crash or instance recovery. Previously, DBAs had to set various parameters (*log_checkpoint_interval*, *log_checkpoint_timeout*, *fast_start_io_target*, and *db_block_max_dirty_target*) to try to control the overall MTTR from an instance or database crash. Setting these parameters tended to be very inexact, and it was hard to really translate them into a target MTTR.

It is for the purpose of being able to define a target MTTR that Oracle9i offers *Fast Start Time–Based Recovery (FSTBR)*. With FSTBR, the DBA defines a desired MTTR for the database in seconds with the parameter *fast_start_mttr_target*. Having set the *fast_start_mttr_target* parameter, Oracle will configure internal database settings to try to maintain this requirement. Note that this parameter provides only an estimated MTTR value, and that several factors such as IO contention can cause the actual recovery time to extend beyond the requested MTTR.

You can set the *fast_start_mttr_target* value anywhere from 0 to 3600 seconds (0 disables the feature, but other parameters such as *log_checkpoint_interval* are still in effect). Note that the lower the value, the more often the database will be checkpointing, which can cause performance issues. So, there is a balancing act that must occur between performance and establishing a reasonable MTTR. Because this parameter is dynamic in nature, you can alter it with the database still operating as you tune this performance/MTTR balance.

The *fast_start_mttr_target* is calculated based on a number of assumptions that Oracle9i makes when it first opens the database. However, the value is dynamic and adaptive, and it will be adjusted over time as the database is used. Therefore, the longer the database is up and running, the better Oracle will be at establishing checkpoint rates that will maintain the requested MTTR.

Oracle9i maintains this target MTTR by continuously checkpointing the database, as required, and advancing the checkpoint counter that indicates the position in the redo log that was last checkpointed. Oracle maintains the checkpointing operation so that it will write out changed data at a rate that maintains the requested MTTR. During instance or crash recovery, Oracle9i will start recovering the database beginning at the checkpoint counter address, rather than at the point of the last normal checkpoint (such as occurs with redo log switches), thus reducing the overall time required to perform recovery.

Fast Start Time–Based, Recovery-Related Parameter Changes

With the introduction of FSTBR, some parameter changes have been affected. The following table indicates the changes that have occurred:

Parameter Name	Change in 9i
db_block_max_dirty_target	This parameter is now obsolete.
fast_start_io_target	If set, overrides values calculated by setting *fast_start_mttr_target*.
log_checkpoint_interval	If set, overrides values calculated by setting *fast_start_mttr_target*.
log_checkpoint_timeout	Unchanged.

FSTBR-Related View Changes

The V$INSTANCE_RECOVERY view has changed in Oracle9i to accommodate the new functionality of FSTBR. New columns include

- **TARGET_MTTR**   The current setting of the *fast_start_mttr_target* parameter value. This might not always be the same as the requested parameter value.

- **ESTIMATED_MTTR**   The current estimate for database MTTR

- **CKPT_BLOCK_WRITES**   The number of blocks written by checkpoint writes to try to maintain the target MTTR

New RMAN Oracle9i Features

RMAN is Oracle's backup and recovery facility. Several changes and new features have been made in Oracle9i's version of RMAN. In this section, we will discuss those changes. First, we will look at features related to management of the RMAN product itself. Second, we will look at changes that relate to backups in RMAN. Finally, we will look at changes and new features for the recovery of databases with RMAN in Oracle9i.

New and Changed Management Features

RMAN has numerous management and reporting commands, such as **list** and **report**, among other commands. Now, with Oracle9i, new commands are introduced, such as the **show** command. Other changes to RMAN include removal of the need for the **run** command in most cases and automatic device allocation. Let's look at the new and changed management features of RMAN in Oracle9i.

Run Command Changes

In previous versions of Oracle9i, **backup**, **restore**, **allocate channel**, and certain other commands had to be enclosed within the confines of the **run** command. This is no longer the case in Orace9i, thus, in most cases, the **run** command is no longer required.

Configure Command

The new **configure** command is used to configure default (or persistent) configuration settings for a specific channel or all channels. Ultimately, this allows the DBA to back up the database by simply using the **backup database** command. Thus, with the database properly configured, you need not issue the **allocate channel** command in many cases. Let's look more at the **configure** command and its new features.

Configure channel Command   Using the **configure channel** command, you can define a specific channel as going to DISK or SBT (tape). You can also define the format of the backup pieces created through that channel and a number of other options. This command also allows you not to include the **allocate channel** command in your backup and recovery commands, as long as you want to use the default values for the given channel allocated to the **backup** or **recover** command (see the "Automatic Channel Allocation" section, later in the chapter, for more on this feature).

Here is an example of the use of the **configure channel** command:

```
CONFIGURE CHANNEL 1 DEVICE TYPE DISK
FORMAT 'd:\oracle\backups\Backup_%t_%u';
```

This particular command defines default values for channel 1. It is assigned to a disk, and the format string defines the name and location of the backup piece. Note that there are several **format** substitution variables available for use. These can be found in the *Oracle Recovery Manager Reference Manual*. If we wanted to define a default value for all channels that might be allocated, the command would look like this:

```
CONFIGURE CHANNEL DEVICE TYPE DISK
FORMAT 'd:\oracle\backups\Backup_%t_%u' MAXPIECESIZE 500M;
```

In this case, all channels that were allocated would, by default, be to disk. In this case, we have also included the *maxpiecesize* parameter, indicating that no one piece of the backup set should exceed 500M.

Configure controlfile Command   The introduction of the **configure** command also includes the capability to configure automated control file backups. When enabled, these automated control file backups will occur any time a **backup** or **copy** command is issued either from the RMAN prompt or within a **run** command block. Within the **run** block, the control file backup will occur only after the last **backup** command in the block has completed. Here is an example of enabling this default using the **configure** command:

```
CONFIGURE CONTROLFILE AUTOBACKUP ON;
```

Another new feature in Oracle9i is the ability to recover the control file backup that was made as the result of an auto backup. You can use the **restore controlfile from autobackup** command. This allows you to restore the control file without a repository.

You can use the **format** clause to define the format of the control file backup, but it must include the %F format in the format string. To define the format for the filename, use the **configure controlfile autobackup** command with the **format** clause, as shown here:

```
CONFIGURE CONTROLFILE AUTOBACKUP FORMAT FOR DEVICE TYPE DISK TO
d:\oracle\backup\controlfile\%F%t.backup';
```

Configure default device type Command   Along with configuration of default channels, you can also configure default devices with the **configure default device type** command. This device configuration will be used when allowing RMAN to automatically allocate a channel (see "Automatic Channel Allocation," later in the chapter).

For example, if we wanted to define the tape drive as the default device, then we would issue the following command:

```
CONFIGURE DEFAULT DEVICE TYPE TO SBT;
```

After this command completes, all automated device allocation will be to tape.

Configure device type...parallelism Command   Along with default device types, you can also define a default level of parallelism that should be applied for any automatic device allocation. The **configure device type...parallelism** command can be used to set the default level of parallelism. Here is an example of using this command that will cause any auto-allocated operation to occur using a parallelism of five:

```
CONFIGURE DEVICE TYPE DISK PARALLELISM 5;
```

Other configure Commands   Other RMAN defaults can be performed with the **configure** command. This includes the following:

- **configure backup copies**   Allows you to specify the creation of identical copies of backup sets.

- **configure exclude**   Allows you to, by default, exclude tablespaces from whole database backups. This allows you to prevent unnecessary backups of read-only or offline tablespaces.

- **configure snapshot controlfile**   Configures the default snapshot control filename.

- **configure auxname**   Sets the default AUXNAME location.

Report and list Command Enhancements

Oracle9i has enhanced both the **report** and **list** commands. In this section, we will look at those enhancements.

Report Command Enhancements   The **report** command has had two enhancements. Both the **report obsolete** and the **report need backup** commands now have been enhanced to take advantage of Oracle9i's new backup retention policies. The **report obsolete** will now report on backups that are obsolete, based on the configured retention policy. This command can be used with the **delete obsolete** command to make management of expired backups much easier.

The **report need backup** command has been enhanced to report on datafiles that have not been backed up within the defined retention policy period. Thus, if the retention policy period was seven days, you could issue a **report need backup** command and RMAN would report all datafiles that were backed up more than seven days ago.

List Command Enhancements   The **list** command now allows two different output orientations. The output can be displayed by backup set or by datafile. The default is **list backup...by backup set**, which will list backups by backup set (this is the old behavior). An additional option **list backup...by file** lists each datafile, and then its associated backup sets. A further option, **list backup...by backup summary** provides a summary of database backup sets.

Command Retooling

Several RMAN commands (**list**, **crosscheck**, **delete**, **expired**, and **change**) have been changed to make them easier to use. Their syntax has been standardized, and the output formats and status codes are more common. However, the old syntax formats have been retained for backward compatibility.

Show Command

The new **show** command displays the current settings defined with the new **configure** commands. You can use the **show** command to display information on the following:

- The retention policy
- The default exclude settings
- The datafile and archive log backup copy settings
- The default device type that had been configured for automated backups
- Channels to be used for automated backup and restore
- Name of the snapshot control file

You can also show all the information reported by the **show** command. Here is an example of the use of the **show** command:

```
RMAN> SHOW ALL;

RMAN configuration parameters are:
CONFIGURE RETENTION POLICY TO REDUNDANCY 1; # default
CONFIGURE BACKUP OPTIMIZATION OFF; # default
CONFIGURE DEFAULT DEVICE TYPE TO DISK; # default
CONFIGURE CONTROLFILE AUTOBACKUP ON;
CONFIGURE CONTROLFILE AUTOBACKUP FORMAT FOR DEVICE TYPE DISK TO '%F'; # default
CONFIGURE DEVICE TYPE DISK PARALLELISM 1; # default
CONFIGURE DATAFILE BACKUP COPIES FOR DEVICE TYPE DISK TO 1; # default
CONFIGURE ARCHIVELOG BACKUP COPIES FOR DEVICE TYPE DISK TO 1; # default
CONFIGURE CHANNEL 1 DEVICE TYPE DISK FORMAT   '/ora01/oracle/admin/test8i/backup
/backup_%t_%u' MAXPIECESIZE 500 M;
CONFIGURE MAXSETSIZE TO UNLIMITED; # default
CONFIGURE SNAPSHOT CONTROLFILE NAME TO '/ora01/oracle/product/9.0.0.0/dbs/snapcf
_test8i.f'; # default
```

Miscellaneous Enhancements

RMAN supports Oracle9*i*'s new multiple-block-size support features. Datafiles of differing block sizes will be put into separate backup sets. Also, RMAN supports Oracle-managed datafiles. When recovering Oracle databases, RMAN will restore the datafiles as OMF datafiles. Also, you no longer need to use the *nocatalog* parameter when starting RMAN, as this is the default mode.

New and Changed Backup Features

Several new backup features and enhancements are introduced in RMAN with Oracle9*i*. These includes backup file optimization, setting backup retention policies, and restartable backups. We will cover backups of archived redo logs as part of one backup operation. Finally, we will look at backing up backup sets and archive log backup enhancements.

Automatic Channel Allocation

We have already discussed the **configure** command and how it is used to define the defaults that will be used by the **allocate** command. This essentially allows you to issue the **backup**, **restore**, and **copy** commands without first issuing an **allocate channel** command. Automated channel allocation features also apply to the allocation of maintenance channels.

When a channel is automatically allocated, it takes a default name of either *ora_sbt_tape_n* or *ora_disk_n*, depending on whether the channel is going to tape or disk. The default maintenance channel is called *ora_maint_disk_n* or *ora_maint_sbt_tape_n*, depending on its destination.

Backup File Optimization

You can reduce overall backup times of your database when you choose not to back up your read-only or offline tablespaces all the time. It used to be a rather tedious task to track these tablespaces to when they were last backed up. In Oracle9i, RMAN offers a new feature—Backup File Optimization (BFO).

With BFO, if RMAN is about to back up a file, and the file has already been backed up by the same device type, the RMAM will skip the backup of that file. This includes both data files and archived redo logs backed up by RMAN. Oracle determines whether the file has changed by comparing the datafile to the header of the backed up datafile. If they match, the file is not backed up.

Before RMAN decides to skip a given datafile, it will determine whether the datafile backup that is available meets the established retention policy (see more on setting a retention policy in the "Configuring Retention Policies Command" section). If the latest backup violates the retention policy, then RMAN will back up the datafile anyway.

There might be cases when you want to back up all tablespaces. In this case, simply use the **force** option of the **backup** command. Use of this option will cause Oracle to back up all datafiles and archived redo logs of the database regarding backup file optimization.

To enable the RMAN optimization feature, use the **configure** command with the **backup optimization** keywords The following examples show you how to use this command:

```
CONFIGURE BACKUP OPTIMIZATION ON;
CONFIGURE BACKUP OPTIMIZATION OFF;
```

The first example enables backup optimization. The second command shown in the previous example shows how to disable optimization.

Configuring Retention Policies Command

When making backups, it's a good idea to define how long you want to keep a given backup set. The policy that revolves around how long backup sets are kept is called a *retention policy*. In Oracle9i, RMAN allows you to define a retention policy regarding backup sets. There are two types of retention policies available in RMAN:

- Recovery window
- Redundancy

These policies are mutually exclusive of each other, and only one policy can be defined at a time. Policies are established with the **configure retention policy** command. Let's look at these different retention policies.

NOTE
Media manager retention policies can cause havoc if they are not properly synchronized with RMAN retention policies! For example, when using optimization, you could have your media manager software remove a backup, and RMAN would not know about it. This might cause the database to be unrecoverable.

Recovery Window Retention Policies   The recovery window retention policy is used to ensure that a backup is available that will facilitate a recovery within the defined time window. For example, if the recovery window is set to seven days, then no backup will be reported as obsolete unless it's older than the defined recovery window retention time.

To set a recovery window retention policy, use the **configure retention policy** command, as shown in the following example:

 CONFIGURE RETENTION POLICY TO RECOVERY WINDOW OF 7 DAYS;

In this case, we have configured a retention policy of seven days. Only backups older than seven days will be reported as obsolete when the **delete obsolete** command is executed. We will discuss the **delete obsolete** command later in this section.

NOTE
If the control_file_record_keep_time database parameter value is less than the time set for the retention policy, you will need to use a recovery catalog.

Redundancy Retention Policies   The redundancy retention policy defines a fixed number of backups that need to be retained by RMAN. If there is a number of backups later than the number defined by the retention policy, then those backups can be deleted using the **delete obsolete** command, which we will discuss in the next section.

To set a redundancy retention policy, use the **configure retention policy** command, as shown here:

 CONFIGURE RETENTION POLICY TO REDUNDANCY 7;

Be careful when choosing your retention policies. While the redundancy policy will work fine if you are sure you will do just a certain number of backups per day, it is possible that you could easily lose backups that you don't intend to if you should back up your database multiple times on the same day (say, for example, because you just upgraded the database). Generally, a recovery window retention policy is best for production databases to assure you can recover to the time you want. Redundancy policies might be more appropriate for test and development environments, in which backup space might be at a premium.

Remove the Retention Policy   If you define a policy and you wish to remove it, you can issue the **configure retention policy** command. To remove the existing retention policy, simply issue the command

 CONFIGURE RETENTION POLICY TO NONE;

Optionally, you can return the retention policy to the default policy, which is one day. To do this, issue the command

CONFIGURE RETENTION POLICY TO DEFAULT;

Delete obsolete Command
The new **rman delete obsolete** command is used in conjunction with the defined retention policy to remove obsolete backups. This example will remove all backups that are obsolete based on the currently existing policy:

DELETE OBSOLETE;

The **delete obsolete** command also can take parameters to define a recovery window or backup redundancy that is different from the existing policy. If your default recovery window is seven days and you want to remove backups that are five days old, then you could issue this command:

DELETE OBSOLETE RECOVERY WINDOW OF 5 DAYS;

Also, the **delete obsolete** command provides a method of removing orphaned backups that were created from a different incarnation of the database. An example of this command would look like this:

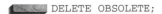 DELETE OBSOLETE ORPHAN;

Keep Clause of the backup Command
You can choose to retain an RMAN backup for a period of time longer than called for by the defined retention policy. This is facilitated through the **keep** clause of the **backup** command. The **keep** clause allows you to use the **until time** keywords to

define a time stamp that indicates the amount of time to keep the backup, or you can indicate to keep the backup indefinitely with the **keep forever** clause.

Restartable Backups

There were hints that this feature would arrive back in the Oracle8 days. When certain RMAN operations would fail, the error messages would indicate that the error was retryable, which it was not. Now, in Oracle9*i*, you can restart a backup that has failed. When you restart the backup, Oracle will proceed to complete the backup. All datafiles not backed up during the failed backup, and any datafile with an incomplete backup, will be backed up. All datafiles successfully backed up will be skipped.

In the event of a failed backup, simply use the **not backed up since time** option of the **backup** command to indicate to RMAN that you wish to restart a backup. When the backup begins, all datafiles not backed up successfully since the time indicated will be backed up. Here is an example of restarting a backup that failed, perhaps the previous night:

```
BACKUP DATABASE NOT BACKED UP SINCE TIME '01-DEC-2001 05:00:00';
```

> **NOTE**
> *If you do not include the **since time** keywords, then only datafiles that have never been backed up will be backed up.*

Backing Up Archived Redo Logs and the Database in One Operation

Now, RMAN allows you to back up your datafiles and archived redo log files in one operation. This feature is supported through the new **plus archivelog** keywords of the **backup** command. An example of this command is shown in the following example:

```
BACKUP DATABASE PLUS ARCHIVELOG;
```

As you would expect, this command will first back up the database. Having backed up the database, RMAN will force a log switch, and back up all the archived redo logs. Oracle will then proceed to do the backup. RMAN will then force another log switch and back up the remaining archived redo logs.

Backing Up Backup Sets

Sounds terribly redundant, doesn't it? Well, Oracle9*i* allows you to back up a backup set to a different device. For example, you might back up your database to disk (because it's faster perhaps and allows for a faster recovery). You might subsequently want to back up that backup set to tape for longer-term storage. In this case, you can use the **backup** command using the new BACKUPSET parameter.

When you back up a backup set, the backup set being backed up must be on a device of *disk*. The source device can be on either *disk* or *tape*. Let's look at an example of such an operation.

```
BACKUP DEVICE TYPE SBT
BACKUPSET COMPLETED AFTER 'SYSDATE - 1';
```

In this example, we are backing up any backup set created a day ago or later. We could have included the **delete input** keywords if we wanted to remove the source backup set after the backup completed. This backup will be made to the tape device.

Archive Log Backup Enhancements

Oracle has long supported multiple archive log directories. Unfortunately, RMAN has not supported this architecture. In Oracle9*i*, RMAN now supports multiple archive log directories. If a failure occurs while backing up archived redo logs, Oracle will use one of the alternative archive log directories—if they are defined. No error is returned as long as all the archived redo logs that could be copied from any one of the destination directories are on the standby sites. If the backup of the archive logs is successful, Oracle will remove the archived redo logs from all the archived redo log directories—if directed to do so.

Block Media Recovery Operations and Restartable Restores

Two new features in Oracle9*i* make the recovery of the Oracle database much easier and quicker. First, restartable restores that allow a failed restore to be restarted are introduced. Also, block media recovery has been introduced to allow for a method of performing block-level recovery of the Oracle database.

Restartable Restores

As with backup file optimization, Oracle9*i*'s RMAN introduces optimizations to the recovery process. When restoring files, RMAN will examine the file headers of the database datafiles. If the file does not need to be restored, then RMAN will not restore it. This feature allows for restartable restore operations.

Block Media Recovery

Oracle9*i* introduces the concept of *Block Media Recovery (BMR)* to the recovery process. The introduction of BMR facilitates database recovery at the block level in certain cases, reducing the database MTTR and improving on database availability. In this section, we will look at the details of BMR, then how to perform BMR.

What is BMR?   Wouldn't you know it? You just got the following Oracle error message:

```
ORA-01578: ORACLE data block corrupted (file # 19, block # 44)
ORA-01110: data file 19: 'd:\oracle\oradata\data\mydb_maintbs_01.dbf'
```

Normally, this would mean that datafile number 19 is likely going to need recovery from your last backup. This means that all the objects contained in datafile 19 are going to be unavailable for the period of the recovery. This also means that your customer isn't going to be happy, because some part of the database is down.

What if, instead, we could just recover the corrupted data blocks from the database backup? Well, with RMAN and Oracle9i, using BMR, you can—in most cases. With BMR, you can restore individual data blocks from your RMAN backups, and recover those blocks to the point of the failure. During the block recovery process, Oracle will continue to allow access to all blocks that are not corrupted, making your customer happier (we hope).

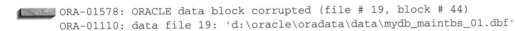

NOTE
BMR applies only to complete recovery because incomplete recovery would leave the database in an inconsistent state.

Performing a BMR Recovery   To perform a BMR recovery, you use the new RMAN command **blockrecover**. You can opt to recover a specific datafile and block by using the **datafile** keyword, or you can recover at the tablespace level if you know the data block address (DBA) by using the **tablespace** keyword. Here are three examples of doing a data block restore:

```
BLOCKRECOVER DATAFILE 19 BLOCK 44;
BLOCKRECOVER DATAFILE 19 BLOCK 44,66,127;
BLOCKRECOVER DATAFILE 19 BLOCK 44 DATAFILE 22 BLOCK 203;
```

The first example will cause Oracle to recover block 44 in datafile 19. Oracle will use the latest backup and required archived redo logs to recover block 44 to the point of failure. If the block in question is corrupt in the last backup, Oracle will cycle through older backups, searching for a noncorrupt block to recover. While this recovery is occurring, the datafile will remain online, and all blocks that are not media corrupted can be read or written to by Oracle processes.

The second example demonstrates the recovery of multiple blocks within the same tablespace, and the last example demonstrates that you can recover multiple blocks in multiple tablespaces in one recovery operation.

Finally, the third example recovers multiple blocks in different datafiles.

Recovering Data Block Corruption Discovered by RMAN Backups   As RMAN backups are made, block corruption can be detected. This corruption of backup sets is reported in V$BACKUP_CORRUPTION or V$COPY_CORRUPTION. Specific block corruption information is stored in the data-dictionary view V$DATABASE_BLOCK_ CORRUPTION. It is likely that you will wish to recover the corrupted blocks. To do so, use the **blockrecover** command, adding the **corruption list restore** option. Here is an example of the use of the command:

```
BLOCK RECOVER CORRUPTION LIST RESTORE UNTIL TIME 'SYSDATE - 5';
```

In this case, we will recover all corrupted blocks. The **until time** keywords indicate that RMAN should use only backups or datafile copies that were created no more than five days ago. Of course, the **until time** command also supports SCN or log sequence numbers as well.

Oracle9i Data Guard

Oracle's standby database architecture is an effective disaster recovery solution for Oracle databases. Oracle has added a number of new modules to the standby database landscape and has enhanced the standby database product itself, all part of a new Oracle9i database feature—Oracle9i Data Guard. The purpose of Data Guard is to provide both a high availability and disaster recovery options. The backup databases are designed to enhance database availability in an environment that is intolerant of extended database outages. Oracle9i Data Guard, alone or in combination with Oracle9i real application clusters, offers robust high availability and recoverability solutions.

The architecture of Data Guard has had several changes made, many of which have been introduced to facilitate a "no data loss" standby database solution. In this section, we will first provide an overview of the new data guard architecture. We will then look in more detail at the new features and components of the data guard architecture.

Oracle9i Data Guard Architecture and Components

In Oracle9i, one of the features Oracle wanted to be able to provide with Data Guard was the ability to offer a no-data-loss standby database architecture. To facilitate this new feature, some changes to Oracle's standby database architecture had to be made. In this section, we will review the overall Oracle9i architecture. The Oracle9i Data Guard architecture consists of the following components:

- **Primary database**   This is the main production database that you wish to protect.

- **LGWR process** The LGWR process can be used in Oracle9i to move database redo, in certain cases, to the standby database.

- **Log transport services** This component previously existed as a part of the RDBMS in standby database configurations in Oracle8i. It has been separated in the standby database architecture, allowing for additional functionality.

- **Oracle Net** This is the replacement for Oracle8i's Net8 network communications layer. It is used to move redo from the primary database to the standby databases.

- **Standby database(s)** Oracle's standby database architecture is for environments that require quick recovery from failure.

- **Log application services** The log application services are used to manage the standby database in various recovery modes.

The relationship of these different components is demonstrated in Figure 3-1. In the following sections, we will look at each of these components in more detail.

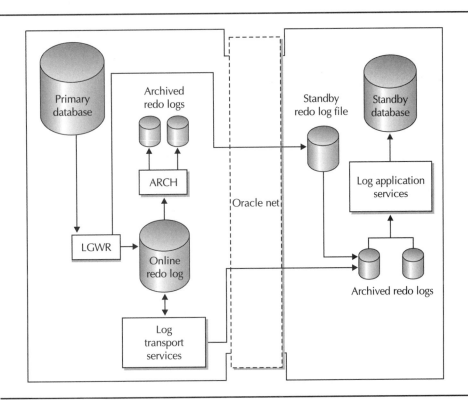

FIGURE 3-1. *Oracle9i Data Guard architecture*

Primary Database

The first component of the Oracle Data Guard architecture is the primary database itself. The primary database is, of course, the real reason that we are using Data Guard in the first place. The primary database is the database that you want to protect from failure and disaster. To use Data Guard, the primary database must be in ARCHIVELOG mode.

Log Transport Services

Oracle physical standby databases (see the "The Physical Standby Database" section, later in the chapter) are updated by virtue of the redo generated by the primary database. This redo is moved to the standby databases by the new Log Transport Services layer.

As with the previous standby database architectures, the generated archived redo logs can be moved to the standby database after they are generated. This movement is facilitated by the ARCH, using Oracle Net (formally called Net8) or another method to move the archived redo logs to the standby databases.

A new feature in Oracle9i Data Guard is the ability to move redo, as it's generated, to the standby database in such a way that zero data loss is guaranteed. When this option is selected, Oracle's LGWR process will control the movement of generated redo from the primary database to the standby databases. We will discuss the log application process on the standby database side later in the "The Log Application Services" section.

The log transport service adds another process in addition to the LGWR and ARCH processes. This new process is the fetch archive log (FAL) process. The FAL process is designed to pull archived redo logs from the primary site to the standby sites. FAL is designed to deal with missing archived redo log sequence gaps. It will perform this activity whenever a gap in the log sequence number gap is detected. There is also an FAL server process on the primary database (or, optionally, on any of the standby database sites). Its purpose is to facilitate requests from the FAL client processes to forward archived redo log files to the standby databases.

The standby database sites can use the FAL server process to obtain missing logs from one of the other standby databases or the primary database. Of course, it is generally preferable for the standby databases to obtain logs from other standby databases for performance reasons.

Other components of log transport servers includes the remote file server (RFS) process, which receives the archived redo logs on the standby database, and the Managed Recovery Process (MRP), which is responsible for applying the redo to the standby database.

Data divergence is the difference in the concurrency of the data between the primary database and the standby database. Oracle supports different levels of data divergence, and offers four different levels of data protection:

- Guaranteed

- Instant

- Rapid

- Delayed

When configuring Oracle9i, one of these data availability modes is established when you set the *log_archive_dest_n* parameters to move the redo to the standby databases. Let's look at each of these modes in a bit more detail.

Guaranteed Data Protection Mode

This mode is designed for architectures that demand zero data loss. This is a new feature in Oracle9i. One of the shortcomings of standby databases prior to Oracle9i was that there was always some opportunity for data loss when failing over to the standby database. guaranteed data protection mode is the solution to this problem.

When used, guaranteed data protection mode guarantees that there will be no data divergence between the primary and standby database(s). When using this mode, redo will be written to the standby database(s) at the same time it is written to the primary database redo logs by the LGWR process. When the standby database architecture is configured in this mode, both redo log writes to the primary and standby database must be successful to at least one standby database for the transaction to succeed. In this mode, if the last remaining standby database becomes unavailable for any reason, the primary database will be shut down until the problem is resolved.

This mode requires the use of standby redo logs on the standby database (see more on standby databases and standby redo logs in the "Standby Redo Logs" section, later in the chapter). This mode might have some performance impacts on the database. This is due to the additional writing, which is synchronous in nature, to the standby databases, and to waiting for the confirmation that the writes to the standby redo logs have been complete. Thus, the cost of this operation mode must be weighed against the benefits of total data protection.

Instant Protection

This mode is much like guaranteed protection mode. Data divergence is allowed up to the point of the last transaction. In this mode, committed transactions will not be returned until the data is written to the standby redo log files at the standby database site. However, the primary database will not be shut down if the standby database becomes unavailable. As with guaranteed data protection mode, the LGWR process is responsible for the movement of redo between the primary database and the standby database sites. As with guaranteed data protection mode, performance might be an issue in this mode as a result of the redo movement process.

Rapid Protection Mode

Perhaps the best balance between data protection and performance is rapid protection mode. In this mode, redo is still sent to the standby database via the LGWR process. However, Oracle does not wait for the redo to be written to the standby redo logs. This mode does allow for the possibility of data loss when failing over to the standby database, and this risk must be considered when designing your high availability and disaster recovery architecture.

Delayed Protection Mode

This is the mode that was previously the only available mode supported by Oracle standby database in Oracle8 and 8i. In this mode, the ARCH process moves over full archived redo logs to the standby databases. The result is potentially significant data divergence between the primary and the standby databases during a failover process.

Implementing a Different Log Transport Service Mode

We have discussed the different log protection modes that you can configure and the benefits of each of these modes. Let's look now at what you need to do to configure these protection modes. First, you must properly set up the log transport services between the primary and the standby databases.

When configuring the log transport service, you will configure it for one of the four protection modes discussed earlier. It is one of the principal jobs of the log transport service to move redo between the primary database and standby databases. Most of the log transport service options are configured in the init.ora parameter file of the primary or standby databases. When configuring a standby database setup, you will need to configure these options:

- Redo log writing process
- Network transmission mode
- Archive log disk writing

The combinations of each of these options have an effect on the overall performance of the primary, and availability and data concurrency of the standby database. Let's look at these options in a bit more detail next.

Redo Log Writing Process Options   The redo log writing process options allow you to define which Oracle server process will be responsible for the writing of redo between the primary and the standby databases. You have two options in Oracle9i.

You can allow the ARCH process to move the archived redo to the standby database, just as Oracle8*i*'s standby database architecture did. Now, in Oracle9*i*, you can also use the LGWR process to move redo to the standby database. Table 3-1 shows each option for writing redo to the standby database, and how that option is defined in the primary database parameter file.

Network Transmission Mode Options   The network transmission mode options indicate how Oracle should treat the movement of redo over the network. There are two network transmission mode options available for use. You can configure your standby database architecture to take advantage of either SYNC or ASYNC mode regarding the movement of the redo to the standby databases. When you choose SYNC, control will not be returned to a user session after a **commit** is issued until the network copy of the redo associated with the user session is complete. This mode is configured using the *log_archive_dest_n* parameter. If the network should become unavailable, or the redo cannot be moved for some other reason, then the user session will hang until the situation is resolved and the redo can be moved. If ASYNC mode is selected (the default), then Oracle will not wait for confirmation of the movement of the redo. Table 3-2 describes each mode and provides an example of how to configure an archive log destination to use that mode.

Redo Log Writing Processes	Description	How to Define, Example
LGWR	The use of LGWR to move redo to standby databases is a new feature in Oracle9*i*. The LGWR process will continuously write online redo logs to the standby databases as the primary database continues to run.	Define how the log transport service should move redo in the primary database init.ora file using *log_archive_dest_n* parameter as seen here: LOG_ARCHIVE_DEST_4= 'service=standby4 LGWR'
ARCH (Default)	The ARCH process moves archived redo logs to the standby databases. The archived redo logs are created and moved to the defined *log_archive_dest_n* locations after a database log switch.	LOG_ARCHIVE_DEST_2= 'LOCATION=d:\oracle\ admin\mydb\arch'

TABLE 3-1.   *Redo Log Writing Process Options*

Mode	Description	Example
Synchronous (default) (SYNC)	This mode causes all redo log write operations and all network IO operations to be performed synchronously. This facilitates movement of redo to the standby database sites and will cause user processes to wait until that redo has been moved over the network to the standby database. This mode is required if you wish to architect a no-data-loss solution.	LOG_ARCHIVE_DEST_4 ='service=stby4 LGWR SYNC'
Asynchronous (ASYNC)	The ASYNC option is available only when the LGWR process is being used as the redo log writing process. This mode facilitates movement of redo without waiting for confirmation of the success of the move.	LOG_ARCHIVE_DEST_4 ='service=stby4 LGWR ASYNC'

TABLE 3-2. *Network Transmission Mode Options*

NOTE
The network transmission mode option applies only to the copying of redo over the network. It does not confirm that disk writes of the redo are complete or that the application of that redo to the standby database is complete.

Archive Log Disk Writing Options   As redo is transmitted over the network to standby sites, you hope that it will be successfully written to disk. The archive log disk writing options that can be configured in Oralce9i Data Guard can ensure that redo is successfully written. This feature, combined with network mode transmission options and redo log writing process options, can be used to ensure a no-data-loss standby database environment. The archive log disk writing options are shown in Table 3-3, along with a description of their use and example settings.

NOTE
*The **affirm** option is for every write of data to the redo logs and does not depend on a user commit. Thus, using **affirm** can have significant performance impacts.*

Effects of the Different Log Transport Options   Table 3-4 provides some insight into the impacts of the different log transport options on Oracle in terms of performance and availability.

Option	Description	Example
AFFIRM	This will cause Oracle to wait for the redo to be written to the standby redo logs of the standby database site (but not applied to the standby database) before it will return a success to the user session issuing the commit. The user session will wait until the redo is written to the standby redo logs of the standby database for every write that the user session causes.	LOG_ARCHIVE_DEST_6 ='service=stby6 LGWR SYNC AFFIRM'
NOAFFIRM (default)	When this setting is enabled, Oracle will not wait for the successful write to disk of the standby database of redo.	LOG_ARCHIVE_DEST_6 ='service=stby6 LGWR SYNC NOAFFIRM'

TABLE 3-3.   *Archive Log Disk Writing Options*

Redo Log Writing Process Options	Network Transmission Mode Options	Archive Log Disk Writing Options	Production DB Performance Impact	Standby DB Data Loss Risk
LGWR	SYNC	AFFIRM	HIGHEST	LEAST
LGWR	SYNC	NOAFFIRM	HIGHER	LOW
LGWR	ASYNC	AFFIRM	HIGH	MODERATE
LGWR	ASYNC	NOAFFIRM	MODERATE	MODERATE
ARCH	SYNC	NOAFFIRM	LOW	HIGH

TABLE 3-4. *Effects on Performance and Data Loss Using Different Log Transport Options*

Oracle Net

Oracle Net is the Oracle networking facility formerly called Net8. This networking architecture can be used to facilitate the movement of generated redo from the primary database to the standby databases. With Oracle9i Data Guard, you can move redo from the primary database to up to 10 standby databases (only 5 databases were supported in Oracle8i).

Physical Standby Database

What was called automated standby database in Oracle8i is now called physical standby database in Oracle9i. This distinction of a physical standby database will become more important in later versions of Oracle9i, as Oracle is planning to introduce a logical standby database in a later release.

You can configure up to nine remote physical standby databases from the primary database using the *log_archive_dest_n* parameter in the init.ora file of the primary database. Oracle9i has introduced several new features that can be used on standby databases, so let's look at those next.

Standby Database File Management   Oracle9i allows you to enable automated file management on Oracle9i standby databases. A new parameter, *standby_file_management*, enables this feature when it is set to AUTO (the default is MANUAL). When automated file management is enabled on standby databases, the creation of a datafile will cause an OMF datafile to be created on the standby database. If the tablespace for that datafile is later dropped, then Oracle will remove the tablespace and datafile on the standby database as well. If you set *standby_file_management* to AUTO, you will not be able to issue several commands on the standby databases. These commands include **alter database rename, alter database add log file, alter database add log file member, alter database drop log file, alter database drop log file member,** and **alter database create datafile.**

NOTE
If the datafile on the standby database is not an
OMF datafile, the Oracle will not drop that datafile.

Of course, you might have some differences in the directory structures between the primary and standby databases. The *db_file_name_convert* and *log_file_name_convert* parameters are still available in Oracle9i to support different directory structures. Oracle9i has enhanced the support provided by these parameters by allowing you to define multiple directory structures within them.

Log Application Services

This service was previously built into the Oracle8i standby database architecture. In Oracle9i, this architecture is still controlled from within the standby database, but it has been split into its own component. This service is responsible for applying the redo from the primary database to the standby databases after it has been moved by the log transport services. In Oracle9i, Oracle standby database log application services support two modes for the standby database that were available in Oracle8i: managed recovery and read-only (although logs cannot be applied in this mode).

Read-Only Mode   Read-only mode allows read-only access to the standby database. This read-only access is at the cost of data divergence between the primary and standby database because a standby database is not updated when it is in read-only mode.

Managed Recovery Mode   Managed recovery mode causes the Oracle9i standby database to be updated with the redo generated from the primary database site. In some configurations, the primary database LGWR process writes redo to standby redo log files, which are then archived on the standby database to the standby database archived redo logs. In other configurations, the primary database ARCH process simply sends archived redo logs to the standby database for processing. In all configurations, the archived redo logs are then applied to the standby database using sustained recovery.

When running the database in managed recovery mode, you can choose to run in either foreground or background mode. The **alter database recover managed standby database** command will start the standby database in foreground managed-recovery mode. New in Oracle9i, the **alter database recover managed standby database disconnect from session** command causes managed standby recovery to occur in the background. You can use the new view, V$MANAGED_STANDBY, to monitor the operations of managed standby database recovery. This view can be used when either foreground or background managed recovery is in use.

Setting the Failure Resolution Policy   Prior to Oracle9i, when the database was in ARCHIVELOG mode, if the ARCH process could not archive the online redo logs, Oracle would simply continue to run until it could no longer find a free online redo log. When this occurred, the database and user sessions froze, and no new users were able to log into the database. This is still the default behavior in Oracle9i.

Now, in Oracle9i, Oracle offers a protected failure resolution policy. When the database is configured for this operational mode, if the LGWR process cannot move the redo information to at least one standby site, the primary database will shut down automatically. You can enable this mode by issuing the **alter database set standby database protected** command. When using this mode, you will need to make sure that the standby database is using two or more standby redo log groups. In addition, you must use LGWR to move the archived redo logs, and you must use the synchronous network transmission mode.

Standby Redo Logs   A new feature in Oracle9i is the standby redo log. The standby redo logs are a separate set of redo logs and are associated with a physical standby database. Like online redo logs, the standby redo log file is preallocated, and can have multiple members for maximal protection. Standby redo logs must be created on standby databases if you wish to implement a no-data-loss standby database architecture.

You can create standby redo logs on the standby database with the **alter database add standby logfile** statement. Just as with normal redo logs, you can add additional members as required for protection of those logs. The **alter database drop standby logfile** command allows you to drop standby redo log files.

NOTE
The standby redo log files count as part of maxlogfiles defined in the control file as part of the create database command.

Standby redo logs will be used when you make LGWR responsible for moving online redo to the standby database. There are other requirements that must be met for standby redo logs to be used. For example, the ARCH process must be active on the standby database, but the standby database need not be in ARCHIVELOG mode. Also, the size of the standby redo logs must match the size of one of the primary database online redo logs, though Oracle suggests you have the same number and size of standby logs as on the primary, or even more.

Oracle9i Standby Database: Role Management and Graceful Failover

Previous to Oracle9i, the only method of switching the primary and standby database was a failover operation, which required the re-creation of the primary database after the failover operation completed. Often, in these cases, this re-created primary database would become the new standby database, and the old standby database would continue in its new role as the primary database. Because the failover required incomplete recovery (due to the use of the **activate standby** command), there was no going back once you switched over to the standby database. Also, in an environment with just one standby server, there was a risk to the system during the period that a new standby database was being created after a failover occurred.

In Oracle9i Data Guard, you have the primary database and one or more standby databases. There might be times that you will want to transfer the roles of a standby database and the primary database, such that the primary becomes the standby and the standby becomes the primary at times other than an unplanned failure. Oracle supports this type of an operation in Oracle9i, using the role management feature. The actual process of changing the role of a given database is called a *switchover operation*. With a switchover operation, you do not need to re-create a new database as you likely would with a failover operation, because the data in both the primary and standby databases is not divergent.

Why might you want to take advantage of graceful switchover? Often, this method can be used to allow for planned hardware down time and maintenance. Also, switchover can be used to diagnose problems and try to deal with logical corruption of data in the primary database.

Switchover operations require planning, and can occur only if specific conditions are met. For a primary database to be switched over as a standby database, the primary must be either mounted or open. There must already be at least one standby database active in your current configuration. That standby database must either be mounted or in read-only mode, and accessible through the network. When you switch the primary database, it must be in ARCHIVELOG mode, and only one session can be active in the instance.

A standby database can be switched over to become a primary database when it is in either read-only mode or mounted. Before being able to complete the switchover, there can be only one active session in the standby instance. Finally, before initiating the switchover, the standby database must have been in managed recovery mode and the switch of the primary database to a standby configuration must be completed.

To facilitate the switchover, use the **alter database commit to switchover** command. If you are switching a physical database to a standby database, then use the command **alter database commit to switchover to physical standby**. If you wish to switch a standby database and make it the primary database, issue the command **alter database commit to switchover to physical primary**. Please refer to the Oracle9i documentation for explicit instructions on switching over your primary or standby databases.

Oracle9i Standby Database Miscelanious Enhancements

Oracle9i has introduced some additional enhancements in Oracle9i Data Guard, including the ability to detect gaps in log-sequence numbers and retrieve redo logs that are needed to deal with those gaps. Also, the DBA can now configure a purposeful delay in the time between the generation of redo and its application on the standby site.

Log Sequence Gap Detection and Recovery

Oracle9i Data Guard provides the ability to determine log sequence gaps. When configured, the Oracle9i standby database can retrieve needed redo logs from the primary database, or another standby database. This functionality is facilitated through two new parameters, both of which need to be configured for the process to work correctly.

- *fal_client* This parameter configures Fetch Archive Log Client (FALC), runs on the standby site, and contains the net service name of the standby database.

- *fal_server* This parameter configures the Fetch Archive Log Server (FALS) process on the standby database site and contains the Net service name for the FAL server.

Oracle provides a new view, V$ARCHIVE_GAP, to help the DBA identify log sequence gap information. See the *Oracle9i Data Guard Concepts and Administration* manual for more information on configuring this feature.

Configurable Log Application Delay

There are environments in which the DBA doesn't want a particular standby database to be in synch with the primary database. This might be because the DBA desires some protection from user errors, or perhaps logical corruption might occur. In Oracle9i, you can configure an individual standby database so that it will have the application of redo from the primary database delayed for a period of time.

This feature can be configured in one of two ways. First, it can be configured using the *log_archive_dest_n* parameter. Alternatively, it can be configured using the **alter database recover managed standby database** command, using the **delay** or **nodelay** keyword. See the *Oracle9i Data Guard Concepts and Administration* manual for more information on configuring this feature.

Support for Single Redo Log Stream

Supporting multiple standby database sites can have performance impacts on the primary database. To mitigate these impacts, you can configure a single redo log stream between the primary database and a single standby database. When properly configured, other standby databases will receive redo from the standby database, freeing the resources of the primary database that would otherwise be tasked with this chore. This option is facilitated through the use of the new *dependency* parameter of the *log_archive_dest_n* parameter. See the *Oracle9i Data Guard Concepts and Administration* manual for more information on configuring this feature.

Support for Establishment of a
Maximum Archive Log Lag Target

In certain configurations, the Oracle9i standby database might well not have any redo applied to it with any great frequency. Consider a primary database with few, small transactions that switches redo logs only every two days. If we are using delayed protection mode, then the standby database will lag behind the primary database by two days. In many environments, this might well be too much of a time lag.

Fortunately, Oracle9i offers a solution to this problem. By configuring the *archive_lag_target* parameter (in seconds), the DBA can configure how often the primary database will perform log switches, which will result in the eventual application of the generated redo log on the standby database.

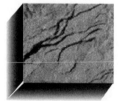

CHAPTER
4

New Oracle9i Database DSS and Data-Warehousing Features

- List partitioning
- Analytical-processing features and enhancements
- View constraints
- New ETL features
- Other data warehouse–related features

ne of the ways that Oracle shines best is in the role of Decision Support System (DSS) or data warehouse. Oracle9i builds on several features of its predecessors in this regard with enhancements to existing features, such as partitioning and query rewrite. It also integrates other features into the RDBMS that were previously facilitated by outside utilities, such as external data loading. In this chapter, we will look at the new features in Oracle9i that relate to DSS and data warehousing databases.

Oracle9i List Partitioning

Oracle9i provides a new method of partitioning objects called *list partitioning.* This partitioning method allows you to take the values in a column and assign a group of those values to individual partitions. In this section, we will look at list partitioning. We will look at how to create a list-partitioned table first. Finally, we will then look at the different maintenance operations that you might need to perform on list-partitioned tables, such as adding, splitting, and dropping partitions.

Creating the List-Partitioned Table

If you were a local retailer, you might have stores in several states. Perhaps you wish to partition your stores into specific regions based on their location within each state, as seen in Table 4-1.

So, we want to partition our store information by region using the list-partitioning method. We use the **create table** command, as seen here:

```
CREATE TABLE store_master
            ( Store_id                 NUMBER,
              Store_address            VARCHAR2(40),
              City                     VARCHAR2(30),
              State                    VARCHAR2(2),
              zip                      VARCHAR2(10),
              manager_id               NUMBER   )
            PARTITION BY LIST (city)
            STORAGE(INITIAL 100k, NEXT 100k, PCTINCREASE 0)
            TABLESPACE store_data
              (
                  PARTITION south_florida
                      VALUES ('MIAMI','ORLANDO')
                      STORAGE(INITIAL 100k, NEXT 100k, PCTINCREASE 0)
                      TABLESPACE store_data_south_florida,
                  PARTITION north_florida
                      VALUES ('JACKSONVILLE','TAMPA', 'PENSACOLA')
                      STORAGE(INITIAL 100k, NEXT 100k, PCTINCREASE 0)
                      TABLESPACE store_data_north_florida,
                  PARTITION south_georga
                      VALUES ('BRUNSWICK', 'WAYCROSS', 'VALDOSTA')
                      STORAGE(INITIAL 100k, NEXT 100k, PCTINCREASE 0)
```

```
            TABLESPACE store_data_south_georga,
        PARTITION north_georgia
            VALUES ('ATLANTA','SAVANNAH', NULL));
```

In this example, we have created a partitioned table with a partition for each of the four regions. We have defined each city in which we have a store as part of one of the partition value lists. A *partition-value list* is simply a list of literal values that will be stored in the partitions of the list-partitioned table. In the case of the first three partitions, we have defined storage characteristics for the partition, as well as assigned tablespaces to the partitions. In the last partition (NORTH_GEORGIA), we have just accepted the default **storage** and **tablespace** settings that are associated with the partitioned table.

A couple of rules regarding list-partitioned tables to note: first, only one column in the table can be defined in the **partition by list** clause. Thus, the partition-value list can contain values from only one column. Second, there is no provision for values in the partitioned table that do not exist in the partition-value list of one of the table's partitions. For example, right now, if you tried to **insert** a row in the STORE_MASTER table with a city name of Dallas, the **insert** would fail because Dallas is not defined in any of the partition-value lists for the partitioned table. This rule also applies to attempts to **update** existing records in a list-partitioned table. Thus, we can't update the Miami record and change the location of the Miami store to Dallas unless Dallas is on a partition-value list somewhere in that partitioned table.

List-Partitioned Table Rules and Features

Several rules and restrictions exist with regard to list-partitioned tables. First of all, this partitioning method supports only heap tables, thus IOTs cannot be list partitioned. Also, the defined literal values used in the partition-value lists must be unique across all defined partitions. Thus, you cannot have Freeman defined in two different partitions. Oracle supports the definition of NULL in the partition-value list, but does not support the use of **maxvalue**. The list literal values must not be larger than 4K, and you must have at least one literal assigned to the partition-value list of each partition.

As with other partitioned tables, there are several pruning options that the Oracle optimizer can take advantage of regarding list-partitioned tables. Three pruning operations are supported by Oracle: equality, **in** clause, and range. Let's look at each of these in a bit more detail next.

Region Name	Location
South Florida	Miami, Orlando
North Florida	Jacksonville, Pensacola, Tampa
South Georgia	Brunswick, Waycross, Valdosta
North Georgia	Atlanta, Savannah

TABLE 4-1. *Sample Store Regions*

NOTE
*Oracle partition pruning for list-partitioned tables
works just fine if you are using literals or bind values
in your SQL statements.*

Equality Partition Pruning

Equality pruning can occur when the **where** clause includes an equality operation on the partition-value list column name that the partitioned table is based on. Based on that part of the **where** clause, Oracle will eliminate all partitions except the partition where the literal value in the **where** clause occurs. Thus, a SQL statement like this,

```
SELECT * FROM store_master WHERE city='Miami';
```

will be able to take advantage of partition pruning because Oracle knows which partition Miami is in, and will eliminate all other partitions from consideration.

In Clause Partition Pruning

Much like the previous example, if that IN clause involves the partition-value list column name, Oracle will look at **in** clauses in the **where** clause. Oracle will then determine which partitions store rows for the literals contained in the **where** clause, and will eliminate all other partitions from consideration. An example of a query that could take advantage of **in** clause partition pruning is shown here:

```
SELECT * FROM store_master WHERE city in ('Miami','Atlanta');
```

Range Partition Pruning

It might seem odd that Oracle can do range partition-pruning with list-partitioned tables. Consider, though, that the values that are contained within the partition-value lists are literal values. As such, Oracle can perform range operations on these values by determining whether the **where** clause contains the partition-value list column, and then determining which partitions contain values that fit within the bounded range defined in the **where** clause. For example, Oracle can perform a range pruning operation on a SQL statement such as this one:

```
SELECT * FROM store_master WHERE city <= 'Brunswick';
```

In the preceding example, Oracle will search only two of the four originally defined partitions, SOUTH_GEORGIA and NORTH_GEORGIA. This is because the SOUTH_GEORGIA partition contains Brunswick, and NORTH_GEORGIA contains Atlanta, which falls within the defined range of the query since Atlanta sorts out as less than Brunswick. The remaining two partitions, NORTH_FLORIDA and SOUTH_FLORIDA, do not contain any cities that would sort as less than Brunswick; thus, those partitions would be eliminated from consideration.

List-Partitioned Table Maintenance

Oracle9i offers several partition-maintenance operations that allow the DBA to maintain the list-partitioned table. In this section, we will look at these operations. including how to add, split, and drop a partition on a list-partitioned table.

Adding a Partition

Let's assume that we have opened a new store in a new region. Given our partitioning scheme, we will need to add a new partition to our partitioned store table. This is done using the **alter table add partition** command. When adding a partition, you need to make sure that the new literal values you will be assigning to the partition are not already assigned to a given partition. If the literal is already assigned to a value, then Oracle will generate an error when it tries to create the partition. In our example, let's assume we have opened a new store in the Las Vegas area (my all-time favorite place in the world!). So, we will now create a new region. Let's call it the SOUTH_NEVADA region. The resulting **alter table** statement would look like this:

```
ALTER TABLE store_master
ADD PARTITION south_nevada VALUES ('Las Vegas')
TABLESPACE south_nevada;
```

In this case, we have added the city Las Vegas to a new partition called SOUTH_NEVADA. We have used the default **storage** characteristics that we defined for the partitioned table, and the partition will be created in the SOUTH_NEVADA tablespace. If we did not define a partition name, Oracle would define one for us. Oracle will automatically update any associated local index partitions. Global indexes will not be affected by this move. Also, during the creation of the new partition, DDL will not be possible on the partitioned table as a whole, though this is generally a fast operation, so the exclusive lock should have a minimal overall impact.

Splitting a Partition

Business is good and we have opened more stores. This might well call for the splitting of an existing partition into two partitions to accommodate the additional data volumes and scale associated with additional user activity. The **alter table split partition** command is provided to allow you to split a list-partitioned table. For example, assume we have some stores in Alaska: one each in Anchorage, Barrow, Juneau, Atka (oddly, our busiest!), and Fairbanks. These stores are just doing a hot bang-up business; and for various reasons, we have decided that we need to split the current Alaska partition into two different partitions—ALASKA_NORTH and ALASKA_SOUTH. To do this, we will use the **alter table split partition** command, taking the current ALASKA partition, and splitting it. Here is the command that is required to perform this action:

```
ALTER TABLE store_master
SPLIT PARTITION alaska
```

```
VALUES ('Anchorage','Atka','Juneau')
INTO (
          PARTITION alaska_south
TABLESPACE alaska_south_tbs,
PARTITION alaska_north
TABLESPACE alaska_north_tbs);
```

In this example, we have indicated that Anchorage, Juneau, and Atka are in the new ALASKA_SOUTH partition, which will be in the ALASKA_SOUTH_TBS tablespace. Thus, the list of values in the **values** clause applies to the first partition defined. All the remaining cities not included in the **values** clause (in this example, Barrow and Fairbanks) will be included in a new partition called ALASKA_NORTH, which will be in the ALASKA_NORTH_TBS tablespace.

As you would expect, if we had not defined partition names, Oracle would assign system-defined names to the partitions. You cannot assign new literal values to a partition when splitting it. This will cause an error to be generated by Oracle. If you do not define physical attributes for the partitions being split, then the undefined attributes will be derived from the attributes of the partition being split. Local indexes will be split in the same operation and will remain usable. Global indexes will be marked UNUSABLE. Finally, as you might expect, after the partition is split, the newly created partitions will have exclusive locks placed on them, restricting DML activity. The table itself will have a row-exclusive lock placed on it.

Merging a Partition

There might be occasions when it will be desirable to merge two existing partitions into a single partition. This procedure can be facilitated using the **alter table merge partitions** command. Let's assume that we have decided to merge the NORTH_FLORIDA and SOUTH_FLORIDA partitions into a single partition called FLORIDA. To facilitate this action, the DBA would issue the following command:

```
ALTER TABLE store_master
MERGE PARTITIONS
    south_florida, north_florida
INTO PARTITION florida
STORAGE (INITIAL 100m) TABLESPACE florida;
```

In this example, we have combined the two Florida partitions into one called FLORIDA, which is in a newly created tablespace called FLORIDA. Note that we have defined the **initial storage** parameter. All other parameters will take the defaults defined for the partitioned table.

In this example, if we had not assigned a partition name to the new partition, then Oracle would have provided a system-generated name for us. Any local indexes that are associated with the partitions being merged will be merged as well, but the resulting index partition will be marked UNUSABLE. Global indexes defined on the tablespaces will be marked UNUSABLE as well. During the **alter table merge partitions** operation, only the partitions being merged will be locked in exclusive mode. The partitioned table will have a shared exclusive lock present on it, which will prevent any DDL changes, but will allow DML to occur on unaffected partitions.

Adding Values to a Partition

Oracle9i allows us to add values to a partition's value list. For example, assume we open a store in Key West, Florida. We will need to add Key West to the partition list for the SOUTH_FLORIDA partition. To do this, we use the **alter table modify partition** command, as shown here:

```
ALTER TABLE store_master
MODIFY PARTITION south_florida
ADD VALUES ('Key West');
```

In this example, the value of Key West is not contained in the partition-value list for the SOUTH_FLORIDA partition. We can now include the Key West store in the STORE_MASTER table. Note that this operation will not make any of the associated local or global indexes UNUSABLE. Also, the partition being modified will have an exclusive lock placed on it for the duration of the operation (which should be quite short).

Removing Values From a Partition

We opened a store in Berkeley some time ago, and, frankly, we got tired of the Neo-Marxists demanding we stock posters of Lenin and Stalin, so we closed the store (but don't tell my publisher this, they have offices in Berkeley). We want to remove Berkeley from the partition called WESTERN_US. To do so, we must first remove all the records that pertain to Berkeley, and then we can drop Berkeley from the partition list using the **alter table modify partition** command, as shown here:

```
DELETE store_master
WHERE city='BERKELEY';

ALTER TABLE store_master
MODIFY PARTITION western_us
DROP VALUES ('Berkeley');
```

When we execute the **alter table** command, it will ensure that there are no records containing Berkeley in the partition we are going to modify. If there are, an error will be generated. Also note that Oracle will not allow you to drop all the literal values from a given partition. One must always remain. If you wish to drop all literal values, then simply drop the partition, as shown here.

```
ALTER TABLE store_master
DROP PARTITION western_us;
```

Be aware that while this operation is running, there is an exclusive lock on the table such that DML operations will be suspended. All related indexes on the table will still be usable and will contain the new partition-value list.

View Constraints

In this section, we will discuss the new Oracle9i view-constraint features. We will review the purpose and benefits of view constraints. We will then look at how to create, modify, and drop view constraints.

Introducing View Constraints

Oracle uses defined referential-integrity (RI) constraint definitions to discover various relationships between fact and dimension tables in a data-warehouse environment. The presence of these constraints (primary key, foreign key, and so on) is important for such Oracle features as query rewrite to work properly. Prior to Oracle9i, however, a problem would arise if the database design called for views to be built on the database's fact or dimension tables. Because you could not define constraints on views, Oracle could not detect the relationships, and, thus, some functionality was lost.

Oracle9i allows constraints to be defined on views, enabling DBAs to place the same constraints on the views that exist on the associated base tables of the views. Collectively, the constraints created on views in Oracle9i are known as *view constraints*. A view that contains view constraints is known as a *constrained view*.

When defined, view constraints can consist of the following types of constraints:

- Primary key

- Unique

- RI

Note that there is no need (nor support for) NOT NULL constraints, as these are inherited from the base table(s) of the view itself.

View constraints are declarative in nature, thus are not enforced by Oracle, and in no way replace the need for constraints on the base tables. View constraints provide no form of data checking or validation (such as would be the case with FK relationships, for example). View constraints always have a status of DISABLE NOVALIDATE.

Finally, view constraints support the use of the **rely** and **norely** states. The use of the **rely** state allows the view to participate in query rewrites when the *query_rewrite_integrity* parameter for a given session is set to TRUSTED.

View constraints are subject to some restrictions (you figured as much, didn't you?). First of all, only primary key, RI, and unique constraints are supported. You cannot define check constraints. A view can be created only as **disable novalidate**. Since the constraints are declarative only, view constraints are never enforced. For the same reason, a view constraint cannot be created with a deferred status. Also, you cannot use the **using index** clause or the **exceptions into** clause as you would with a normal constraint.

Creating View Constraints

You can create a view, and create the view constraints, within the **create view** statement. For example, let's create a view that gives us the average salary for each department. We will define the department number as the primary key for the view, and we will define an FK relationship between the DEPT table and the EMP table column DEPTNO.

```
CREATE VIEW v_emp_dept_view
(deptno, dname, avg_sal)
CONSTRAINT pk_v_emp_dept_view
PRIMARY KEY (dname)
RELY DISABLE NOVALIDATE,
CONSTRAINT fk_v_emp_dept_view_01
FOREIGN KEY (deptno) REFERENCES dept(deptno)
RELY DISABLE NOVALIDATE)
AS SELECT a.deptno, b.dname, AVG(a.sal)
FROM emp a, dept b
WHERE a.deptno=b.deptno
GROUP BY a.deptno, b.dname;
```

Modifying View Constraints

There might be times that you will want to modify a given constraint on a view. This task is accomplished with the **alter view** command. First, you should note that you cannot drop a primary or unique key constraint on a view if it is part of the view's RI constraint (such as a defined foreign-key view constraint). Additionally, you cannot change the state of a primary key or a unique key from **rely** to **norely** if that constraint is part of a foreign key that has a state of **rely**. To change the primary key or unique key state to **norely**, you will need to drop the foreign key or change the state of the foreign key to **norely**.

To add a constraint, simply use the **alter view** command, as shown in this example:

```
ALTER VIEW v_emp_dept_view
ADD CONSTRAINT u_v_emp_dept_view
UNIQUE (dname) RELY DISABLE NOVALIDATE;
```

In this example, we have created a unique constraint on the DNAME column of our view. Of course, we might want to drop this constraint, and, again, we use the **alter view** command, as shown here:

```
ALTER VIEW v_emp_dept_view
DROP CONSTRAINT u_v_emp_dept_view;
```

Dropping the primary key is pretty straightforward as well, as shown here:

```
ALTER VIEW v_emp_dept_view
DROP PRIMARY KEY;
```

There might well be cases when you will want to make the constraint status **rely** or **norely**. This is as simple as issuing the **alter view** command again:

```
ALTER VIEW v_emp_dept_view
MODIFY CONSTRAINT u_v_emp_dept_view NORELY;
ALTER VIEW v_emp_dept_view
MODIFY CONSTRAINT u_v_emp_dept_view RELY;
```

Dropping View Constraints

Normally, to drop a constrained view, you would issue the **drop view** command. When dropping a view that contains defined constraints, you run into some of the same problems that you run into when trying to drop tables that have constraints created on them. That problem is that the view might be referenced by a constraint in another object. In this case, you will need to use the new **cascade constraints** clause of the **drop view** command, as seen in the following example:

```
DROP VIEW v_emp_dept_view CASCADE CONSTRAINTS;
```

New Oracle9i ETL Features

As it has released newer versions of the database, Oracle has added more and more features to support decision support systems (DSS), executive information systems (EIS), and data-warehouse environments. Oracle9i is no exception to this rule. In Oracle9i, Oracle has introduced many new extraction transformation loading (ETL) features into the base database product. The primary purpose of ETL is to allow the loading, validation, cleansing, and transformation of data from external data sources into data-warehouse tables. Generally, the movement of data from external data sources into the Oracle data warehouse is a multi-step process. This process can require a great deal of disk space and significant processing overhead. It is the purpose of the Oracle9i database to reduce this overhead as much as possible and provide a single solution for ETL processing requirements.

One of the features that Oracle ETL processing provides is a method of *pipelining* data from the original data source into the Oracle database. New database features in Oracle9i allow you to streamline the data flow, and offer significant flexibility and functionality. The primary components of the new Oracle9i ETL functionality include the following:

- External Oracle tables
- Table functions
- Multi-table insert statements
- Merge statements

- Oracle change-data capture

- Parallel direct-load enhancements

- Various bulk-bind enhancements

In the following sections, we will look at each of these new features.

Oracle External Tables

Until Oracle9i, the easiest way to load external data into the database was using SQL*Loader. With SQL*Loader, you define the format of the data in the flat file, and then use the SQL*Loader executable to load the data into the database. Oracle9i offers an alternative to SQL*Loader in the form of *external tables*, which we will cover in this section. We will describe what external tables are, and how to create, manage, and use them.

Introducing External Tables

External tables are probably one of the more significant new features in Oracle9i regarding ETL. So, what exactly are they? External tables are read-only Oracle tables in which the data for the table is located outside the Oracle database, stored in flat files. You can query an Oracle external table just as you would a normal Oracle table, using SQL, PL/SQL, or any of the other languages that the Oracle database supports. Other DML operations (**insert**, **update**, and **delete**) are not supported. Also, you cannot create indexes or constraints on external tables. You can query and join multiple external tables, and even join external tables to other Oracle table types (for example, hash or IOTs).

You will define an external table using the **create table** statement, including the **organization external** clause. The syntax for the **create table** statement for the creation of an external table is significantly different from the **create table** statements used to create internal database tables. When you issue a **create table** statement to create an external table, the statement defines the structure of the external data, and looks more like a SQL*Loader control file than a **create table** statement.

External tables are a complement to the Oracle SQL*Loader program. In many cases, external tables can be a more efficient way of loading data into the Oracle database, particularly in cases in which you will be using internal tables in the overall ETL process. External tables do not supplant SQL*Loader, as there might be specific cases when the SQL*Loader load process will be more efficient than the use of external tables. Typically, this will be the case if your overall load process will benefit from an initial load of data into a staging table and subsequent index access to that data.

Creating External Tables

Let's look at creating an external table. Assume that we have an external data source that provides us with a flat file full of data. For the purposes of this example, we will assume we are getting payroll data from our HR system, that this data is comma-delimited, and that there is one record per row in the flat file. Here is a description of the flat file.

Field	Data Type	Description	Sample Data
Employee ID	NUMBER	This is the employee ID.	12345
Pay date	DATE	This is the day the employee was paid.	01-Jan-2001
Check number	NUMBER	This is the check number.	1000
Gross pay	NUMBER	This is the gross amount of the check.	1000.00
Pretax deductions	NUMBER	This is the total amount of pretax deductions.	100.00
Taxes deducted	NUMBER	This is the total amount of taxes that were deducted.	200.00
Net pay	NUMBER	This is the net pay.	700.00
Comments	VARCHAR2(100)	This represents any comments.	This is a comment.

Let's look at an example of our flat file.

```
12345,01-JAN-2001,1000,1000.00,100.00,200.00,700.00
12346,01-JAN-2001,1001,2000.00,200.00,400.00,1400.00
12347,01-JAN-2001,1002,4000.00,400.00,800.00,2800.00
```

Given the format of this flat file, let's now create an external table that will allow us to query this flat file from within the database. Here is the **create table** statement that we will use:

```
CREATE TABLE extrn_pay_amount
( employee_id      NUMBER,
  pay_date         DATE,
  check_number     NUMBER,
  gross_pay      NUMBER,
  pre_tax_ded      NUMBER,
  tax_ded      NUMBER,
  net_pay      NUMBER,
  comments      VARCHAR2(100)
) ORGANIZATION EXTERNAL
(TYPE oracle_loader
DEFAULT DIRECTORY load_dir
```

```
ACCESS PARAMETERS
(  RECORDS DELIMITED BY NEWLINE
    badfile load_dir:'bad_load.fil'
    logfile load_dir:'log_load.fil'
    FIELDS TERMINATED BY ','
    MISSING FIELD VALUES ARE NULL
( employee_id,
    pay_date CHAR date_format date mask "DD-MON-YYYY",
    check_number,
    gross_pay,
    pre_tax_ded,
    tax_ded,
    net_pay,
    comments ) )
LOCATION('salary_paid.out') )
PARALLEL 5
REJECT LIMIT UNLIMITED;
```

Let's look at this statement closely. As you can see, this statement looks more like a SQL*Loader control file than it does a **create table** statement. The first part of the statement looks familiar. Here it is again:

```
CREATE TABLE extrn_pay_amount
(employee_id      NUMBER,
pay_date         DATE,
check_number     NUMBER,
gross_pay        NUMBER,
pre_tax_ded      NUMBER,
tax_ded              NUMBER,
net_pay              NUMBER,
comments         VARCHAR2(100) )
```

Here we have defined several column names and the data types for those columns. This part of the statement really provides the mapping between the data in the external file and the database itself. Let's move on to the next part of the statement:

```
ORGANIZATION EXTERNAL (
TYPE oracle_loader
DEFAULT DIRECTORY load_dir
```

The **organization external** clause indicates that the table we are creating is indeed an external table. Next, we define the access driver with the **type** clause. By default, Oracle uses the SQL*Loader access driver, though Oracle does supply APIs that allow you to create your own access drivers.

After defining the access-driver method to be used, the *default directory* is defined. This parameter defines one or more directories that contain the external file or files containing the external data that the external table will point to. These directories are created prior to the creation of the external table via the **create directory** command.

```
(    RECORDS DELIMITED BY NEWLINE
     badfile bad_dir:'bad_load.fil'
     logfile log_dir:'log_load.fil'
     FIELDS TERMINATED BY ','
     MISSING FIELD VALUES ARE NULL
(  employee_id,
   pay_date CHAR date_format date mask "DD-MON-YYYY",
   check_number,
   gross_pay,
   pre_tax_ded,
   tax_ded,
   net_pay,
   comments ) )
LOCATION('salary_paid.out') )
PARALLEL 5
REJECT LIMIT UNLIMITED;
```

The **access parameters** section defines the format of the external file that Oracle needs to access, and is interpreted only by the access driver. This section looks much like a SQL*Loader control file. We first define that all records are delimited by a newline character (CR-LF), and that all the fields are terminated by commas. Of course, we could have made them fixed-length fields as well, just as you can with SQL*Loader.

Later in the section, we see that the *badfile* and *logfile* parameters are defined, again just like SQL*Loader. Note that we defined the directory that the *badfile* and *logfile* will be written to by using the name of the directory in the parameter. For example, for the *badfile*, we will use the directory called bad_dir, which will need to be defined first with a **create directory** command. Also, the user who will be querying the external table will need **select** access to the directory that contains the external table, and will need write access to the directories that are used for logging.

In this example, the **location** clause indicates the name of the external file that is associated with this external table. This file must reside in the location defined in the default directory location. Of course, this clause is interpreted by the access driver (as are the other clauses in this section), so its meaning might be completely different if you use a custom-made access driver.

Note the **parallel 5** statement. Oracle allows us to make access to external tables parallel, further improving the performance of external tables. Finally, the **reject limit unlimited** clause allows you to indicate how many rows can be rejected before a query against an external table will fail. By default, no errors are allowed; but in our example, we have indicated that an unlimited number of errors may occur. All errors that are generated will appear in the bad file and will be logged in the log file.

Querying the External Table

Now that we have created the external table, let's query it. You simply issue a query as you would for any other table, as seen here:

```
SELECT * FROM extrn_pay_amount;
```

Here is the result:

```
EMPLOYEE_ID PAY_DATE  CHECK_NUMBER  GROSS_PAY PRE_TAX_DED    TAX_DED   NET_PAY
----------- --------- ------------- --------- ----------- ---------- ----------
COMMENTS
-------------------------------------------------------------------------------
      12345 01-JAN-01          1000      1000         100        200       700
      12346 01-JAN-01          1001      2000         200        400      1400
      12347 01-JAN-01          1002      3000         400        800      2800
```

Of course, we can also join data between external tables and internal tables. For example, maybe we want to see the employee name. A simple join of the EMP table to the external EXTRN_PAY_AMOUNT table will give us what we want:

```
SELECT b.employee_id, a.ename, b.gross_pay
FROM emp a, extrn_pay_amount b
WHERE a.empno=b.employee_id;
```

Here are the results of this query:

```
EMPLOYEE_ID ENAME       GROSS_PAY
----------- ---------- ----------
      12345 MILLER           1000
      12346 FORD             2000
      12347 JAMES            3000
```

The ability to join external tables, either with other external tables or internal Oracle tables, makes ETL loading processing much easier to manage and can streamline the ETL load process.

Administering External Tables

As you might expect, you can use the **drop table** command to drop an external table from the database, as seen here:

```
DROP TABLE extrn_pay_amount;
```

The ALTER TABLE command can also be used to change certain characteristics of an external table through the use of the **alter_external_table** clause of the **alter**

table command. Using this clause, you can add, drop, and modify existing columns; and you can change the level of parallelism assigned to the table, the properties of the external data, and the **reject limit** clause.

Oracle has introduced the DBA_EXTERNAL_TABLES and DBA_EXTERNAL_ LOCATIONS views to help you manage external tables in your database. Of course, these views also come in the ALL and USER varieties as well. The DBA_EXTERNAL_ TABLES view provides a list of each external table that is contained in the database. This view contains the owner of the table, its name, the access parameters, and other information about external tables. The DBA_EXTERNAL_LOCATIONS view provides information on the directory names used in each external table definition.

Table Functions

The typical ETL process involves a procedural transformation process on the source data. Usually this transform process can require additional storage, as additional intermediate tables are often required during the data-transform stage. This also requires additional processing time, due to additional scans on the intermediate tables, an increased number of processes that must be executed, and the additional IO costs incurred because of the additional data writes. Oracle9i offers an alternative to this functionality in the form of *table functions*.

Table functions take a set of input, massage it as required, and then return the output in the form of a collection. The input to the table function can be in the form of a collection (such as a VARRAY or a nested table) or a **ref cursor**. We will use a **ref cursor** in our example. The output is in the form of a collection, either a VARRAY or a nested table. We will use a nested table in our example.

The table function can be paralleled, which can speed performance in many cases, as parallelism, along with pipelining, allows streaming of data to consumer processes. When a table function is pipelined, each row of the result set will be returned as soon as it is processed, or the entire row set can be returned after the function is complete. Typically, a table function is pipelined if the data is to be consumed immediately after it is produced. This has the benefit of removing the lag time between the completion of a precursor process and the execution of a subsequent job dependent on the results of the previous job. With pipelining, if the subsequent job depends only on the individual rows returned by the precursor job, then pipelining will allow you to run both jobs at the same time. As the first job returns each row, the second job can process that row. This can significantly reduce the overall processing time for a given process.

Additional benefits of pipelining include the fact that row sets are not stored in memory or some temporary table before being able to be used by a consumer. Pipelining and parallelism of a table function allow multi-threaded and concurrent execution of a table function, and query response times are improved as well.

You call a table function from within the **from** clause of a **select** statement. Table functions can be written from within PL/SQL, Java, and C. There are a number of ways to write table functions, based on your needs. We will provide one example for you here to give you an idea of the power of this feature in Oracle9i. For more information on different options that are available when using table functions, see the Oracle documentation and Oracle Technology Network (technet.oracle.com).

In the following example, we are going to use the external table we created earlier in this chapter called EXTRN_PAY_AMOUNT. We will assume that before we load it into our database, we want to add some text to the comment field indicating when the record was loaded into our database. First, let's look at the code, and then we will break it down into some detail:

```
DROP FUNCTION myTableFunction;
DROP TYPE salaryrecordtable force;
DROP TYPE salaryrecord force;
DROP PACKAGE ref_cur_pkg;

CREATE OR REPLACE TYPE SalaryRecord AS OBJECT
(employee_id      NUMBER,
 pay_date         DATE,
 check_number     NUMBER,
 gross_pay     NUMBER,
 pre_tax_ded        NUMBER,
 tax_ded          NUMBER,
 net_pay          NUMBER,
 comments         VARCHAR2(100) );
/
CREATE OR REPLACE TYPE salaryRecordTable AS TABLE OF SalaryRecord;
/
create or replace package ref_cur_pkg IS
type refcur_t is REF CURSOR RETURN extrn_pay_amount%ROWTYPE;
END;
/
CREATE OR REPLACE FUNCTION myTableFunction (p ref_cur_pkg.refcur_t)
RETURN salaryRecordTable
PIPELINED
PARALLEL_ENABLE (PARTITION p BY ANY)
IS
    out_rec   SalaryRecord := SalaryRecord(NULL,NULL,NULL,NULL,NULL,NULL,NULL,NULL);
    in_rec p%ROWTYPE;
BEGIN
    LOOP
        FETCH p into in_rec;
        EXIT WHEN p%NOTFOUND;
            out_rec:=in_rec;
            out_rec.comments:=in_rec.comments||' Transform Process complete '|| SYSDATE;
            pipe row(out_rec);
    END LOOP;
    CLOSE p;
    RETURN;
END;
/
```

Note how our appended text now appears in the comment column. This same method can be used to transform existing data before it is moved into a staging table. Let's look a little more closely at the table function we just used.

Examining the Table Function

The first thing we do in our example is to create a type called **SalaryRecord**, and then create a nested table called **SalaryRecordTable**. This structure will be used to return the result set back to the **select** query that calls this function. Thus, the transformed output records will be returned in the format defined by the nested table being defined.

Following the creation of the nested table, we create a package called ref_cur_pkg, and create a reference cursor in that package. Later, when we issue our **select** statement, we will use the **cursor** expression in the table function to pass the cursor to the table function for processing.

Following the creation of the **ref_cur_pkg** package, we then create the table function, which we call **MyTableFunction**. This function takes our reference cursor as its sole parameter, and returns the **SalaryRecordTable** nested table. Note the use of the **pipelined** and **parallel_enable** clauses. The **pipelined** clause indicates that the function will pipeline its results out as they are processed, rather than waiting until the entire result set is processed. The **parallel_enable** clause is an optimization hint that indicates that the function can be executed in parallel.

The **partition by** clause can be used only if you are using a **ref cursor** argument type (which you are). Using this clause, we are able to define the partitioning of the inputs to the **ref cursor** argument that affects paralleling of the query. In this case, we have used the **any** argument that allows the data to be partitioned randomly among all the parallel execution servers. Other options are range or hash partitioning, followed by a specific column list. The use of **range** or **hash** will control which data is processed by which parallel server, based on the algorithm of the partitioning method chosen. With range or hash, it is possible to have parallel server processes with uneven load balances, so use these options with care.

Next, in the table function, we define the input record (in_rec) and the output record (out_rec) formats. Following those definitions, we begin the function's procedural section and begin a loop where we fetch each input record and process it. Note that we first move all the records from the input **ref cursor** into the output record with the statement.

```
out_rec:=in_rec;
```

This is done to make sure that all the fields of the record are contained in the output that we are going to generate. In the next section, we modify the comments field, adding some text and the date.

Following the transformation of the data, we issue the pipe row command, which includes the output record's nested table as a parameter. This will cause the record that we just processed to be immediately written out to any waiting consumer process. This is how the pipeline process differs from a normal table function. If we did not include the **pipelined** clause earlier in the function, then we could not use the **pipe row** function, and we would have to wait until the entire row source was processed before we received the output. The rest of the function looks pretty much the same as any other PL/SQL function. Here is the result when we run the function, using the EXTRN_PAY_AMOUNT external table as the source of our data:

```
SELECT * FROM TABLE(myTableFunction(CURSOR(SELECT * FROM extrn_pay_amount) ) );

EMPLOYEE_ID PAY_DATE  CHECK_NUMBER  GROSS_PAY PRE_TAX_DED   TAX_DED    NET_PAY
----------- --------- ------------- --------- ----------- ---------- ----------
COMMENTS
-------------------------------------------------------------------------------
      12345 01-JAN-01          1000      1000         100        200        700
Transform Process complete 15-OCT-01
      12347 01-JAN-01          1002      3000         400        800       2800
Transform Process complete 15-OCT-01
      12346 01-JAN-01          1001      2000         200        400       1400
Transform Process complete 15-OCT-01
```

As you can see from the output, the end result is a transformation of the **comment** column output. While this is a fairly basic example of the power of a table function, it is clear that the table function provides a highly flexible and powerful option that you can take advantage of when designing your data-warehouse ETL architectures.

Other New and Enhanced Data-Warehouse and ETL Features

Several new features and enhancements to existing features have been introduced in Oracle9i, including multi-table **insert** statements and the new **merge** statement. We will also look at the new Oracle change data capture feature, parallel direct-load enhancements, and materialized view changes and enhancements.

Multi-Table Insert Statements

Often during the process of loading data from outside data sources into the data warehouse, data from a given source will need to be loaded into more than one table. Prior to Oracle9i, the only option you had was separate **insert** statements. Running multiple **insert** statements was costly because each execution of the **insert** statement would require parsing of the statement itself, and multiple scans of the source table.

These costs can be eliminated in Oracle9i through the use of multi-table **insert** statements. A multi-table **insert** statement allows you to **insert** the results of a single **select** statement into multiple tables. Parallel **insert** statements can take advantage of parallelism and Oracle's direct-load mechanisms. Another benefit of multi-table **insert** statements is that they can replace programmatic load processes, such as those that use **if...then** type structures to simulate a multi-table **insert** process.

Multi-table insert statements are made possible by some new syntax for the **insert...select** statement. Now, the **insert...select** statement includes one or more **into** clauses that exist within an **into** clause list. Each **into** clause specifies a target object that the row is to be inserted into. The same table can be used in more than one **into** clause.

Oracle9i supports both unconditional and conditional multi-table **insert** statements. If the unconditional form of the **into** clause is used, then each **into** clause in the **into** clause list will be executed for each row returned by the subquery without restriction. When the conditional form of the **into** clause is used, then each **into** clause may contain a **when** clause that determines whether the corresponding **into** clause should be executed.

The format of the **into** clause includes the object that the data should be inserted into, and then the values for that object. There are four kinds of multi-table **insert** statements:

- Unconditional
- Pivoting
- Conditional
- Insert all

Let's look at an example of each of these now.

Unconditional insert Statements

The unconditional **insert** statement begins with the **insert** command, followed by the **all** command, and then the **into** clause list. Following the **into** clause is the **select** statement. Here is an example of an unconditional **insert** statement:

```
INSERT ALL
        INTO salary_deduction_history VALUES (employee_id, ename, pay_date, tax_ded, pre_tax_ded)
        INTO salary_pay_history VALUES (employee_id, ename, pay_date, gross_pay, net_pay)
SELECT a.employee_id, b.ename,  a.pay_date, a.gross_pay, a.pre_tax_ded, a.tax_ded, a.net_pay
FROM extrn_pay_amount a, emp b
WHERE a.employee_id=b.empno;
```

Pivoting insert Statements

A pivoting **insert** statement is used when inserting into the same table multiple times. Again, you use the **insert all** statement, following it with multiple **into** statements to the same table. A pivoting statement serves to take normalized data and denormalize it. Here is an example of a pivoting multi-table **insert** statement that takes the data from a denormalized external table and reformats it into the normalized style of the destination table:

```
INSERT ALL
        INTO all_paycheck VALUES (emp_id, 'JAN', net_pay_jan)
        INTO all_paycheck VALUES (emp_id, 'FEB', net_pay_feb)
        INTO all_paycheck VALUES (emp_id, 'MAR', net_pay_mar)
```

```
      INTO all_paycheck VALUES (emp_id, 'APR', net_pay_apr)
      INTO all_paycheck VALUES (emp_id, 'MAY', net_pay_may)
      INTO all_paycheck VALUES (emp_id, 'JUN', net_pay_jun)
SELECT emp_id, net_pay_jan, net_pay_feb, net_pay_mar, net_pay_apr,
net_pay_may, net_pay_jun
FROM combined_paycheck_report;
```

Conditional insert Statements

The **when** clause can be used in a multi-table **insert** statement to provide for conditional control of each individual insert. The **when** clause supports subqueries, equivalency checks, and ordered **when** clause evaluation. The action of the **when** clause is determined by the use of either the **insert all** or **insert first** command. Let's look at an example of both an **insert all** and an **insert first** multi-table **insert** statement.

Insert all

The use of the **insert all...select** statement allows you to control multi-table **inserts** using conditional **when** statements. With **insert all**, each **when** statement will be evaluated, regardless of the results of the evaluation of the previous **when** statement:

```
INSERT ALL
WHEN emp_id in (select emp_id FROM emp where title='MANAGER')
INTO manager_pay_history VALUES (employee_id, ename, pay_date, gross_pay, net_pay)
WHEN pay_type='BONUS'
INTO bonus_pay_history VALUES (employee_id, pay_date, gross_pay, net_pay)
INTO all_pay_history VALUES (employee_id, pay_date, gross_pay, net_pay)
SELECT a.employee_id, a.pay_date, a.pay_type, a.gross_pay, a.net_pay
FROM extrn_pay_amount a, emp b
WHERE a.employee_id=b.empno;
```

In this example, we have two **when** clauses, and each is evaluated independent of the other. The first **when** statement checks the employee title in the EMP table. If the employee is a manager, then that record is written into the MANAGER_PAY_HISTORY table. Then the next **when** clause is evaluated. This time, if the **pay_type** column has a value of BONUS, then a record is written to the BONUS_PAY_HISTORY table. Finally, in all cases, a record is written to the ALL_PAY_HISTORY table. Now, let's look at using an ordered **when** clause evaluation.

Insert first

The **insert first** multi-table **insert** statement allows for conditional execution of an **insert** statement based on a series of **when** clauses. The primary difference between **insert all** and **insert first** is that only the first **when** clause that evaluates to TRUE will be executed. Any subsequent **when** clause will not be evaluated. Additionally, an **else** clause is available to allow for default processing if none of the **when** clauses evaluate to TRUE. Here is an example of an **insert first** statement:

```
INSERT FIRST
    WHEN emp_id > 10000 THEN
        INTO hire_2001_pay_history VALUES (employee_id, pay_date, gross_pay,
```

```
        net_pay)
    WHEN emp_id > 9000 THEN
        INTO hire_2000_pay_history VALUES (employee_id, pay_date, gross_pay,
        net_pay)
    WHEN emp_id > 8000 THEN
        INTO hire_1999_pay_history VALUES (employee_id, pay_date, gross_pay,
        net_pay)
    ELSE
        INTO hire_before_1999_pay_history VALUES (employee_id, pay_date, gross_pay,
        net_pay)
SELECT a.employee_id, a.pay_date, a.pay_type, a.gross_pay, a.net_pay
FROM extrn_pay_amount a, emp b
WHERE a.employee_id=b.empno;
```

In this example, it appears that the employee ID is somehow related to the hire date. Based on the employee number, the employee pay record is written to one of several tables that store pay records for employees based on when the employee is hired. Oracle will evaluate each **when** clause, from top to bottom, until one of the **when** clauses evaluates to TRUE.

Merge Statements

During data load operations, it might be that you will want to **insert** a row in a table if the primary key of the correct row does not exist, or you might wish just to update the row. To deal with this, Oracle9i provides a new **merge** command. The **merge** command allows you to conditionally **insert** a row into the database if it doesn't exist, or **update** an existing row.

Using the **merge** command improves database performance because it reduces the overall number of table scans that Oracle would otherwise have to complete. Also, the use of the **merge** statement can reduce the need to write more complex PL/SQL code to accomplish the same type of operation.

To use the **merge** command, you generally have a large fact table in a data warehouse and a smaller table that contains just the changes to be made to the fact table or a delta table. The **merge** command will scan the delta table, and based on a defined join between the tables, the **merge** command will determine whether the records in it need to be Inserted into the main table or just updated. Here is an example of the use of the **merge** command:

```
MERGE INTO employee_information A
USING emp_delta B
ON (a.emp_id = b.delta_emp_id)
WHEN MATCHED THEN
    UPDATE SET a.address=b.address, a.city=b.city, a.state=b.state, a.zip=b.zip,
        a.phone=b.phone;
WHEN NOT MATCHED THEN
    INSERT (emp_id, address, city, state, zip)
    VALUES (b.emp_id, b.address, b.city, b.state, b.zip);
```

In this example, Oracle will scan the EMP_DELTA table, looking for matching records between it and the EMPLOYEE_INFORMATION table. Oracle will look for matches based on the EMP_ID column in the EMPLOYEE_INFORMATION table and the DELTA_EMP_ID column in the EMP_DELTA table. If there is a matching record, then an **update** operation occurs, otherwise, an **insert** operation occurs.

Oracle Change Data Capture

Oracle9i offers a change data capture (CDC) facility that can be used to extract information on recent data changes. CDC captures DML that occurs on Oracle database tables, and these changes are stored in database change tables (not unlike the idea behind a snapshot or materialized view log). As the CDC information is collected, various views can be used to track the changes made to tables being tracked. These changes can also be propagated through a publish and subscribe mechanism.

NOTE
To use the CDC feature, Java must be enabled in the database.

To use CDC, you must first create a change table on each table you wish to track changes on. This change table will track all the deltas that then occur on the source table. Changes are tracked automatically by Oracle using internal triggers; so the recording of the deltas is very quick, but can still have some performance impacts on the database—depending on number and size of the changes that are occurring on the source table.

Tracking Table Changes

You create a change table by using **dbms_logmnr_cdc_publish**, the new Oracle9i package that has been provided specifically for CDC. The procedure **create_ change_table** will create the change data table. An example of running this procedure follows:

```
EXEC DBMS_LOGMNR_CDC_PUBLISH.CREATE_CHANGE_TABLE
(owner => 'scott', change_table_name=>'dept_changes',
change_set_name=>'SYNC_SET', source_schema=>'scott',
source_table=>'dept', column_type_list='deptno number(2), dname varchar2(14),
loc varchar2(13)', capture_values=>'both', rs_id='y', row_id='y',
user_id='n',timestamp='n', object_id=>'n', source_colmap='y',
target_colmap='y', options_string=>NULL);
```

Look in the Oracle documentation for the various option settings for the **dbms_ logmnr_cdc_publish.create_change_table** procedure. This particular statement creates a change table called DEPT_CHANGES in the SCOTT schema.

Publish and Subscribe to Change Data

Having created change tables, Oracle allows you to publish the changes to be used by those who wish to subscribe to the changes and apply those changes elsewhere.

See the *Oracle9i Data Warehousing Guide* for more information on how to publish and subscribe to the CDC data. During the subscribe-publish process, Oracle creates a change table, also called a *change source*. The various change sources are collectively known as a *change set*. Each individual subscriber view is built off the change set.

Oracle provides separate subscription windows for each subscriber, thus allowing each subscriber to use the change and apply the change deltas at different times. As each subscriber finishes with the current subscription window, a procedure is executed to purge the window and prepare it for the next set of CDC deltas to be added to that table.

CDC-Related Views

Several views have been added to Oracle9*i* to support CDC. The views are seen in Table 4-2.

View Name	Description
ALL_PUBLISHED_COLUMNS	Displays information on all published source table columns for which the subscriber has privileges
ALL_SOURCE_TABLES	Displays information on the published source tables for which the subscribers have privileges to subscribe
CHANGE_SETS	Displays information on existing change sets
CHANGE_SOURCES	Displays information on existing change sources
CHANGE_TABLES	Displays information on existing change tables
DBA_PUBLISHED_COLUMNS	Displays information on all the existing (published) source table columns
DBA_SOURCE_TABLES	Displays information on all the existing (published) source tables
DBA_SUBSCRIBED_COLUMNS	Displays information on all columns of published tables to which subscribers have subscribed
DBA_SUBSCRIBED_TABLES	Displays information on all published tables to which subscribers have subscribed
DBA_SUBSCRIPTIONS	Displays information on all subscriptions

TABLE 4-2.   *CDC-Related Views*

View Name	Description
USER_PUBLISHED_COLUMNS	Displays information on all the published source table columns for which the user has privileges
USER_SOURCE_TABLES	Displays information on the published source tables for which this user has privileges to subscribe
USER_SUBSCRIBED_COLUMNS	Displays information on all columns of published tables to which the subscriber has subscribed
USER_SUBSCRIBED_TABLES	Displays information on all published tables to which the subscriber has subscribed
USER_SUBSCRIPTIONS	Displays information on all current subscriptions

TABLE 4-2. *CDC-Related Views* (continued)

Oracle9i Parallel Direct Load Enhancements

Previous to Oracle9i parallel direct-load **insert** operations on partitions were limited to a single parallel-slave process per partition. Now, in Oracle9i, multiple slave processes are able to update a single partition. This can help improve results of direct load **insert** operations, particularly if data to be inserted into partitions is particularly skewed to favor one or a few specific partitions, causing the load to be unbalanced.

Oracle9i Summary Management Changes

Several changes have been made to materialized views (MViews) in Oracle9i. These include the **explain materialized view** command, the **explain query rewrite** command, and enhancements to MView fast refreshes.

Explain Materialized View

With MViews, it is sometimes difficult to know whether a given materialized view can or will be able to be fast-refreshed. Oracle9i provides a new procedure within the **dbms_mview** package, **dbms_mview.explain_mview**, that provides information on the ability of the MView to fast-refresh, and also what types of query rewrite can be done on the MView.

Prior to running **dbms_mview.explain_mview**, you must first make sure that the script $ORACLE_HOME/rdbms/admin/utlxmv.sql has been executed in the schema that you are going to run the procedure in. Next, you will run the **dbms_mview.explain_mview** procedure, passing as a parameter either the name of an MView or the **select** SQL statement for a potential MView that you want analyzed. Once the procedure has completed running, you can view the results of the procedure by querying the view MV_CAPABILITIES_TABLE, or you can store the results in a VARRAY.

Let's look at an example. Suppose we are planning to create an MView that summarizes employee salary by pay week. We want to analyze the MView we are getting ready to create to see whether it will be fast-refreshable, and whether it will be able to be used with query rewrite. So, we execute the **dbms_mview.explain_ mview** procedure and review the results. Note that when we run the **explain_mview** procedure, we assign a statement ID to the statement (in this case, 123). This allows us to easily identify the results of the command in the MV_CAPABILITIES_TABLE that we will query for the results of the execution of **explain_mview**. The command we used to analyze the MView statement and the results are as follows:

```
exec DBMS_MVIEW.EXPLAIN_MVIEW('SELECT pay_date, SUM(net_pay) FROM sal GROUP BY pay_date',123);
SELECT capability_name, possible, related_text, msgtxt
FROM mv_capabilities_table
WHERE statement_id='123'
ORDER BY seq;


CAPABILITY_NAME         P RELATED_TEXT  MSGTXT
-------------------- - ------------- ------------------------------
PCT                     N
REFRESH_COMPLETE        Y
REFRESH_FAST            N
REWRITE                 Y
PCT_TABLE               N SAL           relation is not a partitioned
                                        table
REFRESH_FAST_AFTER_I N SCOTT.SAL       the detail table does not have
INSERT                                  a materialized view log
REFRESH_FAST_AFTER_O N SUM(NET_PAY)    SUM(expr) without COUNT(expr)
NETAB_DML
REFRESH_FAST_AFTER_O N                 see the reason why REFRESH_FAS
NETAB_DML                              T_AFTER_INSERT is disabled
REFRESH_FAST_AFTER_O N                 COUNT(*) is not present in the
NETAB_DML                               select list
REFRESH_FAST_AFTER_O N                 SUM(expr) without COUNT(expr)
NETAB_DML
REFRESH_FAST_AFTER_A N                 see the reason why REFRESH_FAS
NY_DML                                 T_AFTER_ONETAB_DML is disabled
REFRESH_FAST_PCT        N              PCT is not possible on any of
                                       the detail tables in the
                                       materialized view
REWRITE_FULL_TEXT_MA Y
TCH
REWRITE_PARTIAL_TEXT Y
_MATCH
REWRITE_GENERAL         Y
REWRITE_PCT             N              general rewrite is not possible
                                       and PCT is not possible on
                                       any of the detail tables
```

In this example, we find that there are some operations that can be done on the proposed MView, and others that cannot. For example, we see that the view can have complete refreshes done on it (as seen from the **refresh_complete** row in the CAPABILITY_NAME column), but that fast refreshes (the **refresh_fast** row) are not possible. Why is it that fast refreshes are not available on this MView? One clue comes from the **refresh_fast_after_insert** row. This row indicates that a snapshot log does not exist, which certainly would disqualify this MView from being able to do fast refreshes.

NOTE
PCT, which is referenced several times in this view, stands for partition change tracking. *This will be discussed in the "MView Fast-Refresh Enhancements" section.*

Explain Query Rewrite

Along with the ability to explain the capabilities of MViews, Oracle9*i* introduces the ability to explain query rewrite results. In Oracle8*i*, it was often difficult to figure out why query rewrite was not working. So many different factors come into play with query rewrite—dimensions, constraints, the query rewrite integrity modes of the database, and several others. Oracle9*i* offers the ability to analyze a given query and advise whether it will be eligible for query rewrite.

This functionality is provided through the **dbms_mview** package, using the **explain_rewrite** procedure. As with the **explain_mview** procedure previously discussed, you must first execute a script to create a table called **rewrite_table** by using the $ORACLE_HOME/rdbms/admin/utlxrw.sql script.

Having executed the utlxrw.sql script, we are ready to use the **explain_rewrite** procedure to see whether a given SQL statement is rewritable. First, let's look at the syntax for this procedure:

```
PROCEDURE DBMS_MVIEW.EXPLAIN_REWRITE
(   query          IN VARCHAR2,
    mv             IN VARCHAR2,
    statement_id   IN VARCHAR2);
```

Optionally, you can direct the output of **explain_rewrite** to a VARRAY, instead of a table. In this event, the procedure should be called as follows:

```
DBMS_MVIEW.EXPLAIN_REWRITE
(   query          IN VARCHAR2(2000),
    mv             IN VARCHAR2(30),
    msg_array      IN OUT SYS.RewriteArrayType);
```

In this next example, we will create a materialized view, MY_SAL, and then issue a call to **dbms_mview.explain_rewrite** to determine whether a query will be fast-refreshable by the MY_SAL materialized view. We will then look at the EXPLAIN_REWRITE view to review the results.

```
CREATE MATERIALIZED VIEW my_sal REFRESH FAST AS
SELECT a.empno, b.ename, c.dname, SUM(a.net_pay)
FROM sal a, emp b, dept c
WHERE a.empno = b.empno and a.empno = b.empno
AND   b.deptno=c.deptno
GROUP BY a.empno, b.ename, c.dname;DECLARE
     my_query     VARCHAR2(200):= 'SELECT a.empno, b.ename, c.dname,
     SUM(a.net_pay)
     FROM sal a, emp b, dept c
     WHERE a.empno = b.empno
     AND a.empno = b.empno
     AND b.deptno=c.deptno
     GROUP BY a.empno, b.ename, c.dname';
BEGIN
     DBMS_MVIEW.EXPLAIN_REWRITE(my_query,'MV_SAL','100');
end;
/
SQL> select message from rewrite_table;

MESSAGE
-------------------------------------------------------------------
QSM-01002: no query rewrite when OPTIMIZER_GOAL is rule based
```

In this example, we see that we cannot rewrite the query because the database appears to be in the rule-based *optimizer_goal*, which does not support query rewrite. Once we have corrected this problem, we would want to run the **explain_rewrite** procedure, as there might be other issues that will prevent the query from being rewritable. For example, even if the *optimizer_goal* was set at the default of CHOOSE, the materialized view would not work without analyzing the materialized view.

MView Fast-Refresh Enhancements

Materialized views are most effective if they can be fast-refreshed. If a materialized view is fast-refreshable, then the opportunity for data divergence between the MView and its base tables is much less pronounced. There were several restrictions on fast refresh in Oracle8*i*. Oracle9*i* has enhanced MView fast-refresh capabilities to allow fast refreshes of MViews that include aggregation and joins, as well as inline views, **cube**, **rollup**, and **grouping** operations in MViews. Finally, MViews can now be fast-refreshed after partition maintenance operations such as **drop partition** and **exchange partition**.

To support enhanced MView fast-refresh operations, a new keyword, **sequence**, has been added to the **create materialzed log** command. When used, this command facilitates the creation of a sequence column in the MView log. This allows Oracle to track the sequence of DML operations in a given table. The **sequence** keyword allows for mixed DML to occur in the tables at the base of the MView log. When a table is involved in mixed DML, this means that it is involved in a diverse number of **insert**, **update**, and **delete** operations.

If your MView is built on more than one table that involves mixed DML, then each table that the MView is built on will need to include the **sequence** keyword when creating the MView logs for that table. This is required to be able to fast-refresh an MView built on tables that involve mixed DML. Also, if the tables are subject to direct loads and normal DML, then it will need an MView log that is built with the **sequence** keyword.

Partition Change Tracking

Prior to Oracle9i, if a partition in a table that an MView was built on become stale (or was changed in some way), then, depending on the setting of the *query_rewrite_integrity* parameter, the related MViews would be considered stale and would not be considered for query rewrite.

Oracle9i maintains partition staleness at a more granular level. In Oracle9i, staleness is tracked at a partition level, using partition change tracking. If the databases *query_rewrite_mode* is set in TRUSTED or ENFORCED mode, then as long as the rows in a specific partition are considered FRESH (unchanged), then a query can be rewritten to use the MView rather than the underlying table.

For example, assume you have a partitioned table with two partitions and your *quert_rewrite_mode* is set to TRUSTED. Assume further that there is an MView that is built using this partitioned table. Finally, assume that a change has been made to the first partition of the table, but that it did not affect the second.

Given this example, if a query was issued against the table, and it involved rows in the first partition or in both partitions, then the query could not be rewritten because the partition is stale. If the query used only the rows in the second partition, then it would be able to be rewritten using the MView, since the second partition has not been modified. See the Oracle documentation for more details on this new feature of Oracle9i.

CHAPTER
5

Miscellaneous Oracle9i
Features and Enhancements

- New Oracle9i security features and enhancements
- NLS and globalization support enhancements
- Enhancements to Oracle9i configuration programs
- Miscellaneous new Oracle9i features and enhancements
- Oracle9i parameter and view changes

n this chapter, we have piled several different categories of changes into one big bucket we call miscellaneous. These include security features, National Language support, and other enhancements that didn't belong in the other chapters. Rather than having several short chapters, we opted just to put them here. You will find them ordered, though; first we discuss security issues, then NLS issues. We will move on to some of the external configuration programs and conclude with parameter changes that might interest you.

Removal of connect internal and Server Manager

Oracle has long warned of the removal of Server Manager (SVRMGR) product as well as the ability to issue **connect internal**. In Oracle9i this is finally realized. Oracle9i does not ship with SVRMGR at all, and the use of connect internal is no longer allowed. You will need to use SQL*Plus or Oracle Enterprise Manager to manage your database now. Note that with the removal of **connect internal** that access to manage the database requires connecting as a privileged user. To do so, you will need to use the *as sysdba* parameter when connecting to the database, as shown in the following examples:

```
sqlplus "sys as sysdba"
sqlplus "sys as sysoper"
SQL> connect sys as sysdba
SQL> connect sys as sysoper
SQL> sqlplus "sys@test as sysDBA"
```

Virtual Private Database Enhancements

Oracle9i introduces new features and functionality to its virtual private database (VPD) functionality. This includes the introduction of the Oracle Policy Manager (OPM), which is an Oracle Enterprise Manager (OEM) graphical interface to VPD. Also, VPD now provides a global application context, as well as partitioned fine-grained access control (FGAC). Let's look at each of these features.

Oracle Policy Manager

OPM is a new tool provided in OEM to ease the administration of Oracle's security features, such as VPD, application context, and label security. It is installed automatically when you install OEM. To be able to use the tool in a given database, some setup is required. Depending on which security features you wish to use, the database account that OPM will use (assuming it's not SYS or SYSTEM) will need to be granted certain roles, and will require other privilege grants. These requirements are summarized in the following table:

Security Feature	Required Role	Required Grants
Label Security	LBAC_DBA	**execute** on the following packages: **sa_sysdba**, **sa_components**, **sa_label_admin**, **sa_user_admin**, and **sa_session**.
VPD		**execute** on **dbms_rls** package, **select** on ALL_POLICIES and ALL_POLICY_GROUPS views.
Application context		**select** on ALL_POLICY_CONTEXTS, DBA_CONTEXT views.

Global Application Contexts

Global application contexts (GAC) in Oracle9*i* allow you to use connection pooling and VPD, providing additional scalability for high-velocity applications, such as web-based applications. With GAC, the middle tier (for example, the application server) associates a common application context for each user session, rather than setting up a specific per-session application context. This context is then stored in the SGA of the database instance and applied to the user session when it is created on the database. This GAC will then be the context that the user session will use.

To facilitate GAC, new procedures in **dbms_session** have been added. These new procedures include

- **set_context**   Used to set the application context for a specific client ID.

- **clear_context**   Used to clear the application context for the client ID.

- **set_identifier**   Used to define the ID for the application session. Once this has been executed, **sys_context** calls will use only the context associated with the set identifier defined.

- **clear_identifier**   Clears the identifier set with the **set_identifier** procedure.

How GAC Works

We've discussed GAC in general principles. Let's look at how it might be used in real life. One of the places where GAC might be used is with a web application. In our example, to be able to use a GAC, we would first need to create a *global-context namespace*. This is created with the **create context** command, as seen here:

```
CREATE CONTEXT report_context USING report_own.init ACCESSED GLOBALLY;
```

This context creates a global-context namespace called **report_context**. The **using** clause argument, **report_own.init**, defines a procedure that will be called when we want to set the context (we will discuss this shortly). The **accessed globally** keyword indicates that this is a global context being allocated.

Now, we will fire up our application server to do some business. The application server will connect to the database at this time, using a management account that we have created. Let's call it WEBADM.

Our web user, Eliza, surfs over to our application server. As the connection is made, the application server authenticates the connection by Eliza, and a temporary session ID is assigned to this connection. Assume, for this example, that the ID is 9999. Note that each session ID is unique. This session ID will be returned through Eliza's browser, or a cookie might be used. The application server will also initialize the GAC to Eliza, calling a package we have already created, **report_own.init**. Note that this is the same package we associated with the GAC. This package actually is used to assign the needed context variables to the GAC. For example, **report_own.init** might execute these statements:

```
DBMS_SESSION.SET_CONTEXT('report_context','id','ELIZA','WEBADM',9999);
DBMS_SESSION.SET_CONTEXT('report_context','r_level','1','WEBADM',9999);
```

Note that the parameter *webadm* in the calls above is important from a security prospective. This limits the ability to access the GAC to a specific user. Thus, if a DBA were to log in to the database as SYS, the DBA would not be able to see the GAC from the SYS account because the GAC defined is limited to the WEBADM account and session identifier 9999 (which we will discuss next). If the application contexts were instead set like this,

```
DBMS_SESSION.SET_CONTEXT( 'report_context','id','ELIZA',NULL, 9999);
DBMS_SESSION.SET_CONTEXT('report_context','r_level','1', NULL,9999);
```

then any session would be able to see the GAC—provided they had set their session identifier to 9999. You can also set the client_id to NULL, which, in effect, provides for a globally accessible context (for those sessions not assigned a client ID).

Now, the application server will create the database session and initialize the context for the session by issuing a **dbms_session.set_identifier(9999);**. This command establishes the session's *client ID*. The client ID is used to uniquely identify a specific session and its associated global context. At this point, any **sys_context** calls will return the context values associated with that specific session. So, if the session issues a call **sys_context('report_own', 'r_level')**, then it would return 1 for Eliza's session. Once the session is complete, the application server would issue a call to clear the session identifier, using **dbms_session.clear_identifier**.

Partitioned Fine-Grained Access Control

In Oracle8*i*, it was often a complicated endeavor to create fine-grained access control (FGAC) policies for individual applications. This would often require parallel development of access policies, which could be a difficult process. The combinations of possible restrictions that would have to be programmed for also could become quite complex and sophisticated.

Oracle9*i* solves this problem by allowing the definition of application-specific contexts, along with the definition of a default policy that enforces policies that should always be applied to the object.

To use partitioned FGAC, you define an application context for each application. Depending on which application context is set, different access policies and the default policy combine to provide the overall access policy for the given application.

An example of the use of partitioned FGAC would be a central data-hosting environment. For example, say your company provides central processing facilities for several banks. Let's assume we have a single table called CUSTOMERS that contains customer records for each bank account for each customer. The first requirement here is that we want a given bank to be able to see only its own customers. Thus, we will create a default policy that restricts a bank to its own records.

The banks use several applications to access the data in these accounts. One of the applications provides customer information from the CUSTOMERS table on customers of each of the branches. Another application provides customer information from the CUSTOMERS table for customers of the trust department. The rule is that the branches cannot see trust-department customer information, but that the trust department can see both their information and branch information. Further, a given branch can see only its individual customer information, and cannot see the customers of another branch.

In this example, you would create a default policy to control the overall access to the data by the different banks. Then you would define policies for each application group. Finally, you would create application contexts, which are called the *driving contexts*. Driving contexts are associated with a group of FGAC policies. When the query against the CUSTOMERS table is executed, Oracle will execute the default policy and then check the driving context, which was set by the application, and execute any policies assigned with that driving policy. The result is that each application will have access only to the data it is supposed to have access to.

Other Security Improvements

Oracle9i introduces additional security enhancements, including Label Security, improvements to the **dbms_obfuscation** package, as well as the introduction of fine-grained auditing. Let's look at these items next.

Label Security

Oracle Label Security is available only for the Enterprise Edition of the product. It is an optional, add-on product and does not install when doing a default Oracle9i install. Rather, you will need to use the custom install option when installing the Oracle RDBMS software from the Universal Installer and select the Label Security check box to ensure it is installed.

Label Security is an alternative to fine-grained access control (FGAC), though Label Security, at its core, uses FGAC. Label Security does not require the creation of security policy packages to enforce row-level security. Thus, Label Security removes the programming requirement that is present with FGAC.

With Label Security, DBA-defined labels determine the sensitivity of rows of Oracle data. To take advantage of Label Security, a column is added to each table that the DBA wishes to secure. This column is then checked by the database and compared to the user's assigned security level. If the user is assigned a security level that permits access to the row, they will be able to access it.

DBMS_OBFUSCATION Enhancements

The **dbms_obfuscation** package allows you to encrypt and decrypt sensitive information, essentially providing a method of doing column-level encryption. In Oracle9i, the **dbms_obfuscation** package includes a random number generator that is FIPS-140 certified. With this random number generator, the number generated is always randomized, regardless of the key provided.

Fine-Grained Auditing

Fine-grained auditing (FGA) is a new feature of Oracle9i Enterprise Edition that allows you to audit **select** statements. This auditing occurs with the creation of *audit policies* that define a criterion for a given column in the object to be audited, which determines when auditing should and should not take place. The criterion can be based on the selection of the column at any time, or based on specific values or a range of values in the column that might be of interest. Once the criterion is established, Oracle will evaluate any **select** statement that an audit policy is defined on to see if the auditing criterion is met. If the auditing criterion is met, then information about that SQL statement is recorded in an audit log for later review.

NOTE
You should use FGA only when using cost-based optimization. Rule-based optimization can cause unexpected results when row filtering is applied.

Enabling an Audit Policy

As an example, assume that we have a table that is tracking the schedule of the President of the United States. The Secret Service has requested that we track any time that someone queries this table and, specifically, looks for the travel plans for the President. For the purposes of our example, our table looks like this:

```
CREATE TABLE itineraries
( travel_record_number    NUMBER,
person_traveling          VARCHAR2(40),
traveling_from            VARCHAR2(40),
traveling_to              VARCHAR2(40),
Depart                    date,
Arrive                    date);
```

To meet this important request, we could create an auditing policy using FGA. To do so, we would use the **dbms_fga** package to create the audit policy. Here is an example of the creation of the audit policy that will allow us to know whether the President's travel plans have been queried:

```
DBMS_FGA.ADD_POLICY(
object_schema   =>   'TRAVEL',
object_name     => 'ITINERARIES',
policy_name     => 'CHECK_PRESIDENT_QUERIES',
audit_condition => 'PERSON_TRAVELING = ''PRESIDENT''',
audit_column    => 'DEPART');
```

Let's look at what we have done in this SQL statement. First, we have created a security policy called check_president_queries, as defined by the *policy_name* parameter. Further, the *object_name* parameter defines that this policy is assigned to the ITINERARIES table. This policy applies to the DEPART column, as shown by the *audit_column* parameter. Note here that an audit policy can apply to only one column, though a given table can have multiple audit policies assigned to it. Next, the *audit_condition* parameter defines the conditions in which we want Oracle to produce an audit record. In this case, any time a SQL statement queries values from the *audit_column* (in this case, departure time), and if the **person_traveling** is the PRESIDENT, an audit record will be created.

Each row that is returned based on this audit policy is called an *interested row*. Note that only one audit record is generated for each interested row returned by a single SQL statement execution; so, if a query returns 50 interested rows, only one audit trail record is written. Finally, when the audit condition is reached, the auditing record is created by an autonomous transaction. This is also true with the execution of the event handler, which we will discuss next.

NOTE
The user creating the policies will need **execute** *privileges to use the* **dbms_fga** *package.*

Audit Event Handler

Let's assume that the Secret Service wants to be notified by e-mail any time that the President's travel plans are queried. To facilitate this, you can add an audit event handler. The audit event handler will be executed each time an audit record is executed. The procedure could be written to send the e-mail requested by the secret service. To have the audit event handler execute, you will need to identify it when creating the security policy. Here is an example:

```
DBMS_FGA.ADD_POLICY(
    object_schema    =>    'TRAVEL',
    object_name      => 'ITINERARIES',
    policy_name      => 'CHECK_PRESIDENT_QUERIES',
    audit_condition  => 'PERSON_TRAVELING = ''PRESIDENT''',
    audit_column     => 'DEPART'
    handler_schema   =>    'TRAVEL',
    handler_module   =>    'EMAIL_SS',
    enable           =>    TRUE );
```

The audit policy handler is a procedure that is sent three parameters when it is called by Oracle. This includes the schema name of the table being queried, the table name itself, and the name of the policy that is calling the policy handler procedure. Here is an example of such a procedure (assuming that the function p_send_email has already been written):

```
CREATE OR REPLACE PROCEDURE travel.email_ss
(schema VARCHAR2, table VARCHAR2, policy VARCHAR2)
AS
    v_msg := varchar2(100);
BEGIN
    -- Using a procedure we have created to send email from the database,
send the SS an
    -- email about this access attempt.
    v_msg:='The Presidents schedule has been looked at.';
    P_SEND_EMAIL(send_to=>'SServiceAgent', sub=>'Presidents Travel',
msg=>v_msg);
END;
```

Audit Trail

Audit records are written to the table DBA_FGA_AUDIT_TRAIL. Here is a query against DBA_FGA_AUDIT_TRAIL that shows a user querying the President's schedule and the resulting audit record:

```
SELECT travel_record_number, person_traveling, depart
FROM itineraries WHERE traveler='PRESIDENT';

RECORD_NUMBER      PERSON_TRAVELING     DEPART
-------------      ----------------     ---------
            1           PRESIDENT       01-NOV-01

SQL> SELECT sql_text FROM dba_fga_audit_trail;

SQL_TEXT
----------------------------------------------------------------------
--------------------
select travel_record_number, person_traveling, depart from travel where
traveler='PRESIDENT';
```

Just as with the SYS.AUD$ audit table, you will want to move the base table of the DBA_FGA_AUDIT_TRAIL view from the SYSTEM tablespace to its own tablespace. Use the **alter table move** command to move this table (sys.fga_log$). This will reduce I/O on the SYSTEM tablespace, as well as fragmentation. The DBA will also need to manage the growth of the audit records in this table.

Security on Oracle Database Default Accounts

When you create an Oracle database, it may be created with a number of default accounts. Prior to Oracle9i, these accounts would be created with default passwords, and would be available for immediate use. In Oracle9i, all default accounts except SYS, SYSTEM, and SCOTT will be created as locked accounts. To unlock the accounts, use the **alter user account unlock** command. You should always change the passwords of these accounts, and unlock them if they will be needed.

NLS and Globalization Support Enhancements

Several enhancements to Oracle NLS and globalization features are present in Oracle9i. In this section, we will look at some of these improvements, including the use of character and byte semantics in the database, changes to NCHAR data types, and issues relating to time zones and daylight saving time in the United States. We will also review the new time stamp and interval data types introduced in Oracle9i.

Character Versus Byte Semantics

In Oracle8i, you defined the size of CHAR, VARCHAR2, CLOB, and LONG data types in terms of bytes. Thus, a VARCHAR2(10) indicated that storage of 10 bytes, rather than 10 characters, was to be allocated. In single-byte character sets, this had little impact because a single character was a byte in size. In multi-byte character sets, however, this could become a problem because a given character that you wanted to store could be larger than 10 bytes.

Oracle9i offers a solution to this problem by allowing you to define SQL character types in terms of either bytes or characters. This is known as *byte or character semantics*. Now, you can define each character storage type using either byte or character semantics when you create that column. Here is an example of such an operation:

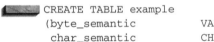

```
CREATE TABLE example
(byte_semantic          VARCHAR2(50 BYTE),
 char_semantic          CHAR(100 CHAR) );
```

You can also use the new *nls_length_semantics* setting to define the default semantic setting (byte or char) to be used when creating objects. This parameter can be set in the database initialization file, or changed using the **alter system** or **alter session** commands. Two options are available for you to use, byte or char. Thus, if you wish the table columns in your database to use character semantics by default (byte is the default), then set *nls_length_semantics*=char in the database parameter file. Note that changing this parameter will have no impact on objects that are already defined in the database.

Some changes to the data dictionary have been made that will allow you to determine whether a given column is defined using byte or character semantics. The USER_TAB_COLUMNS and ALL_TAB_COLUMN data-dictionary views contain two new columns. The first is the **char_length** column, which defines the maximum character length of a given column. The **char_used** column defines whether a given column is using byte semantics (shown by a *B* in the column) or character semantics (shown by a *C* in the column).

The DBA_IND_COLUMNS, USER_IND_COLUMNS and ALL_IND_COLUMNS data-dictionary views also have the **char_length** column added to them to indicate the maximum character length of the given column.

NCHAR Data Type Changes

The NCHAR data type (NCHAR, NVARCHAR and NCLOB) has changed in Oracle9i. Previously, the NCHAR data type (introduced in Oracle8) allowed a number of different character sets to be stored in columns of this type, as well as the character set the database was created with. This allowed for the storage of different character sets that were multi-byte, such as Asian character data.

Oracle9i has changed the NCHAR data type, limiting it to support only Unicode character sets (UTF8 and AL16UTF16). Other character sets, including Asian character sets, are no longer supported by NCHAR data types.

If you were using NCHAR data types to store non-Unicode data types, you have a migration issue that you will need to deal with. Oracle provides the following migration process:

1. Export all objects with NCHAR columns from the Oracle8 database.

2. Drop the NCHAR columns in the Oracle8 database.

3. Upgrade the database to Oracle9i.

4. Create a temporary schema.

5. Import the objects with NCHAR columns back into the upgraded Oracle9i database using the temporary schema.

6. Re-create the NCHAR columns in the original table.

7. Move the NCHAR columns from the temporary schema back into the original table.

You can also use the utlnchar.sql script at the end of an Oracle8i to 9i upgrade script to convert Oracle8 NCHAR columns to the new Oracle9i NCHARs.

Once the columns have been modified, you will not be able to downgrade the data in those columns. Instead, you will need to drop the NCHAR columns, downgrade the database, and then re-import the columns, using the export you took of the original Oracle8i database.

Changing Database Character Sets

Oracle9i allows you to change the database character set via the **alter database character set** command. You can use this command if, for example, you wish to move from a single-byte character set to a multi-byte character set.

If you are migrating or converting your database character sets via the **alter database character set** command, you will want to investigate the new character-set scanning utility called csscan. It can be used to scan the database to find areas of possible character-set conversion issues including issues that might cause data truncation. Also, this utility will advise you if certain column widths should be expanded prior to modifying the database character set.

Please refer to the Oracle9i documentation for more information on converting the database character set.

Time Zones and Daylight Saving Time

Oracle9i now allows you to define a time zone for the database as a whole, as well as at a session level. Time-zone settings apply only to objects with columns that use the new Oracle9i data type, **timestamp with local timezone**. If you do not set a database time zone, then Oracle will use the time zone setting of the operating system.

Oracle allows you to define time zones as offsets of universal coordinated time (UTC), or you can use named regions. To set the time zone for the entire database, either you establish the database time zone when creating the database by using the **set time_zone** clause of the **create database** command, or you use the **alter database** command. Here is an example of each of these options:

```
CREATE DATABASE mydb
SET TIME_ZONE='-05:00';
```

Note that when defining a time zone in this manner, you define it as an offset to UTC. Thus, in this example, we are setting the time zone for eastern standard time, which is five hours earlier than UTC.

The database time zone can be redefined using the *time_zone* parameter of the **alter database** command. This offset is based on a UTC offset again, as shown here:

```
ALTER DATABASE SET TIME_ZONE= '-08:00';
```

Also, you can use named regions when setting time zones, both for the database and when using the ALTER SYSTEM command. In this example, we are setting the database time zone to central standard time using the **alter database** command:

```
ALTER DATABASE SET TIME_ZONE= 'CST';
```

You can also change the time zone setting for a given database session using the **alter session** command, as shown here:

```
-- This sets the session time zone to use the OS Local Time Zone.
ALTER SESSION SET TIME_ZONE =  local;
-- This sets the session time zone to use the database time zone.
ALTER SESSION SET TIME_ZONE= 'CST';
```

New Date-and-Time Data Types

Some new date-and-time data types have been added in Oracle9i, including TIMESTAMP, TIMESTAMP WITH TIME ZONE, and TIMESTAMP WITH LOCAL TIME ZONE. Note that TIMESTAMP and TIMESTAMP WITH TIME ZONE are also literals that you can use. Also, a new data type, an INTERVAL data type, has been added to Oracle9i. Let's look at each of these in more detail.

New TIMESTAMP Data Types

There are three new **timestamp** data types in Oracle9i. Each of these represents a different data type. Two of the new **timestamp** data types provide time-zone offset information, in two different ways. Let's look at the three new **timestamp** data types in a bit more detail in Table 5-1.

Data Type	Storage Size	Fields	Notes
TIMESTAMP [(*fractional_seconds_ precision*)]	11 bytes	Year, Month, Day, Hour, Minute, Second	The *fractional_seconds_ precision* parameter represents the number of digits in the fractional part of the SECOND field. Valid values are 0 to 9 (default is 6). An example of a time stamp is 2001-01-01 01:00:01.115.
TIMESTAMP [(*fractional_seconds_ precision*)] WITH TIME ZONE	13 bytes	Year, Month, Day, Hour, Minute, Second, Time Zone displacement value	The *fractional_seconds_ precision* parameter represents the number of digits in the fractional part of the SECOND field. Valid values are 0 to 9 (default is 6). An example of a time stamp with time zone is 2001-01-01 01:00:01.115+03:00.
TIMESTAMP [(*fractional_seconds_ percision*)] WITH LOCAL TIME ZONE	11 bytes	Year, Month, Day, Hour, Minute, Second	The *fractional_seconds_ precision* parameter represents the number of digits in the fractional part of the SECOND field. Valid values are 0 to 9 (default is 6).

TABLE 5-1.   *TIMESTAMP Data Type Summary*

Let's look at a couple of examples of the use of these new data types. First, let's create a table using a **timestamp** column:

```
CREATE TABLE login_logout
(username      VARCHAR2(30),
 timein        TIMESTAMP(3),

 timeout       TIMESTAMP(3) );

-- Insert a record

INSERT INTO login_logout VALUES
('Robert Freeman','01-JAN-01 06:00:00.010 AM', '01-JAN-01 06:00:00.010 AM');

-- Now, let's look at the record

SELECT * FROM login_logout;

USERNAME             TIMEIN                    TIMEOUT
---------------      ------------------------  ------------------------
Robert Freeman       01-JAN-01 06:00:00.010 AM 01-JAN-01 06:00:00.010 AM
```

Now let's look at a **timestamp with time zone** example:

```
CREATE TABLE login_logout
(username      VARCHAR2(30),
 timein        TIMESTAMP(0) WITH TIME ZONE,
 timeout       TIMESTAMP(0) WITH TIME ZONE);

-- Insert a record

INSERT INTO login_logout VALUES
('Robert Freeman','01-FEB-01 06:00:00.010 AM', '01-FEB-01 09:00:00.010 AM');

-- Now, let's look at the record

SELECT * FROM login_logout;

USERNAME             TIMEIN                           TIMEOUT
---------------      -----------------------------    ------------------------
Robert Freeman       01-FEB-01 06:00:00.00 AM -05:00  01-FEB-01 09:00:00.00 AM -05:00
```

The real difference between the **with time zone** and **with local time zone** data types is that, with the former, the time-zone offset is separately listed in the output. With the **local time zone**, the time-zone offset is calculated in the returned time. Thus, if the stored time is 17:00 in the database and you are in a time zone three hours earlier, then the data type will return a value of 14:00, which would represent the local time stamp based on the time stamp of the data in the column.

The offset being reported is based on UTC and the session **time_zone** setting. Now, let's look at an example of the **timestamp with local time zone** data type:

```
CREATE TABLE login_logout
(username     VARCHAR2(30),
timein        TIMESTAMP(3) WITH LOCAL TIME ZONE,
timeout       TIMESTAMP(3) WITH LOCAL TIME ZONE,);

-- Insert a record .. database is on EST time zone

INSERT INTO login_logout VALUES
('Robert Freeman','01-FEB-01 06:00:00.015 AM', '01-FEB-01 09:00:00.015 AM');

SELECT * FROM login_logout;

USERNAME          TIMEIN                          TIMEOUT
---------------   -----------------------------   ------------------------
Robert Freeman    01-FEB-01 06:00:00.00 AM        01-FEB-01 09:00:00.00 AM


-- Now, let's look at the record
ALTER SESSION SET time_zone='PST';
Session Altered

SELECT * FROM login_logout;

USERNAME          TIMEIN                    TIMEOUT
---------------   ------------------------  ------------------------
Robert Freeman    01-FEB-01 03:00:00.00 AM  01-FEB-01 06:00:00.00 AM
```

New INTERVAL Data Types

The new **interval** data types are used to store a period of time. With the **interval year to month** data type, you can store a period of time consisting of months and years (for example, three years and four months). This data type takes 5 bytes for each value.

With the **interval day to second** data type, you can store a period of time in days, hours, minutes, and seconds. This data type requires 11 bytes of storage for each value.

Let's look at some examples of the use of these data types. We'll create a table called subscription that keeps track of how long a given subscriber's subscription is:

```
CREATE TABLE subscription
(subscriber_name  VARCHAR2(30),
 time_to_expire   INTERVAL YEAR TO MONTH);
```

In this case, I have a year and a half on my subscription:

```
INSERT INTO subscription VALUES ('Robert Freeman','1-6');
SELECT * FROM subscription;
```

Daylight Saving Time

Within a given time zone, Oracle determines whether daylight saving time (which is used in most of the U.S.) is in effect, and returns the time based on whether it is or not. When daylight saving time is in effect, the time jumps from 1:59:59 A.M. to 03:00 A.M. on the first Sunday in April. Also, in this case, values between 2:00 A.M. and 2:59:59 A.M. are considered invalid.

During the last Sunday in October, the time jumps from 2:00 A.M. to 01:00:01 A.M. Caution should be used with values between 01:00:01 A.M. and 02:00 A.M., as the period of time between these values will occur twice.

Enhancements to Oracle9i Configuration Programs

Several enhancements have been added to the Oracle Universal Installer (UI), as well as the Database Configuration Assistant (DCA). Let's look at those quickly.

Oracle Universal Installer Enhancements

In Oracle9i, the UI is now directory enabled, allowing it to take advantage of LDAP directory servers (such as Oracle Internet Directory). Other improvements include general enhancements to the interface itself, reduced memory requirements, and reduced overall installation times. Also, the Oracle UI inventory mechanism has been improved to allow concurrent installations of different products on the same target machine.

Enhancements to Database Configuration Assistant

The Oracle9i DCA offers some new features. Probably the most interesting is the ability to create a database based on an existing database. The DCA allows you to fully customize the attributes of the database including the tablespaces, datafile, redo log, and control file information and initialization parameters of the database. Further, you can run custom scripts when creating a database, if you like.

With templates, you can use an existing database to clone a new database and its objects (tables, indexes, rollback segments, and so on). Optionally, the DCA can clone the entire database and its data (or without data) as well. Further, you can save the source database structure as a template to use when creating a database later. Also, the DCA allows you to edit existing database creation templates and save them for later use.

The DCA lets you fully configure the database you are going to create. You can create as many tablespaces and datafiles as you need through the DCA now. The same is true with redo log groups and members. The DCA will allow you to define the setting of any initialization parameter, and you can choose specific values for memory settings (such as the shared pool), or you can direct the DCA to allocate a percentage of available memory to the SGA instead.

Miscellaneous New Oracle9i Features and Enhancements

In this section, we will cover several miscellaneous topics regarding Oracle9i. This includes changes to the installation of advanced replication, converting existing LONG columns in tables to LOB data types, and database flash freeze.

Advanced Replication Installed by Default

Now, with Oracle9i, you do not need to run catrep.sql to install advanced replication. While the script is still required, it is now automatically executed as a part of catproc.sql. This will result in catproc.sql taking a bit longer to execute than you might have previously experienced in Oracle8i.

Converting LONGs to LOB Data Types

In Oracle9i, the **alter table** command has been enhanced to allow you to modify a LONG column to a CLOB data type. Also, you can modify a LONG_RAW column to a BLOB data type. Also, during the conversion process, the NULL or NOT NULL constraints of the column are preserved. This new feature has implications, for example, with replication. This is because you cannot replicate objects with LONG columns, but you can replicate objects with LOB column types. Also, if you have materialized views built on the table that you are migrating, you will need to rebuild those materialized views.

During the move process, the entire table is moved. This can result in a significant, but temporary, need for additional disk space. Once the table is copied and the LONG column converted in the process, the old table will be removed. Here is an example of converting a LONG column into a CLOB:

```
ALTER TABLE long_table MODIFY (my_long_column CLOB);
```

NOTE
VARCHAR and RAW columns cannot be converted into LOBs using this method.

Database Flash Freeze

Sometimes things just are not working right, say, a database will start to demonstrate a certain problem intermittently. Often, since you don't really know what's causing the problem, it's hard to diagnose. Sometimes, when the problem happens, you would like to be able to collect database state information (or Oracle support would like you to collect this). Unfortunately, even when you are looking for it, sometimes by the time the problem is discovered, the database has gone on its own merry way and you have no way to tell what was going on when the problem began.

Oracle9i flash freeze locks a database when specific error conditions occur. When the database is locked, it will not allow any further activity to occur, except for privileged accounts. This allows you to run your diagnostic checks and collect any debugging information that Oracle support might wish you to collect, before you reopen the database to the user community.

When the database is flash-frozen, the contents of memory, process, and resource states, and other database-related information, is frozen for analysis. Each process is halted during the flash-freeze process until the database is signaled by the DBA to restart those processes.

Flash freeze, in and of itself, is not really a new feature. It was available in previous Oracle versions, but it had to be manually executed. Oracle9i allows event-driven flash freezes. Now, the DBA can define that various conditions, such as internal errors or external events or error codes, will cause flash freeze to occur automatically.

Flash-freeze events can be set either in the database parameter file or via the **alter system set event** command. Here is an example:

```
ALTER SYSTEM SET EVENT = "600 flashfreeze on error 1521, proc=PMON";
```

In this example, we have identified that an occurrence of event 1521, associated with PMON, should cause the system to flash-freeze.

> **NOTE**
> *Generally, you will not set your system to flash-freeze unless Oracle support requests such an action.*

Oracle9i Parameter and View Changes

Several parameters in Oracle9i have been added, renamed, or made obsolete. The same is true with views. This section will document these changes for you.

Obsolete Database Parameters

The following Oracle8i (8.1.7) database parameters are no longer valid in Oracle9i. You will need to remove them from your database parameter file during an upgrade from 8i to 9i. If you fail to do so, the database will open, but Oracle will generate an error.

always_anti_join	*always_semi_join*	*db_block_lru_latches*
db_block_max_dirty_ target	*db_file_direct_io_count*	*gc_defer_time*
gc_releasable_locks	*gc_rollback_locks*	*hash_multiblock_io_ count*
instance_nodeset	*job_queue_interval*	*lm_locks*
lm_ress	*optimizer_percent_parallel*	*sort_multiblock_read_ count*
text_enable		

Renamed Parameters

The names of some parameters (particularly those relating to MTS) have been changed. Here is a list of the changed parameters in Oracle9i.

Old Parameter Name	New Parameter Name
ops_interconnects	*cluster_interconnects*
parallel_server	*cluster_database*
parallel_server_instances	*cluster_database_instances*
mts_circuits	*circuits*
mts_dispatchers	*dispatchers*
mts_max_dispatchers	*max_dispatchers*
mts_max_servers	*max_shared_servers*
mts_servers	*shared_servers*
mts_sessions	*shared_server_sessions*
ope_interconnects	*cluster_interconnects*

New Parameters in Oracle9i

Several new parameters have been added in Oracle9i. Here is a list of those parameters. Please consult the *Oracle9i Reference Guide* for further information on these parameters.

archive_lag_target	db_nk_cache_size	db_cache_advice
db_cache_size	db_create_file_dest	db_create_online_log_ dest_n
db_keep_cache_size	db_recycle_cache_size	drs_start
fal_client	fal_server	fast_start_mttr_target
global_context_pool_ size	log_archive_dest_n (n = 6, 7,...10)	log_archive_dest_state_n (n = 6, 7,...10)
logmnr_max_persistent_sessions	nls_length_semantics	nls_nchar_conv_excp
nls_timestamp_format	nls_timestamp_tz_format	pga_aggregate_target
plsql_compiler_flags	plsql_native_c_compiler	plsql_native_library_ dir
plsql_native_library_ subdir_count	plsql_native_linker	plsql_native_make_file_name
plsql_native_make_ utility	remote_archive_enable	remote_listener
sga_max_size	shared_server_sessions	spfile
standby_file_ management	standby_preserves_names	trace_enabled
undo_management	undo_retention	undo_suppress_errors
undo_tablespace	workarea_size_policy	

New Data-Dictionary Views in Oracle9i

Several new dynamic performance views have been added to Oracle9i. Here is a list of those views. See the *Oracle9i Reference Manual* for a description of each.

ALL_AUDIT_POLICIES	ALL_BASE_TABLE_MVIEWS	ALL_EXTERNAL_LOCATIONS
ALL_EXTERNAL_TABLES	ALL_INDEXTYPE_COMMENTS	ALL_JOIN_IND_COLUMNS
ALL_LOG_GROUP_COLUMNS	ALL_LOG_GROUPS	ALL_MVIEW_LOGS
ALL_OPERATOR_COMMENTS	ALL_PENDING_CONV_ TABLES	ALL_POLICY_CONTEXTS
ALL_POLICY_GROUPS	ALL_PROCEDURES	ALL_SECONDARY_OBJECTS
ALL_SOURCE_TAB_ COLUMNS	ALL_SOURCE_TABLES	ALL_SQLJ_TYPE_ATTRS

ALL_SQLJ_TYPE_METHODS	ALL_SQLJ_TYPES	ALL_STORED_SETTINGS
ALL_SUBSCRIBED_COLUMNS	ALL_SUBSCRIBED_TABLES	ALL_SUBSCRIPTIONS
ALL_TYPE_VERSIONS	DBA_APPLICATION_ROLES	DBA_ATTRIBUTE_TRANSFORMATIONS
DBA_AUDIT_POLICIES	DBA_BASE_TABLE_MVIEWS	DBA_EXTERNAL_LOCATIONS
DBA_EXTERNAL_TABLES	DBA_FGA_AUDIT_TRAIL	DBA_GLOBAL_CONTEXT
DBA_INDEXTYPE_COMMENTS	DBA_JOIN_IND_COLUMNS	DBA_LOG_GROUP_COLUMNS
DBA_LOG_GROUPS	DBA_MVIEW_LOGS	DBA_OPERATOR_COMMENTS
DBA_PENDING_CONV_TABLES	DBA_POLICY_CONTEXTS	DBA_POLICY_GROUPS
DBA_PROCEDURES	DBA_PROXIES	DBA_REPCAT_EXCEPTIONS
DBA_REPEXTENSIONS	DBA_REPSITES_NEW	DBA_RESUMABLE
DBA_SECONDARY_OBJECTS	DBA_SNAPSHOT_LOG_FILTER_COLS	DBA_SOURCE_TAB_COLUMNS
DBA_SOURCE_TABLES	DBA_SQLJ_TYPE_ATTRS	DBA_SQLJ_TYPE_METHODS
DBA_SQLJ_TYPES	DBA_STORED_SETTINGS	DBA_SUBSCRIBED_COLUMNS
DBA_SUBSCRIBED_TABLES	DBA_SUBSCRIPTIONS	DBA_TEMPLATE_REFGROUPS
DBA_TEMPLATE_TARGETS	DBA_TRANSFORMATIONS	DBA_TYPE_VERSIONS
DBA_UNDO_EXTENTS	USER_APPLICATION_ROLES	USER_ATTRIBUTE_TRANSFORMATIONS
USER_AUDIT_POLICIES	USER_BASE_TABLE_MVIEWS	USER_EXTERNAL_LOCATIONS
USER_EXTERNAL_TABLES	USER_INDEXTYPE_COMMENTS	USER_JOIN_IND_COLUMNS
USER_LOG_GROUP_COLUMNS	USER_LOG_GROUPS	USER_MVIEW_LOGS
USER_OPERATOR_COMMENTS	USER_PENDING_CONV_TABLES	USER_POLICY_CONTEXTS
USER_POLICY_GROUPS	USER_PROCEDURES	USER_PROXIES
USER_RESUMABLE	USER_SECONDARY_OBJECTS	USER_SOURCE_TAB_COLUMNS
USER_SOURCE_TABLES	USER_SQLJ_TYPE_ATTRS	USER_SQLJ_TYPE_METHODS
USER_SQLJ_TYPES	USER_STORED_SETTINGS	USER_SUBSCRIBED_COLUMNS
USER_SUBSCRIBED_TABLES	USER_SUBSCRIPTIONS	USER_TRANSFORMATIONS
USER_TYPE_VERSIONS		

Renamed Data-Dictionary Views in Oracle9i

Some of the dynamic performance views in Oracle9i have had their names changed. Here is a list of the old view names prior to Oracle9i and the new view names in Oracle9i.

Old View Name	Oracle9i New View Name
ALL_REGISTERED_SNAPSHOTS	ALL_REGISTERED_MVIEWS
ALL_SNAPSHOT_REFRESH_TIMES	ALL_MVIEW_REFRESH_TIMES
DBA_REGISTERED_SNAPSHOT_GROUPS	DBA_REGISTERED_MVIEW_GROUPS
DBA_REGISTERED_SNAPSHOTS	DBA_REGISTERED_MVIEWS
DBA_SNAPSHOT_LOG_FILTER_COLS	DBA_MVIEW_LOG_FILTER_COLS
DBA_SNAPSHOT_REFRESH_TIMES	DBA_MVIEW_REFRESH_TIMES
USER_SNAPSHOT_REFRESH_TIMES	USER_MVIEW_REFRESH_TIMES
USER_REGISTERED_SNAPSHOTS	USER_REGISTERED_MVIEWS

New Dynamic-Performance Views in Oracle9i

Several new dynamic performance views are introduced in Oracle9i. You will find a list of these views in the following table. Refer to the *Oracle9i Reference Manual* for more information on these views.

GV$ACTIVE_SESS_POOL_MTH	GV$ARCHIVE_DEST_STATUS	GV$ARCHIVE_GAP
GV$ENQUEUE_STAT	GV$GCSHVMASTER_INFO	GV$GCSPFMASTER_INFO
GV$GLOBALCONTEXT	GV$HVMASTER_INFO	GV$LOGMNR_CALLBACK
GV$LOGMNR_LOGFILE	GV$LOGMNR_PROCESS	GV$LOGMNR_REGION
GV$LOGMNR_SESSION	GV$LOGMNR_TRANSACTION	GV$LOGSTDBY
GV$LOGSTDBY_STATS	GV$MANAGED_STANDBY	GV$MVREFRESH
GV$PGASTAT	GV$QUEUEING_MTH	GV$REPLPROP
GV$REPLQUEUE	GV$RESUMABLE	GV$RMAN_CONFIGURATION
GV$SPPARAMETER	GV$SQL_PLAN	GV$SQL_REDIRECTION
GV$SQL_WORKAREA	GV$SQL_WORKAREA_ACTIVE	GV$STANDBY_LOG
GV$TIMEZONE_NAMES	GV$UNDOSTAT	GV$VPD_POLICY
V$ACTIVE_SESS_POOL_MTH	V$ARCHIVE_DEST_STATUS	V$ARCHIVE_GAP
V$ENQUEUE_STAT	V$FILESTATXS	V$GCSHVMASTER_INFO
V$GCSPFMASTER_INFO	V$GLOBALCONTEXT	V$HVMASTER_INFO

V$LOGMNR_CALLBACK	V$LOGMNR_LOGFILE	V$LOGMNR_PROCESS
V$LOGMNR_REGION	V$LOGMNR_SESSION	V$LOGMNR_TRANSACTION
V$LOGSTDBY	V$LOGSTDBY_STATS	V$MANAGED_STANDBY
V$MVREFRESH	V$PGASTAT	V$QUEUEING_MTH
V$REPLPROP	V$REPLQUEUE	V$RESUMABLE
V$RMAN_CONFIGURATION	V$SPPARAMETER	V$SQLXS
V$SQL_PLAN	V$SQL_REDIRECTION	GV$ACTIVE_SESS_POOL_MTH
GV$ARCHIVE_DEST_STATUS	GV$ARCHIVE_GAP	GV$ENQUEUE_STAT
GV$GCSHVMASTER_INFO	GV$GCSPFMASTER_INFO	GV$GLOBALCONTEXT
GV$HVMASTER_INFO	GV$LOGMNR_CALLBACK	GV$LOGMNR_LOGFILE
GV$LOGMNR_PROCESS	GV$LOGMNR_REGION	GV$LOGMNR_SESSION
GV$LOGMNR_TRANSACTION	GV$LOGSTDBY	GV$LOGSTDBY_STATS
GV$MANAGED_STANDBY	GV$MVREFRESH	GV$PGASTAT
GV$QUEUEING_MTH	GV$REPLPROP	GV$REPLQUEUE
GV$RESUMABLE	GV$RMAN_CONFIGURATION	GV$SPPARAMETER
GV$SQL_PLAN	GV$SQL_REDIRECTION	GV$SQL_WORKAREA
GV$SQL_WORKAREA_ACTIVE	GV$STANDBY_LOG	GV$TIMEZONE_NAMES
GV$UNDOSTAT	GV$VPD_POLICY	V$ACTIVE_SESS_POOL_MTH
V$ARCHIVE_DEST_STATUS	V$ARCHIVE_GAP	V$ENQUEUE_STAT
V$FILESTATXS	V$GCSHVMASTER_INFO	V$GCSPFMASTER_INFO
V$GLOBALCONTEXT	V$HVMASTER_INFO	V$LOGMNR_CALLBACK
V$LOGMNR_LOGFILE	V$LOGMNR_PROCESS	V$LOGMNR_REGION
V$LOGMNR_SESSION	V$LOGMNR_TRANSACTION	V$LOGSTDBY
V$LOGSTDBY_STATS	V$MANAGED_STANDBY	V$MVREFRESH
V$PGASTAT	V$QUEUEING_MTH	V$REPLPROP
V$REPLQUEUE	V$RESUMABLE	V$RMAN_CONFIGURATION
V$SPPARAMETER	V$SQLXS	V$SQL_PLAN
V$SQL_REDIRECTION	V$SQL_WORKAREA	V$SQL_WORKAREA_ACTIVE
V$STANDBY_LOG	V$TEMPSTATXS	V$TIMEZONE_NAMES
V$UNDOSTAT	VVPD_POLICYSQL_WORKAREA	V$SQL_WORKAREA_ACTIVE

Renamed Dynamic-Performance Views in Oracle9i

A number of dynamic performance views have had their names changed in Oracle9i. The old names are still available for backward compatibility. Here is a list of the views whose names have been changed.

Old View Name	New Oracle9i View Name
GV$BSP	GV$CR_BLOCK_SERVER
GV$CLASS_PING	GV$CLASS_CACHE_TRANSFER
GV$DLM_ALL_LOCKS	GV$GES_ENQUEUE
GV$DLM_CONVERT_LOCAL	GV$GES_CONVERT_LOCAL
GV$DLM_CONVERT_REMOTE	GV$GES_CONVERT_REMOTE
GV$DLM_LATCH	GV$GES_LATCH
GV$DLM_LOCKS	GV$GES_BLOCKING_ENQUEUE
GV$DLM_MISC	GV$GES_STATISTICS
GV$DLM_RESS	GV$GES_RESOURCE
GV$DLM_TRAFFIC_CONTROLLER	GV$GES_TRAFFIC_CONTROLLER
GV$FILE_PING	GV$FILE_CACHE_TRANSFER
GV$LOCK_ELEMENT	GV$GC_ELEMENT
GV$LOCKS_WITH_COLLISIONS	GV$GC_ELEMENTS_WITH_COLLISIONS
GV$MTS	GV$SHARED_SERVER_MONITOR
GV$PING	GV$CACHE_TRANSFER
GV$TEMP_PING	GV$TEMP_CACHE_TRANSFER
V$BSP	V$CR_BLOCK_SERVER
V$CLASS_PING	V$CLASS_CACHE_TRANSFER
V$DLM_ALL_LOCKS	V$GES_ENQUEUE
V$DLM_CONVERT_LOCAL	V$GES_CONVERT_LOCAL
V$DLM_CONVERT_REMOTE	V$GES_CONVERT_REMOTE
V$DLM_LATCH	V$GES_LATCH
V$DLM_LOCKS	V$GES_BLOCKING_ENQUEUE

Old View Name	New Oracle9i View Name
V$DLM_MISC	V$GES_STATISTICS
V$DLM_RESS	V$GES_RESOURCE
V$DLM_TRAFFIC_CONTROLLER	V$GES_TRAFFIC_CONTROLLER
V$FILE_PING	V$FILE_CACHE_TRANSFER
V$LOCK_ELEMENT	V$GC_ELEMENT
V$LOCKS_WITH_COLLISIONS	V$GC_ELEMENTS_WITH_COLLISIONS
V$MTS	V$SHARED_SERVER_MONITOR
V$PING	V$CACHE_TRANSFER
V$TEMP_PING	V$TEMP_CACHE_TRANSFER

Obsolete Dynamic-Performance Views in Oracle9i

The GV$TARGETRBA and V$TARGETRBA dynamic performance views are obsolete in Oracle9i.

CHAPTER
6

Oracle9i SQL, PL/SQL
New Features

- Oracle9i ANSI/ISO SQL 1999 compliance
- Constraint enhancements
- New SQL and PL/SQL functionality
- Oracle9i object enhancements
- Changes to internet packages in Oracle9i

hapter 6 covers several new features and enhanced functionality in Oracle9i SQL and PL/SQL. This includes changes to support the ANSI/ISO SQL 1999 standards, constraint enhancements, and various other new SQL and PL/SQL features. We will also cover Oracle9i Object enhancements as well as changes to the internet packages in Oracle9i.

New Operators: CROSS JOIN, NATURAL JOIN, USING, ON, and JOIN

The **cross join**, **natural join**, **using**, **on**, and **join** operators introduced in Oracle9i provide functionality that already existed in Oracle8i. Table 6-1 provides an example of the use of the new functionality as well as a compatible Oracle statement not using these functions.

Statement Name	Description	Example Using Statement	Example Without Statement
cross join	Produces cross product of two tables, resulting in a Cartesian join.	SELECT empid, deptno FROM emp CROSS JOIN dept;	SELECT empid, deptno FROM emp, dept;
natural join	Performs join based on like columns in two tables. The like columns must be of the same name and data type.	SELECT empid, deptno, dname FROM emp NATURAL JOIN dept;	SELECT a.empid, a.deptno, b.dname FROM emp a, dept b WHERE a.deptno=b.deptno;
using	Allows specification of columns to be used as the equijoin when performing a JOIN. This type of join uses the **join** clause, rather than the **natural join** clause. Note that use of the **natural join** and **using** clauses are mutually exclusive.	SELECT empid, dname FROM emp JOIN dept USING (deptno);	SELECT empid, dname FROM emp a, dept b WHERE a.deptno=b.deptno;

TABLE 6-1. *New Oracle9i Operators*

Statement Name	Description	Example Using Statement	Example Without Statement
on	Much like the **where** clause, can be used to restrict the result set returned. One major benefit is that **on** can be used to join columns that are named differently. Also allows multiple predicates, much like a **where** clause with **and** and **or** clauses.	`SELECT empid, dname FROM emp a JOIN dept b ON (a.deptno = b.department_no AND a.empid < 20);`	`SELECT empid, dname FROM emp a, dept b WHERE a.deptno=b.department_no AND a.empid < 20;`

TABLE 6-1.   *New Oracle9i Operators* (continued)

New Outer-Join Operations

Oracle has always allowed outer joins in SQL through the use of the (+) syntax, and this is still supported in Oracle9i. The problem is that this is not SQL 1999 compliant. In this section, we will look at the new outer-join directives, starting with **left outer join** and **right outer join**. Then we will look at the **full outer join** directive and its new functionality.

Left Outer Join and Right Outer Join

Oracle9i now allows the use of one of two directives, **left outer join** and **right outer join**. Here is an example of the use of each of these commands:

NOTE
This example, and the others in this chapter, use the sample tables created in the demo scott/tiger schema. Some of the output has been modified to fit the page.

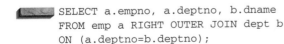

```
SELECT a.empno, a.deptno, b.dname
FROM emp a RIGHT OUTER JOIN dept b
ON (a.deptno=b.deptno);
```

```
    EMPNO     DEPTNO DNAME
---------- ---------- --------------
      7369         20 RESEARCH
      7521         30 SALES
      7566         20 RESEARCH
      7654         30 SALES
      7698         30 SALES
      7782         10 ACCOUNTING
      7788         20 RESEARCH
      7839         10 ACCOUNTING
      7844         30 SALES
      7876         20 RESEARCH
      7900         30 SALES
                      TEST
                      OPERATIONS
SELECT a.empno, a.deptno, b.dname
FROM emp a LEFT OUTER JOIN dept b
ON (a.deptno=b.deptno);

    EMPNO     DEPTNO DNAME
---------- ---------- --------------
      7839         10 ACCOUNTING
      7782         10 ACCOUNTING
      7876         20 RESEARCH
      7788         20 RESEARCH
      7566         20 RESEARCH
      7369         20 RESEARCH
      7900         30 SALES
      7844         30 SALES
      7698         30 SALES
      7654         30 SALES
      7521         30 SALES
      7499         90
```

In the first case, we will get all rows in the department table, even if there is not a matching row in the employee table. With the second example, we will discover all employees that are not currently assigned to a department.

Full Outer Joins

The **full outer join** command will essentially produce the equivalent of a **right outer join** and **left outer join** of both tables. Previously, this type of functionality was possible only through the use of a **union** statement. Here is an example of the use of the **full outer join** command, along with an example of the statement that includes all employees, including those not assigned to departments, and including departments that are t assigned to any employees. Also, we have provided an example of the type of statement that would have to be run prior to Oracle9i to produce the same result.

```
-- 9i statement using the FULL OUTER JOIN syntax
SELECT a.empno, a.deptno, b.dname
FROM emp a FULL OUTER JOIN dept b
ON(a.deptno=b.deptno);
```

EMPNO	DEPTNO	DNAME
7369	20	RESEARCH
7499	90	
7521	30	SALES
7566	20	RESEARCH
7654	30	SALES
7698	30	SALES
7782	10	ACCOUNTING
7788	20	RESEARCH
7839	10	ACCOUNTING
7844	30	SALES
7876	20	RESEARCH
7900	30	SALES
7902	20	RESEARCH
7934	10	ACCOUNTING
		OPERATIONS
		TEST

```
-- Prior to 9i statement..
SELECT a.empno, a.deptno, b.dname
FROM emp a, dept b
WHERE a.deptno=b.deptno(+)
UNION
SELECT a.empno, a.deptno, b.dname
FROM emp a, dept b
WHERE a.deptno(+)=b.deptno;
```

Case Expression Enhancements

Previous to Oracle9i, simple **case** statements were already supported. In Oracle9i, support for the remaining types of **case** statements is provided. In ANSI SQL 1999, there are four types of **case** statements:

- Simple
- Searched
- NULLIF
- COALESCE

In this section, we will discuss these **case** statement types and how they are used.

Simple case Statements

Simple **case** statements are much like the **decode** statement. They can be used to search and then replace a given value within a given SQL statement. Here is an example:

```
SELECT ename,
(CASE deptno
   WHEN 10 THEN 'ACCOUNTING'
   WHEN 20 THEN 'RESEARCH'
   WHEN 30 THEN 'SALES'
   WHEN 40 THEN 'OPERATIONS'
   ELSE 'Unassigned'
   END ) as Department
FROM emp;

ENAME       DEPARTMENT
----------  ----------
SMITH       RESEARCH
ALLEN       Unassigned
WARD        SALES
JONES       RESEARCH
MARTIN      SALES
BLAKE       SALES
CLARK       ACCOUNTING
SCOTT       RESEARCH
KING        ACCOUNTING
TURNER      SALES
ADAMS       RESEARCH
JAMES       SALES
FORD        RESEARCH
MILLER      ACCOUNTING
```

In this example, if the DEPTNO column has a 10 in it, the SQL query will return the value *accounting* rather than the number 10. If the deptno is not 10, 20, 30, or 40, then the **case** statement will fall through to the **else** clause, which will return *unassigned*. Note that with a simple **case** statement, no comparison operators can be used.

Searched case Statements

The searched **case** statement is the much more powerful cousin of the simple case statement. The searched **case** statement is like an **if...then...else** structure, and can be used to conditionally search and replace values using logical operators and multiple conditions. Let's look at an example:

```
SELECT ename, sal, deptno,
CASE
 WHEN sal <= 500 then 0
 WHEN sal > 500 and sal<1500  then 100
 WHEN sal >= 1500 and sal < 2500  and deptno=10 then 200
 WHEN sal > 1500  and sal < 2500 and deptno=20 then 500
 WHEN sal >= 2500 then 300
 ELSE 0
END "bonus"
FROM emp;
```

ENAME	SAL	DEPTNO	bonus
SMITH	800	20	100
ALLEN	1600	90	0
WARD	1250	30	100
JONES	2975	20	300
MARTIN	1250	30	100
BLAKE	2850	30	300
CLARK	2450	10	200

In this example, we are trying to determine how much of a bonus each employee is eligible for. The bonus amount is based on the salary of the employee, but notice that we have also added some conditions based on what department number the employee is in. You can see that a searched **case** statement can have many different **when** clauses, and that you can apply many criteria in those clauses to get the answers you need.

Nullif and coalesce

To further comply with SQL 1999, the **nullif** and **coalesce** statements have been added to Oracle9i. The **nullif** statement is very simple. It takes two arguments. If they are equivalent, then the result is a NULL. If they are not equivalent, then the first argument is returned by the function. Here is an example of a **nullif** statement:

```
SELECT ename, NULLIF (comm, 0) COMM FROM emp;
```

ENAME	COMM
SMITH	
ALLEN	300
WARD	500
JONES	
MARTIN	1400
BLAKE	
CLARK	
SCOTT	

In this example, if the COMM column (which is the commission for an employee) has a 0 value, it will be returned as a NULL, as shown in the sample output.

The **coalesce** statement is a bit like the Oracle **nvl** function. Given an unlimited number of arguments, it will return the first non-null value in those arguments. Here is an example:

```
SELECT ename, COALESCE(comm, 0) COMM FROM emp;
ENAME           COMM
----------      ----------
SMITH                    0
ALLEN                  300
WARD                   500
JONES                    0
MARTIN                1400
BLAKE                    0
CLARK                    0
SCOTT                    0
```

In this case, if the COMM column is NULL, a 0 value will be returned. Note that with **coalesce**, there is no implicit type conversion of the arguments passed to it, so the following code would not work:

```
SELECT ename, COALESCE(comm, 'None') FROM emp;
```

The following code, however, would work:

```
SELECT ename, COALESCE(to_char(comm), 'None') COMM FROM emp;
ENAME           COMM
----------      ----------
SMITH           None
ALLEN           300
WARD            500
JONES           None
MARTIN          1400
BLAKE           None
CLARK           None
SCOTT           None
```

Scalar Subqueries

A *scalar subquery* expression is a subquery that returns exactly one column value from one row. The returned value of the scalar subquery expression is the return value of the selected list item of the subquery. If zero rows are returned by the subquery, then the value of the scalar subquery expression is NULL; and if the subquery returns more than one row, then Oracle returns an error.

Limited scalar subqueries were allowed in Oracle8i. Oracle9i allows more. Be careful when using scalar subqueries though. They tend to be resource intensive. There are often more efficient ways of getting at the data you are interested in than using a scalar subquery.

Let's look at some of the scalar subqueries possible in Oracle9i. First, here is an example of a scalar subquery used in the **select** clause of a SQL statement:

```
SELECT empno,
(SELECT ename FROM emp b WHERE b.empno=a.mgr) manager
FROM emp a
ORDER BY mgr;

    EMPNO MANAGER
---------- ----------
     7788 JONES
     7902 JONES
     7499 BLAKE
     7521 BLAKE
     7839
```

In this example, we are basically creating a join between a table called EMP and itself so that we can display the name of the employees' managers. Of course, a regular join in this case would probably be more efficient. Here is another example, a scalar subquery in the **where** clause:

```
SELECT ename, sal, comm
FROM emp a
WHERE ( (SELECT comm FROM bonus z where
                z.empno=a.empno) >
(SELECT AVG(bonus) from historical_bonus WHERE year = 1999 ) );

ENAME           SAL       COMM
---------- ---------- ----------
FORD           3000        600
MILLER         1300        600
```

In this example, we are printing the employee name and salary for all employees who are getting bonuses that are larger than the average of all 1999 bonuses. Again, a join here would probably be much more efficient. A scalar subquery can also be used in an **order by** clause, as shown in this example:

```
SELECT empno, ename, deptno
FROM emp a
ORDER BY (SELECT dname FROM DEPT b where a.deptno=b.deptno);
```

```
    EMPNO ENAME          DEPTNO
---------- ---------- ----------
      7782 CLARK              10
      7839 KING               10
      7934 MILLER             10
      7369 SMITH              20
      7876 ADAMS              20
      7902 FORD               20
      7788 SCOTT              20
      7566 JONES              20
      7521 WARD               30
      7698 BLAKE              30
      7654 MARTIN             30
```

In this case, we ordered the output by department name, a column that is not readily available in the EMP table, and not even one we have displayed in the query (we do display the department numbers just so you can see that they were sorted).

Note that scalar subqueries are still not valid in Oracle9*i* in the following cases:

- As default values for columns

- As hash expressions for clusters

- In the **returning** clause of DML statements

- In function-based indexes

- In **check** constraints

- In **when** conditions of **case** expressions

- In **group by** and **having** clauses

- In **start with** and **connect by** clauses

- In statements that are unrelated to queries, such as **create profile**

Constraint Enhancements

Several new enhancements have been added in Oracle9i regarding constraints. These include improvements in the locking strategy regarding nonindexed foreign keys, primary key caching, constraint-related index-management features, and the ability to do index-only scans on function-based indexes.

Locking and Nonindexed Foreign Keys

Prior to Oracle9i, changes to data in a parent table in a nonindexed foreign key relationship would require, at a minimum, a share lock of the child table (where the foreign key is defined). Certain operations were even more restrictive, taking table-level share-subexclusive locks on the parent table. These kinds of locks allowed only reading, and prohibited all DML activity. Prior to Oracle8i, the DBA would have to create indexes on the keys involved in the foreign key relationship to avoid these problems.

Oracle9i still requires these locks, but they are taken for only a very short time and then released for each row. This can significantly improve overall performance. If you are updating multiple rows, then the lock will be obtained and released once for each row. DML activity on the child table requires no locks on the parent table at all.

Primary Key Caching During FK Creation

In Oracle9i, the creation of foreign key records requires the lookup of the primary key in the parent table. This can be an expensive operation. Oracle9i creates a cache of primary key values after the second row lookup in a multi-row operation in an attempt to speed up the primary key lookup operation.

Constraint-Related Index-Management Features

In Oracle9i, the **create index** clause can be used within the **create table** statement to create either a primary key index or a unique index. Also, parallel and partitioning clauses are supported at this level. Here is an example of creating a table with both a **create index** clause for the primary key and the creation of a unique key.

```
CREATE TABLE my_table
(id                  NUMBER
 PRIMARY KEY USING INDEX (CREATE INDEX ix_my_table ON my_table(id) ),
 table_identifier    NUMBER,
 table_information   VARCHAR2(30) ,
CONSTRAINT my_table_unique
UNIQUE(table_identifier)
USING INDEX (CREATE INDEX my_table_idx ON my_table(table_identifier) ) );
```

You can also choose to drop or keep indexes when using the **alter table** command to drop or disable a given constraint, as shown in this example:

```
ALTER TABLE my_table
DROP PRIMARY KEY KEEP INDEX;

ALTER TABLE my_table
DISABLE CONSTRAINT my_table_unique
CASCADE DROP INDEX;
```

Index-Only Scans on Function-Based Indexes

Prior to Oracle9i, index-only scans on function-based indexes could not be used except for expressions that disallowed the return of NULL values from the index. Now, in Oracle9i, you can mark the columns that the expression is built on as NOT NULL, and Oracle will be able to do an index-only scan on the function-based index because Oracle will know that the result is guaranteed to be NOT NULL.

New SQL Functionality

Oracle9i introduces new SQL functionality that you can take advantage of. First, you will learn about default column values and the **default** keyword. Next, we will cover **select for update...wait**, followed by the new Oracle9i date-time functions.

Explicit Column-Value Defaults

Oracle9i now allows you to define a default value for a given column through the use of the new default keyword. When a default column is defined, the default value will be used when no value is defined for that column in an **insert** or **update** statement.

Creating Tables with Default Values

You define a default value when you issue a **create table** statement, as shown here:

```
CREATE TABLE my_table
( id          NUMBER          PRIMARY KEY,
  uname       VARCHAR2(30)    DEFAULT  'UNKNOWN');
```

In this case, we have defined a default value for the UNAME column. This default value will be used only if the **default** keyword is used in an **insert** or **update** of the column (we will see examples of this shortly).

You can also change an existing column in a table to use a default value by using the **alter table** command. Note that if you do this, any existing columns using a previously defined default value will not be changed. Here is an example of altering a table to use a default value:

```
ALTER TABLE my_table MODIFY (uname DEFAULT 'UNDEFINED');
```

So, in this example, any future **insert** or **update** statements indicating that the default value should be used will now use **undefined** as the default value.

Using default in insert and update Statements

To use the **default** value established for a given column in a table, you need to use the **default** keyword in an **insert** or **update** statement. Here are a couple of examples:

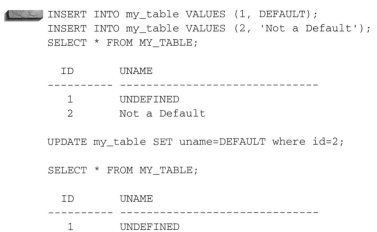

```
INSERT INTO my_table VALUES (1, DEFAULT);
INSERT INTO my_table VALUES (2, 'Not a Default');
SELECT * FROM MY_TABLE;

    ID      UNAME
---------- -----------------------------
    1       UNDEFINED
    2       Not a Default

UPDATE my_table SET uname=DEFAULT where id=2;

SELECT * FROM MY_TABLE;

    ID      UNAME
---------- -----------------------------
    1       UNDEFINED
    2       UNDEFINED
```

Select for update wait

Oracle9i has enhanced the **wait** clause to the **select for update** command. Now the **Wait** clause allows you to define a period of time (in seconds) that the command must wait to be able to access locked rows. Using **wait** without any specified time will result in the query indefinitely waiting until the row is unlocked. The default behavior is **wait**, in which case the statement will not wait for any row that is locked, and will fail. Here is an example:

```
SELECT * FROM my_table FOR UPDATE WAIT 3;
```

New Date-Time Functions

We have already talked about the new date-time data types introduced in Oracle9i. Also, there have been several new date-time functions added in Oracle9i as well. Each of these data types can also be used in PL/SQL as parameters and variables, and to provide return values for functions. Table 6-2 summarizes these functions, and their purposes.

Function Name	Purpose
current_date	Returns the current date for the session time zone in **date** data-type format.
current_timestamp	Returns the current date based on the session time zone using a **timestamp with time zone** data type.
localtimestamp	Returns the current date and time using the session time zone. The time value is returned using a **timestamp** data type.
dbtimezone	Returns the value of the database time zone.
from_tz	Converts a time stamp value to a **timestamp with time zone** value.
sessiontimezone	Returns the value of the current session's time zone.
to_dsinterval	Converts a character string (**char, varchar2, nchar,** or **nvarchar2**) to an **interval day to second** data type.
to_yminterval	Converts a character string (**char, varchar2, nchar,** or **nvarchar2**) to an **interval year to month** data type.
to_timestamp	Converts a character string (**char, varchar2, nchar,** or **nvarchar2**) to a **timestamp** data type.
to_timestamp_tz	Converts a character string (**char, varchar2, nchar,** or **nvarchar2**) to a **timestamp** data type, along with the time-zone value.
tz_offset	Returns the time-zone offset for the value entered.
extract	Returns the value of a specific date-time field from either a date-time or an interval expression.
sys_extract_utc	Extracts the UTC from a given date-time input with the time-zone displacement.
systimestamp	Returns the system date, including fractional seconds and time zone of the database.

TABLE 6-2. *New Date-Time Functions*

Let's look at a few quick examples:

```
SELECT sessiontimezone, to_char(current_date, 'mm/dd/yyy hh24:mi:ss')
current_d
FROM dual;

SESSIONTIMEZONE      CURRENT_D
-------------------- ------------------
-05:00               06-NOV-01 17:14:20


ALTER SESSION SET TIME_ZONE='-4:0';

SELECT sessiontimezone, to_char(current_date, 'mm/dd/yyy hh24:mi:ss')
current_d
FROM dual

SESSIONTIMEZONE      CURRENT_D
-------------------- ------------------
-04:00               06-NOV-01 18:14:20
```

Note that in the first example, the session time-zone offset changes from –5:00 to –4:00 and the current date is changed to reflect the new time-zone offset. Here is an example of using the **dbtimezone** function:

```
SELECT DBTIMEZONE FROM DUAL;

DBTI
----
PST

SELECT SESSIONTIMEZONE FROM DUAL;

SESSIONTIMEZONE
--------------------
-04:00
```

Here we see that the database time zone is set to Pacific standard time, and the session time zone is set –4 hours from UTC. The system time-zone value, returned as a time-zone offset, is based on the database time zone as last set via the **create database** or **alter database** commands. The session time-zone value is based on the session setting, either the default or as established via the **alter session set time_zone** command.

Now let's look at the **to_dsinterval** function. This function converts a given string (CHAR, VARCHAR2, NCHAR or NVARCHAR2) to a data type of INTERVAL DAY TO SECOND. In the following example, we will take the system date and add seven days and 12 hours to it.

```
SELECT SYSDATE + TO_DSINTERVAL('7 12:00:00') FROM dual;

SYSDATE+T
---------
14-NOV-01
```

Also, there is the TO_YMININTERVAL function that converts a character string to an INTERVAL YEAR TO MONTH. Here is an example:

```
SELECT SYSDATE + TO_YMININTERVAL.\ ('01-00') FROM dual;

SYSDATE+T
---------
06-NOV-02
```

In this case, we have added a year to today's date. You can also extract specific components from date-time and interval data types with the **extract** function. Here is an example:

```
SELECT extract(year from
       SYSTIMESTAMP) year,
       extract(month from
       SYSTIMESTAMP) month
FROM DUAL;

      YEAR      MONTH
---------- ----------
      2001         11
```

Note in the example that we have also used the **systimestamp** function to extract the current system time-stamp value.

New PL/SQL Functionality

Oracle9i offers new and enhanced PL/SQL functionality, which is the subject of this section. First, the common SQL parser will be addressed, followed by the PL/SQL CASE statement. Then, we will close with seamless support for Oracle LOB data types in PL/SQL.

The Common SQL Parser

Previously, during the PL/SQL analysis phase, the Oracle PL/SQL engine used a different SQL parser than that of the Oracle RDBMS. This led to conditions in which certain new SQL features would not be available in PL/SQL, and also eliminated bugs that would occur due to the presence of the different SQL engines. Oracle9i has changed PL/SQL so that it now uses the RDBMS SQL parser to do PL/SQL compile-time analysis, eliminating the PL/SQL compile-time analysis of SQL statements.

It is possible that certain PL/SQL program units will not work after an upgrade or migration to Oracle9i because of the move to the common SQL parser. While this should be a rare situation, you should be prepared to deal with this possibility when testing after migrating or upgrading to Oracle9i.

NOTE
You will notice that with the move to the common parser, PLS errors that used to be generated now become ORA errors.

The case Statement and Expression

We have already discussed the simple and searched **case** statement in Oracle9i SQL, and PL/SQL also offers the **case** constructs in a couple of different flavors:

- Simple case expression

- searched case expression

- Simple case statement

- searched case statement

The syntax of these **case** statements and expressions comply with SQL: 1999 with an addition of a slight extension to support labeling of **case** statements. Let's look at the different kind of case statements in Oracle9i PL/SQL.

First, a **case** expression (simple or searched) begins with a **case** statement and ends with the end statement. A simple **case** expression cannot contain any comparison operators, but a searched **case** expression can. Also note that you can only compare one value with a **case** expression. Here is an example of a simple **case** expression:

```
CREATE OR REPLACE FUNCTION my_function (p_input  NUMBER)
RETURN NUMBER
IS
v_return NUMBER;
BEGIN
    v_return:= CASE p_input
                    WHEN .10 then 10
                    WHEN .25 then 25
                    ELSE 50
                END;
    RETURN v_return;
END;
/
```

A searched **case** expression is much more flexible. In it, you can do comparisons, and the **when** clause can contain multiple variables to compare against. Here is an example of a searched **case** expression:

```
CREATE OR REPLACE FUNCTION my_function (p_input  NUMBER)
RETURN NUMBER
IS
```

```
v_return NUMBER;
BEGIN
     v_return:= CASE
                        WHEN   p_input < 1000
                               THEN 0
                        WHEN   p_input BETWEEN 1000 AND 10000
                                 THEN 1000
                        ELSE
                                 2000
                END;
     RETURN v_return;
END;
/
```

A **case** statement (simple or searched) is more like an IF...THEN...ELSE statement construct and is more sophisticated than a **case** expression. Also, in a **case** statement, you can assign values to variables within the case structure. The **case** statement begins with the **case** command, and ends with an **end case** command. Here is an example of a simple **case** statement:

```
CREATE OR REPLACE FUNCTION my_function (p_input  NUMBER)
RETURN NUMBER
IS
v_return NUMBER;
BEGIN
 CASE p_input
      WHEN .10 THEN
            v_return := 10;
      WHEN .25 THEN
            v_return := 25;
      ELSE
            v_return := 50;
  END CASE;
     RETURN v_return;
END;
/
```

Note in this example that we are able to assign a value to v_return, which we were not able to do in the **case** expressions previously. Finally, here is an example of a searched **case** statement:

```
CREATE OR REPLACE FUNCTION my_function (p_input  NUMBER)
RETURN NUMBER
IS
v_return NUMBER;
BEGIN
     CASE
          WHEN   p_input < 1000
                THEN v_return := 0;
```

```
            WHEN  p_input BETWEEN 1000 AND 10000
                THEN v_return := 1000;
            ELSE
                v_return := 2000;
        END CASE;
        RETURN v_return;
END;
/
```

Seamless Support for LOBs

Oracle9i offers seamless support for Large Object (LOB) data types. For example, functions such as **substr**, **rtrim**, or any other character-based function will now work on LOBs. Also, CHAR and VARCHAR variables can be assigned back and forth to LOB variables.

There are several functions in the **standard** package that take LONG or LONG RAW data types, as arguments now support LOB data types as well. Also, Oracle will implicitly convert LOBs to VARCHAR or RAWS and the reverse in assignments when passing any parameters.

Oracle9i Object Enhancements

Let's dive into Oracle9i objects now. Oracle9i really completes Oracle's drive toward making its flagship RDBMS a capable object-oriented database. The principle attribute of object inheritance is now fully employed within the Oracle database. Type inheritance is provided, making the maintenance of the Oracle9i object database much easier to deal with. Finally, multi-level collection types are now supported in Oracle9i. Let's look at each of these new features in some more detail.

Inheritance

Oracle9i Objects now supports object inheritance. This serves to complete the object functionality of the Oracle database. Now in Oracle9i, you can create a parent object type, called a *supertype*. Having created that parent object, you can then create one or more objects that inherit(s) the attributes and methods of that supertype object. These objects are called *subtypes*. The subtype objects have all the attributes of the supertype, plus you can add additional attributes or methods to them, making the subtypes more specialized objects. You can then create additional subtypes from these subtypes as required. The connection of supertypes to subtypes is called a *type hierarchy*.

Type Evolution

One of the problems with Oracle objects prior to Oracle9i was that there developed a hierarchy of objects. A type could be present in another type, which could be present in a collection, which could be present in a table. Previous to Oracle9i, if you wished to change a supertype, you would have to drop all the subtypes first, change the supertype, and then re-create the subtypes. This was fairly inconvenient, to say the least.

Oracle9i removes this requirement and allows you to make changes to a type anywhere along the type hierarchy. Those changes will then propagate to schema objects that reference that type. Thus, with Oracle9i, you can now add, drop, and modify attributes and methods of object types at will.

Multi-Level Collections

Oracle now allows you to create multi-level collections for PL/SQL tables, VARRAYS, and while doing native dynamic SQL. This, in essence, allows you to create multi-dimensional arrays in Oracle. Here is an example:

```
DECLARE
-- Create the VARRAYS
TYPE md_varray_1 IS VARRAY(10) OF INTEGER;
TYPE md_varray_2 IS VARRAY(10) of md_varray_1;

-- Initialize the VARRAYS
mem_1   md_varray_1 := md_varray_1(1,2,3);
mem_2   md_varray_2 := md_varray_2(mem_1, md_varray_1(12,24,36),
                       md_varray_1(5,10), mem_1);
v_int   INTEGER;
mem_val  md_varray_1;
BEGIN
    -- Now, get the 2,3 value of md_varray_2
    v_int := mem_2(2)(3);
    DBMS_OUTPUT.PUT_LINE(v_int);

    -- Add a record
    mem_2.EXTEND;
    mem_2(5):=md_varray_1(100,200);

    -- Replace a record
    mem_2(4):= md_varray_1(100,300,0,0);

    -- Let's add an element to the 4th element
    mem_2(4).extend;

    -- Add a value to the newly added element
    mem_2(4)(4):=101;
END;
/
```

The same types of multi-dimensional nested-table operations apply to nested table use.

Bulk-Bind Improvements

Oracle9i bulk binding has been enhanced. First, Oracle9i now allows you to use bulk binding with Oracle collection types with the **select** and **fetch** clauses. Bulk binding of records used in **insert** and **update** statements is also supported.

Error processing for bulk binds has been much improved. Previously, errors during bulk-bind operations would cause the operation to stop, and an exception would be raised. Oracle has provided the ability to allow the application to handle the error and continue the bulk-bind process. Errors are collected during the operation and returned when the bulk-bind operation is complete.

Bulk error handling is provided through the use of the new **save exceptions** keyword in a **forall** statement. All errors will be stored in a new Oracle cursor attribute, **%bulk_exceptions**. This cursor stores the error number and message within it for each SQL error. The total number of errors is also stored as an attribute of **%bulk_exceptions (%bulk_exceptions.count)**. As a result, the number of subscripts within **%bulk_exceptions** will naturally be one to **%bulk_exceptions.count**. Failure to use **save exceptions** will cause the bulk-bind operation to operate as it always has, stopping at the first error that occurs. You can still check **%bulk_exception** for the error information in this case. Here is an example of a bulk-bind operation that uses the **save exceptions** clause:

```
v_count number;
TYPE t_salary IS TABLE OF NUMBER;
TYPE t_empno IS TABLE OF NUMBER;
v_salary t_salary:=t_salary(1000,2000,3000,4000,5000);
v_empno t_empno:=t_empno(100,101,102,103,104);
BEGIN
    FORALL v_count IN 1..5
    SAVE EXCEPTIONS
    INSERT INTO salary (pay_date, pay_amount, empno) VALUES
    (SYSDATE, v_salary(v_count)/12, v_empno(v_count) );
    DBMS_OUTPUT.PUT_LINE('Count = '||v_count);
    EXCEPTION
    WHEN OTHERS
    THEN
    DBMS_OUTPUT.PUT_LINE('Number of errors recorded: '||
        SQL%BULK_EXCEPTIONS.COUNT);
    FOR counter IN 1..SQL%BULK_EXCEPTIONS.COUNT
    LOOP
        DBMS_OUTPUT.PUT_LINE('Record Number: '||Counter);
        DBMS_OUTPUT.PUT_LINE('Error Code: '||
                SQL%BULK_EXCEPTIONS(counter).error_code);
        DBMS_OUTPUT.PUT_LINE('Error Message: '||
                SQLERRM(SQL%BULK_EXCEPTIONS(counter).ERROR_INDEX) );
    END LOOP;
END;
/
```

Native Dynamic SQL Enhancements

Native dynamic SQL was introduced in Oracle8i as an easier method of implementing dynamic SQL from within PL/SQL. Oracle9i enhances native dynamic SQL by implementing bulk dynamic SQL. With bulk dynamic SQL, performance of dynamic SQL is improved because multiple rows can be processed by a single call to the database. This leads to much fewer context switches, which also improves execution times.

Oracle9i has enhanced native dynamic SQL, adding bulk fetch support for cursors, and support for **bulk execute immediate** and **execute** for dynamic SQL. Further support for the **forall** statement, including the **collect into** and **returning into** clauses, is extended to support dynamic SQL. Let's first look at an example of bulk binding with Dynamic SQL:

```
DECLARE
TYPE v_number_table IS TABLE OF NUMBER;
v_num_list  v_number_table;
BEGIN
    EXECUTE IMMEDIATE
    'SELECT empno FROM emp WHERE deptno = 10'
    BULK COLLECT INTO v_num_list;
END;
/
```

In this example, we are loading the contents of an entire SQL query into a nested table for later processing if we like. If that isn't enough just to make you wet your lips with anticipation of the possibilities, then how about bulk binding for input variables? Here is an example:

```
DECLARE
    TYPE t_id_table IS TABLE OF NUMBER;
    TYPE t_date_table IS TABLE OF DATE;
    TYPE t_trans_code_table IS TABLE OF NUMBER;

    v_id_table t_id_table := t_id_table (1,2,3,4,5);
    v_date_table t_date_table :=
    t_date_table(SYSDATE, SYSDATE, SYSDATE, SYSDATE, SYSDATE);
    v_trans_code_table t_trans_code_table :=
        t_trans_code_table(66,44,55,33,11);
BEGIN
    FORALL looping IN 1..5
        EXECUTE IMMEDIATE
        'INSERT INTO transaction_table
        (transaction_id, transaction_date, transaction_code)
        VALUES (:1, :2, :3)'
```

```
            USING v_id_table(looping), v_date_table(looping),
            v_trans_code_table(looping);
END;
/
```

In this example, we have used **execute immediate** to perform an **insert**
statement that passes three collection variables via the **using** clause. This PL/SQL
statement will make just one database call for all the inserts that are to occur.

Changes to Internet Packages in Oracle9i

If you have used some of the Oracle Internet-related packages, such as **utl_http**,
utl_smtp, **utl_tcp**, or **utl_inaddr**, then there are a few changes to these packages that
you will be interested in. First, these packages no longer require that Java be loaded
into the database to execute them. They are now loaded at database creation time
(via catproc.sql). Finally, their performance has been improved because they now
run natively within the database.

Additional improvements include support for HTTP cookies, control over HTTP
conversations, addition of the ability of PL/SQL applications to retrieve web pages
and interact with other HTTP applications, support for POST and other HTTP request
methods, and HTTP 1.1 persistent connection support.

New Optimizer and Statistics-Gathering Options

Some new options are offered in Oracle9i regarding the optimizer and gathering
database statistics, and we will look at these options in this section. First, new
first_rows optimization options are available to help the optimizer choose better
execution plans. New statistics-gathering options also are available. Oracle9i now
allows you to gather system-level statistics as well. These statistics provide even
more information to the optimizer so that it will pick an optimal execution plan.
Changes to the **analyze...validate structure** command also make it easier to use
on active systems.

New *first_rows* Optimization Options

Oracle9i offers new options regarding *first_rows* optimization. Now, you can
define for the optimizer that a specific number of rows that you want returned by
using the *first_rows_n* parameter. The optimizer will then try to create a plan that

optimizes for the return of the first *n* number of rows. This new *first_rows_n* optimization method is more efficient than the old *first_rows* option, which is still available. Generally, the optimizer will generate a better plan when the optimizer uses the *first_rows_n* optimization mode rather than *first_rows*.

These new optimization modes can be defined by setting the *optimizer_mode* parameter to one of four new values:

- *first_rows_1*

- *first_rows_10*

- *first_rows_100*

- *first_rows_1000*

In addition to setting the *optimizer_mode*, you can also use the new **first_rows(*n*)** hint in SQL queries. The *n* parameter supports any numeric argument, and will cause the optimizer to produce a plan optimized for the fastest return of the number of rows defined. If the old *first_rows* optimizer mode is defined, or the **first_rows** hint is used without an argument, then the old, default, *first_rows* optimization method will be used.

New Statistics-Gathering Options

If you use the **dbms_stats.gather_schema_stats** procedure, you have some new options to choose from. Now Oracle9i can actually decide on the percentage of rows that need to be analyzed to gather accurate statistical information. This allows DBAs to use estimated statistics with more confidence and reliability.

Also, when DBAs use histograms, new options are available to indicate how many buckets must be built when analyzing the table. These new options are

- **REPEAT**   This simply rebuilds the histogram buckets based on the previous number of buckets.

- **AUTO**   This will build new histograms. Oracle will choose a number of buckets to use based on the data distribution in the table and application workload. This depends on Oracle9i's ability to capture workload information, and is more efficient after the database and the application have been running for a sufficient time. If this is not the case, you should use the SKEWONLY option.

- **SKEWONLY**   This will build new histograms. Oracle will choose a number of buckets to use based on the data distribution in the table.

An example of the use of the **gather_schema_stats** procedure using the new options is shown here:

```
EXEC DBMS_STATS.GATHER_SCHEMA_STATS ( -
ownname => 'SCOTT', -
estimate_percent => DBMS_STATS.AUTO_SAMPLE_SIZE, -
method_opt => 'for all columns size REPEAT');
```

Oracle9i also offers the *gather auto* option, which is equivalent to running both the *gather stale* and *gather empty* options. The *gather auto* option makes the gathering of statistics at the schema level easier. Here is an example of the use of this option:

```
EXEC DBMS_STATS.GATHER_SCHEMA_STATS ( -
ownname => 'SCOTT',  -
options => 'GATHER AUTO');
```

New Optimizer Options

The CBO now gives more meaningful cost estimates. Oracle has added new columns to the PLAN_TABLE table:

- **CPU_COST**   The estimated CPU cost for the operation

- **IO_COST**   The estimated IO cost for the operation

- **TEMP_SPACE**   An estimate of temporary space that will be required by the operation

Further, the new features added to the CBO allow it to account for the effects of caching on the performance of nested-loop joins and index prefetching when costing out an execution plan.

Gathering System Statistics

Oracle9i has further enhanced the CBO so that it will consider the system's own performance statistics when costing plans. To take advantage of this new feature, you must first gather system statistics. Much like gathering object statistics, you must collect system statistics on a regular basis to derive the maximal benefit of this new feature. This is because CPU and IO footprints fluctuate over time.

As you gather system statistics, you can identify each statistic run with a specific statistic ID. This allows you to track system costs based on the query type footprint that the system is experiencing. Thus, you might track system statistics during the day for OLTP operations, and during the night for reporting operations, using different statistics IDs.

Note that SQL statements are not invalidated when system statistics are generated; thus, only newly parsed SQL statements will benefit from the new statistics that are gathered. Oracle has added three new procedures to gather system statistics. These are

- **dbms_stats.gather_system_stats**
- **dbms_stats.set_system_stats**
- **dbms_stats.get_system_stats**

Let's quickly look at each of these.

The dbms_stats.gather_system_stats Package

This procedure is used to collect system statistics for a given period of time. Here is the syntax diagram of the procedure:

```
PROCEDURE DBMS_STATS.GATHER_SYSTEM_STATS
( gathering_mode   VARCHAR2 DEFAULT 'INTERVAL',  -- Valid Values INTERVAL,START, STOP
  interval         INTEGER  DEFAULT 60,          -- In Seconds
  stattab          VARCHAR2 DEFAULT NULL,        -- Statistics Table
  statid           VARCHAR2 DEFAULT NULL,        -- Statistics collection ID
  statown          VARCHAR2 DEFAULT NULL);       -- Owner of the stats table
```

Here is an example of the use of this package:

```
EXEC DBMS_STATS.GATHER_SYSTEM_STATS(gathering_mode=>'INTERVAL', -
interval=>120, statid=>'OLTP');
```

In this example, we are collecting stats for a specific time as defined by the *gathering_mode* parameter. INTERVAL is the default value for this option. We also could have used the value START to begin collecting system statistics, followed by the same call using the STOP value to stop statistics collection when we wanted.

The interval parameter defaults to 60 seconds, and, in our example, we have increased the collection interval to 120 seconds. In this example, we could have defined the name of a statistics table (using the stattab parameter) that we could use to store the statistics in, as opposed to the default option, which is the data dictionary. If we wish to send the statistic to a separate statistics table, then we will need to use the **dbms_stats.create_stat_table** procedure to create the statistics table first. Optionally, you can include the schema owner of the table in the call, as you can see from the syntax diagram. Finally we have assigned an ID to the statistics that are to be collected of OLTP. If we were to generate reports in the evening, we might instead assign an ID of REPORTS to those system statistics, since the system footprint is likely to be much different.

NOTE
*To successfully gather system statistics, you will
need to have the* job_queue_processes *parameter set
to a value greater than zero.*

The dbms_stats.set_system_stats Package

This procedure allows you to set system statistics explicitly. Here is the syntax for this procedure:

```
PROCEDURE DBMS_STATS.SET_SYSTEM_STATS
(    pname              VARCHAR2,
     pvalue             NUMBER,
     stattab     IN     VARCHAR2 DEFAULT NULL,
     statid      IN     VARCHAR2 DEFAULT NULL,
     statown     IN     VARCHAR2 DEFAULT NULL);
```

With this procedure, you can set one of three system statistic parameters, as defined by the *pname* parameter. These statistics and their associated codes are shown in Table 6-3.

Statistic Pname Parameter Name	Description
sreadtim	Wait-time to read a single block, in milliseconds
mreadtim	Wait-time to read a single multiblock, in milliseconds
cpuspeed	CPU clock cycles per second, in millions

TABLE 6-3. *System Statistic Codes and Descriptions*

The dbms_stats.get_system_stats Package

This procedure is used to verify system statistics contained in the statistics table. Here is the syntax for the procedure:

```
PROCEDURE DBMS_STATS.GET_SYSTEM_STATS
(   status    OUT   VARCHAR2,
    dstart    OUT   DATE,
    dstop     OUT   DATE,
    pname           VARCHAR2,
    pvalue    OUT   NUMBER,
    stattab   IN    VARCHAR2 DEFAULT NULL,
    statid    IN    VARCHAR2 DEFAULT NULL,
    statown   IN    VARCHAR2 DEFAULT NULL);
```

Please see the *Oracle9i Reference Manual* for complete details of the possible values that are returned by this procedure. Basically, you use this procedure to report the status of a specific set of statistics in your statistics table. Here is an example:

```
DECLARE
v_status_out    VARCHAR2(50);
v_dstart_out    DATE;
v_dstop_out     DATE;
v_pname_out     VARCHAR2(50):='SREADTIM';
v_pvalue_out    NUMBER;

BEGIN
DBMS_STATS.GET_SYSTEM_STATS
( status=>v_status_out,
  dstart=>v_dstart_out,
  dstop=>v_dstop_out,
  pname=>v_pname_out,
  pvalue=>v_pvalue_out,
  statid=>'OLTP');

DBMS_OUTPUT.PUT_LINE('Status is : '||v_status_out);
DBMS_OUTPUT.PUT_LINE('Stats collection started : '||v_dstart_out);
DBMS_OUTPUT.PUT_LINE('Stats collection ended   : '||v_dstop_out);
DBMS_OUTPUT.PUT_LINE('Stats Parameter Value is : '||v_pvalue_out);
END;
/
```

Once you have gathered the various system statistics, you can then import the statistics you need into the database. For example, for daytime operations, you might use the **dbms_stats.import_system_stats** command to move the OLTP system statistics gathered during the daytime hours into the database. Here is an example:

```
EXEC DBMS_STATS.IMPORT_SYSTEM_STATS('MYSTATS_TAB','OLTP');
```

During the night, you would want to load the statistics run in the evening during report generation, so, again, you would use the **dbms_stats** package, as shown here:

```
EXEC DBMS_STATS.IMPORT_SYSTEM_STATS('MYSTATS_TAB','REPORT');
```

Note that, in this case, the OLTP stats will be overwritten by the REPORT stats. You could, of course, automate this process using the Oracle job scheduler.

Online analyze...validate Structure

You can now validate the structure of an object online using the **analyze...validate object** command (this was previously possible only with the **dbms_stats** package). While this command is running, DML operations on the object being validated can continue, though there will be additional overhead associated with the validation operation.

Examining Cached Execution Plans

As a DBA, you are familiar with the execution plans created with the results of the **explain plan** SQL command and *tkprof*, as well as the use of the SQL*Plus **set autotrace on** commands. If you have used these tools much, no doubt you will have noticed that the execution plans generated are not always accurate if the statements generating those plans contain bind variables. This is because the Oracle optimizer will quickly look at the value of the bind variables the first time a SQL statement is executed to determine the correct execution plan for a given statement. The optimizer does this only the first time a like statement is optimized, and it assumes that the plan generated for that statement will be efficient for any like-generated statement.

This knowledge of the values of the bind variables makes the resulting execution plan more efficient, but causes *tkprof* and **set autotrace on** to give incorrect execution plan results. This is because the resulting execution plan generated by *tkprof* and **set autotrace on** have no ability to look at the value of the bind variable that is being used.

Oracle9i provides a new view, V$SQL_PLAN, to provide more accurate execution-plan information for the DBA trying to tune a SQL statement. This new view contains the actual execution plan for the SQL statement cached in the shared pool. This view is useful for more than just tuning SQL statements. You can use this view if you want to find cursors that are using specific types of access paths, such as sort merge joins or nested loops, finding which indexes are in use in the cursors that are cached.

Another good use for V$SQL_PLAN is to save old SQL statements and cached execution plans before you make database architecture plans. Having made your changes (for example, added or dropped an index), rerun the cached SQL statements again and determine whether the execution plans remain unchanged. This is a much faster and more accurate alternative to running mass **explain plan** or **set serveroutput** on tests, and will probably give you a heads-up if some significant change has occurred. Execution-plan comparison also is helpful after running an **analyze** command to see whether the execution plans have changed because of changes in the nature of the data.

Here is an example of a query against the V$SQL_PLAN view and the SQL query that the output was generated for:

```
-- Execute the query (we removed the output for brevity…
SELECT * FROM EMP;

-- Look at the real life execution plan for this query
PROMPT Enter address from V$SQLAREA for SQL Statement
SELECT DECODE(id,0,'',
       LPAD('        ',2*(level-1))||level||'.'||position)||' '||operation||
       DECODE(id,0,'',' Option: ')||options||
       DECODE(id,0,'',' Object Name: ')||DECODE(id,0,'',NVL(object_name, 'None'))||
       DECODE(id,0,'',' Object Number: ')||DECODE(id,0,'',NVL(TO_CHAR(object#), 'None' ))||
')||DECODE(id,0,'',NVL(TO_CHAR(object#), 'None' ))||
       DECODE(id,0,'Cost = '||position)
       SQL_Query_plan
       FROM v$sql_plan
       CONNECT BY prior id = parent_id
       AND address = upper('&&SQLADDRESS')
       START WITH id =0 AND address = upper('&&SQLADDRESS');


SQL_QUERY_PLAN
----------------------------------------------------------------
 DDL STATEMENT Cost = 0
  2.1 PARTITION RANGE Option: ALL Object Name: None Object Number: None
    3.1 TABLE ACCESS Option: FULL Object Name: EMP Object Number: 5272
```

Note that the V$SQL_PLAN view requires the address of the SQL statement, which is available from V$SQLAREA. Of course, there are other ways that you might approach the use of the table. You could pull all execution plans that include a given object, for example, and determine just how often that object is being queried and how.

CHAPTER 7

Oracle9i Real Application Clusters

- Installation and configuration
- Oracle9i new Cache Fusion implementation
- HA features
- ORAC management and diagnostics
- Supported platforms

ince companies must always be prepared to serve their customers around the clock, this expanded reach makes it more costly when service is not available, either planned or unplanned. High availability (HA) is becoming a critical requirement for e-businesses that cannot afford costly system downtime.

Oracle Real Application Clusters (ORAC) is the multi-node extension to Oracle database server that enables e-businesses to build highly available and highly scalable database servers across multiple nodes. The new ORAC architecture makes it possible to scale the most demanding e-business applications with intensive transaction loads, and thus support large populations of Internet users.

This chapter concentrates on the new features of ORAC that exceed the capabilities of previous Oracle cluster software releases. It starts with new terminology and continues by discussing enhancements in ORAC that distinguish it from previous cluster systems.

New Terminology

ORAC introduces a number of terms to reflect new functionality more accurately, including the following:

- **Massively Parallel Processing (MPP)**   Commonly understood as computing that uses many separate CPUs running in parallel to execute a single program. Oracle parallel server (OPS) reflected the MPP concept in previous releases of Oracle cluster software. Oracle9i real application clusters is a broader term and encompasses MPP notation.

- **Oracle Parallel Fail Safe (OPFS)**   Replaced by ORAC guard, which is an integral part of ORAC.

- **OPSCTL utility**   Replaced by SRVCTL.

- **Oracle Parallel Server Communications Daemon (OPSD)**   Replaced by the global services daemon (GSD).

- **Oracle Parallel Server Management (OPSM)**   Replaced by server management (SRVM).

- *Parallel Cache Management (PCM) is obsolete.* These operations have been replaced by *global cache service* (GCS) block requests.

NOTE
For example, if your sessions hang indefinitely, now you have to pay attention at a global cache lock wait event rather than a PCM one.

■ *Non-PCM is obsolete.* The *Global Enqueue Service* (GES) now implements the resource management.

■ *Lock mastering is obsolete.* The equivalent function in real application clusters is resource mastering.

■ *Lock database is obsolete.* The equivalent functions are handled by the global resource directory (GRD).

■ *The term Distributed Lock Manager (DLM) is obsolete.* The background processes that were formerly aggregated under the DLM in previous cluster software products still exist, but the DLM no longer manages resources in ORAC. The GCS and GES now handle the management functions that had been handled by the DLM in earlier Oracle cluster software releases.

Installation and Configuration

The ease with which you can administer cluster software is, to a large degree, a function of how well it is configured. The resulting system must be

■ **Maintainable**   The DBA has flexibility to apply patches, relocate tables, and so on, without requiring changes to application code or changes to the cluster parameters.

■ **Robust**   Highly available.

Oracle9i real application clusters has substantially improved installation and configuration processes while adding the following new requirements:

■ You must create a shared raw device to store ORAC server configuration information. In previous versions, Oracle stored this information in the db_name.conf file on UNIX and in the Registry on Windows NT platforms.

■ If you need to Migrate an existing database in an ORAC environment, you must also create the following shared raw devices, which were optional in previous products:

   ■ Oracle9i sample schemas

   ■ Online analytical processing (OLAP)

■ Oracle9i interMedia

■ Automatic undo management feature

These requirements are in addition to previous raw device requirements such as those for the SYSTEM, USERM, TEMP, and other tablespaces.

The Oracle Universal Installer and Database Configuration Assistant (DBCA) have been enhanced to offer simplified software installation and database creation for ORAC. The Oracle DBCA will create a seed database expecting the following configuration:

Create a Raw Device for...	...with File Size	Sample Name
SYSTEM tablespace	400M	db_name_raw_system_400
Server parameter file	5M	db_name_raw_spfile_5
USERS tablespace	120M	db_name_raw_users_120
TEMP tablespace	100M	db_name_raw_temp_100
UNDOTBS tablespace per instance	500M	db_name_raw_undo_500
OEMREPO tablespace	20M	db_name_raw_oemrepo_20
EXAMPLE tablespace	160M	db_name_raw_examples_160
INDX tablespace	70M	db_name_raw_indx_70
TOOLS tablespace	12M	db_name_raw_tools_12
DRSYS tablespace	90M	db_name_raw_dr_90
First control file	110M	db_name_raw_control01_110
Second control file	110M	db_name_raw_control02_110
Two redo log files for each instance	120M (per file)	db_name_thread_lognumb_120
srvcfg configuration raw device	100M	db_name_raw_srvmconf_100

The Oracle Universal Installer offers the following database configuration types: general purpose, transaction processing, data warehouse, customized, and software only. The customized database configuration type replaces the custom installation type.

NOTE
An option to Upgrade or Migrate an existing database is presented. Do not select this option! Currently, the Oracle migration utility is not able to Upgrade an ORAC database, and will cause an error if selected to do so.

The DBCA templates named General Purpose, Transaction Processing, and Data Warehousing correspond to the installer's configuration types. In addition, the DBCA has a New Database template that does not include datafiles and that is fully customizable.

NOTE
To simplify installation, you can select the general-purpose, transaction-processing, or data-warehousing configuration type in the Universal Installer's Database Configuration screen. Providing you have configured your shared raw devices, after completing the remaining installer screens, the installation and DBCA database creation processes continue without further user input.

The raw partition tablespaces require greater capacities than the values that were published in documentation for previous versions.

ORAC now supports Cluster File Systems (CFS) to simplify ORAC installation and management. You have to use the Oracle managed-files option, your hardware server platform must support a CFS, and this CFS must be supported by Oracle. The Oracle managed-files feature automatically creates and deletes files that Oracle requires to manage the database.

NOTE
At this time, CFS is available only on Compaq Tru64 and VMS.

The Oracle Cluster Setup Wizard is available to install the operating system–dependent (OSD) layer software on Windows NT and Windows 2000 operating systems.

■ ORAC and Oracle fail safe are integrated with Microsoft's Cluster Server (MSCS). This enables more flexibility in configuring them on Windows NT. They also make use of Internet protocol (IP) failover and Microsoft's cluster management utilities.

■ The Oracle DBCA has administrative features such as instance and template management. You can use the template management feature to manage and customize database creation scripts. As part of creating databases, DBCA can create and display the contents of server parameter files (SPFILEs).

NOTE
Oracle recommends that you use SPFILEs when you implement ORAC, and that you modify the default file location for SPFILEs for ORAC environments if you are using raw devices.

Beginning with Oracle9i, all default database user accounts except SYS, SYSTEM, SCOTT, DBSNMP, AURORAJISUTILITY$, AURORA$ORB$UNAUTHENTICATED, and OSE$HTTP$ADMIN are locked and expired on an initial database installation via DBCA. To activate a locked account, a DBA must manually unlock it and reassign it a new password.

NOTE
We recommend that you change the password immediately after you unlock the account.

New Oracle9i Cache Fusion Implementation

In Oracle8i parallel server, as in Oracle9i real application clusters, a particular data block can be modified by only one instance at a time. The first instance must write the block to disk before the requesting instance can read it. This constitutes the forced disk write to a block, or pinging.

Pinging blocks via disk to get read-consistent views of the blocks on a remote instance caused major system performance degradation. Oracle8i parallel server was the first version to introduce the Cache Fusion concept to reduce performance overhead. The Cache Fusion mechanism greatly reduced pinging when selecting data from an instance whose lock element was in use by another instance. The instance-owning dirty buffer was no longer forced to write its changes to disk (forced disk-write or ping). Instead, Cache Fusion created a read-consistent copy of the buffer and shipped it across the interconnect to the instance that was selecting the data. Although Oracle8i Cache Fusion addressed read-write contention, in the situation when instance had to change the block that was held on the remote instance, it had to go through the same ping mechanism and write the block to disk.

Oracle9i real application clusters enhanced the Cache Fusion functionality by addressing write-write contention. This substantially improves system throughput and utilization. With ORAC Cache Fusion, Oracle has taken further steps to reduce the amount of I/O contention by virtually eliminating the need to ping blocks to disk for locks that are in use but are requested for write access on the remote instance. The owning instance can ship copies of dirty buffers to remote instances for write access. This functionality is available by default in Oracle9i real application clusters. You can override Cache Fusion by setting GC_FILES_TO_LOCKS in your initialization parameter file to 1. This tells Oracle to use pre-ORAC behavior to force disk writes for cross-instance modification requests. Oracle does not recommend this in most circumstances. Hashed locks still use the ping mechanism for write-write contention, and fixed locks have been eliminated in Oracle9i real application clusters.

With OPS, some applications did not scale well because disk block transfers affected performance and could cause I/O bottlenecks. To avoid this, data, application, or the users across instances had to be optimally partitioned. This always affected development costs associated with modifying the data or the application. By providing block transfers without forced disk writes, Cache Fusion avoids the need for partitioning and allows any application to take advantage of the scalability offered by ORAC.

Cache Fusion Architectural Concepts

Oracle9i real application clusters Cache Fusion introduced more robust and accurate concepts to manage collaboration between multiple instances. The GCS and GES now handle the management functions that had been handled by the DLM in earlier Oracle cluster software releases. A global cache element is an Oracle-specific data structure representing a *Cache Fusion resource*. There is a 1:1 corresponding relationship between a global cache element and a Cache Fusion resource in the GCS.

Oracle9i uses a messaging mechanism to maintain resource statuses. Both GCS and GES use messages containing information to ensure that the current block image can be located. These messages also identify block copies being retained by any specific instance for use by the recovery mechanisms. The recovery-specific information contains sequence numbers to identify the order of changes made to that block since it was read from disk. The GRD is a repository of information about current status of resources shared by the instances. The GRD contains two groups of resources: enqueue resources, managed by the GES, and buffer cache resources, managed by the GCS. GCS and GES maintain contents of GRD.

The GCS evolves various background processes such as the *GCS processes* (LMSn) and *GES daemon* (LMD).

The LMSn are the processes that handle remote GCS messages. The current release of Oracle9i real application clusters software provides for up to 10 GCS processes. The number of LMSn processes varies, depending on the amount of messaging traffic among nodes in the cluster. LMD is the resource-agent process that manages GES resource requests, such as deadlock detection of GES requests.

GES and GCS

The GES coordinates enqueues that are shared globally.

The GCS is the controlling mechanism that implements Cache Fusion. It is responsible for block transfers between instances. In Oracle 8i, each Cache Fusion resource could be held by an instance in one of three lock modes: null (N), shared (S), or exclusive (X). The GSC introduces expanded notation of Cache Fusion resource mode.

Three characters are required to distinguish resources. The first actually characterizes traditional *resource type:* N, S, or X. The second is new to Oracle9i. It represents a *role*. There are two roles:

- **Local (L)** The blocks associated with the resource can be manipulated without further reference to GCS or other instances. For example, when a resource is acquired for the first time, it is acquired with a local role.

- **Global (G)** The blocks covered by the resource might not be usable without further information from the GCS or other nodes. For example, if the resource is acquired and it already has dirty buffers on a remote instance, then it takes on a global resource role.

If the resource is in exclusive mode and has a local role, then the following rules apply:

- Only one instance can have the resource in exclusive mode.

- All unwritten changes must be in local cache.

- At checkpoint, instance can write changed blocks to disk without confirmation from GCS.

If the resource is in exclusive mode and has a global role, then the following rules apply:

- The associated block can be modified in the current cache.

- The status of associated block on disk is unknown (it might or might not be current).

- The associated block can be served to another instance.

- The associated block cannot be written without GCS approval.

The third character represents a notion called *Past Image (PI)*. It can have two meanings: 0 (current image of block) and 1 (past image of block). A Past Image is a copy of a globally dirty block image maintained in the instance cache. A PI must be maintained by an instance until it, or a later version of the block, is written to disk. The GCS informs an instance that its PI is no longer needed after another instance writes the block. Past Images are discarded when an instance writes a current block image to disk. Such writes occur to satisfy normal Database Writer (DBWR) activity, checkpoint requests, and so on, not to transfer blocks between instances. When an instance needs to write a block—to satisfy a checkpoint request, for example—the instance checks the role of the resource covering the block. If it is global, the instance must notify the GCS. The GCS finds the most current block image and informs the instance holding that image to perform the block write. After saving the block, the GCS then informs all holders of the global resource that they can release the buffers holding the PI copies of the block. Cache Fusion resource modes are presented in the Table 7-2.

Mode	Definition	Description
NL0	Null local 0	The same as N in Oracle8i OPS
SL0	Shared local 0	The same as S in Oracle8i OPS
XL0	Exclusive local 0	The same as X in Oracle8i OPS
NG0	Null global 0	Instance owns current block image.
SG0	Shared global 0	Instance owns current block image and the resource can be shared with the other nodes. Can write current image.
XG0	Exclusive global 0	Instance owns current block image for modification. Can write current image.
NG1	Null global 1	Instance owns past block image. Can write PI image.
SG1	Shared global 1	Instance owns past block image and the resource can be shared with the other nodes. Can write current and PI images.
XG1	Exclusive global 1	Instance owns past block image for modification. Can write current and PI images.

TABLE 7-2.   *Cache Fusion Resource Modes*

Writing Block and Recovery Considerations

For recovery purposes, instances that have Past Images will keep these Past Images in their buffer cache until notified by the master instance of the resource to release them. A *Block Written Record* (BWR) is placed in its redo log buffer when an instance writes a block covered by a global resource or when it is told it can free a PI buffer. This record indicates to the recovery process that redo information for the block is not needed by this time. Although the BWR makes recovery more efficient, the instance does not force a flush of the log buffer after creating it because it is not essential for accurate recovery.

Each block PI has a *system change number (SCN)*. Instances regularly synchronize their SCNs, and PI SCN is guaranteed to be later than the previous modification performed on this block and earlier than modifications performed by the next instance. When a write completes, the writer updates the GRD with write completion and the new SCN information. The GCS requests instances to flush all PIs having earlier SCNs than the one in the block written to disk.

Typical ORAC Block Transfer Scenarios

Let's assume there is a four-node ORAC cluster (instances A, B, C, and D), and the resource master is located on instance D.

Scenario 1: Obtaining Resource with No Block Transfer

Instance C issues a select against a block with SCN 123.

Step 1   Instance C requests resource from resource master on instance D.

Step 2   Instance D grants the resource, and resource status on instance C changes from NL0 to SL0.

Step 3   Instance C initiates I/O request to the disk.

Step 4   Block gets delivered to instance C. Instance C now holds the block with SCN 123 using an SL0 resource.

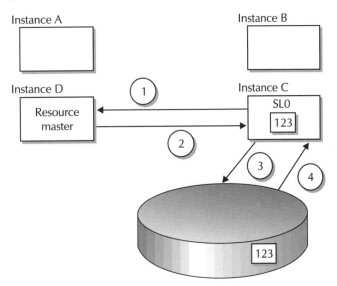

Scenario 2: Obtaining Resource with Block Transfer in Read-Read Situation

Instance B issues a select against a block with SCN 123.

Step1   Instance B requests resource from resource master on instance D via GCS.

Step 2 The GRD contains the status of the resource for block with SCN 123. It indicates that resource was granted to instance C with SL0 mode. The GCS requests shared resource and block transfer to instance B.

Step 3 Instance C ships the copy of the block to instance B via fast interconnect.

Step 4 Instance B receives the block image along with the SL0 resource. Instance B sends a message to the GCS to notify about newly acquired resource. The GCS is now responsible for recording this information at GRD.

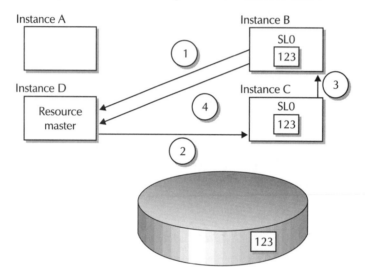

Scenario 3: Obtaining Resource with Block Transfer in Read-Write Situation

Instance A issues a *Data Manipulation Language* (*DML*) statement requiring exclusive resource against the block with SCN 123.

Step 1 Instance A requests resource from resource master on instance D.

Step 2 The GRD contains the status of the resource for the block with SCN 123. It indicates that resource was granted to instances C and B with SL0 mode. The GCS requests from instance C to transfer the block with SCN 123 to instance B for exclusive access. At the same time, it requests instances B and C to close their shared resource on the block.

Step 3 Instance C ships the copy of the block to instance B via fast interconnect. Both instances B and C release the resource.

Step 4   Block gets delivered to instance A. Instance A can now modify the block.
The block SCN becomes 124.

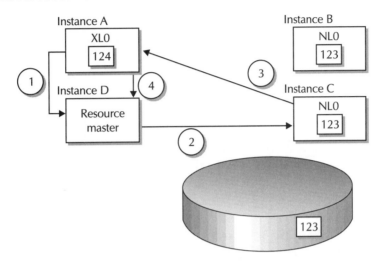

Scenario 4: Obtaining Resource with Block Transfer in Write-Write Situation

Instance C issues a DML statement requiring exclusive resource against the block
with SCN 123. The copy of the block on disk is still at SCN 123.

Step 1   Instance C requests resource from resource master on instance D.

Step 2   The GRD contains the status of the resource for the block with SCN 124.
It indicates that resource was granted to instance A with XL0 mode. The GCS
requests from instance A to transfer block with SCN 124 to instance C for exclusive
access and release its resource. The request message may be queued until the GCS
can process the request.

Step 3   Instance A completes its work on the block, logging all the changes and
forcing a log flush if this has not occurred, converting its resource to NG1, and
shipping the copy of the block image with SCN 124 to instance C.

Step 4   Block gets delivered to instance C. After receiving the image, instance
C sends an acknowledgment message notifying the GCS that instance C has the
resource with an XG0 status, and that instance A, the previous holder of the
exclusive resource, now holds a PI version at SCN 124. To make its own changes
to the block, instance C acquires new SCN 131.

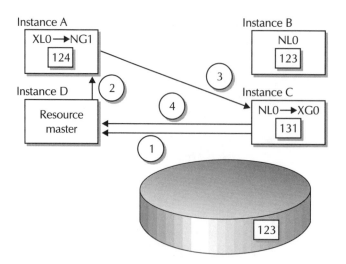

Scenario 5: Obtaining Resource with Block Transfer in Write-Read Situation

Instance B issues a select statement against the block with SCN 131 that is held by instance C.

> **NOTE**
> *This will require instance C to build a read-consistent block image before shipping it to instance B.*

Step 1   Instance B requests shared resource from resource master on instance D.

Step 2   The GRD contains the status of the resource for the block with SCN 131. It indicates that the resource was granted to instance C with XG0 mode. The GCS requests from instance C to transfer block with SCN 131 to instance B for shared access. Again, the request message may be queued until the GCS can process the request.

Step 3   As in previous scenarios, instance C completes its work on the block, logging all the changes and forcing a log flush—if this has not already occurred; and, downgrading its resource to SG1, it ships the copy of the block image with SCN 131 to instance. The copy of the block will be a read-consistent version of the block with SCN 123.

Step 4   Block gets delivered to instance B. After receiving the image, instance B sends an acknowledgment message notifying the GCS that instance B has the resource with SG0 status, and instance C, the previous holder of the exclusive resource, now holds a PI version of a block with SCN 131 for a shared access.

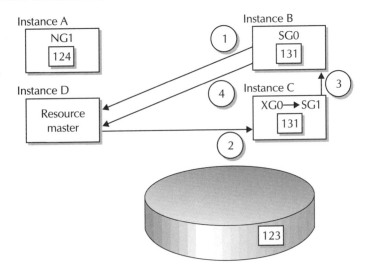

Scenario 6: Writing Dirty Buffer

This instance configuration is similar to the one we discussed in Scenario 4. To simplify, assume instance C has a resource mode XG1, rather than XG0, and instance A has a checkpoint request.

Step 1 Instance A sends a write request to write at SCN 124 or higher to resource master on instance D.

Step 2 The GCS selects the node to perform the actual write: either the current node or the node holding the most recently granted resource. In this scenario, it is instance C that holds the latest PI of the block. Instance D sends a write request message to instance C.

Step 3 Instance C writes the block to a disk.

Step 4 Having received the write completion notification, instance C logs the completion and the version written with a BWR and advances its checkpoint, but does not force a log write.

Step 5 Instance C sends notification to GCSs about I/O completion. The resource role on instance C changes to local because DBWR wrote the current image.

Step 6   Having received the write completion notification, GCS requests from all instances holding PI to flush the PI. It also requests from instance C to change resource role to local (all Past Images of the block no longer exist).

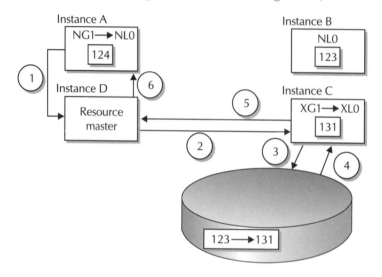

HA Features

As more and more critical commercial applications move to the Internet, providing highly available services becomes increasingly important. One of the advantages of a clustered system is that it has hardware and software redundancy. HA can be provided by detecting node or daemon failures and reconfiguring the system appropriately so that the workload can be taken over by the remaining nodes in the cluster.

Cache Fusion for HA

In earlier implementations of Oracle cluster software, the operating system was responsible for such detection and reporting to the database. To minimize downtime caused by the instance failure, Oracle9i, *cluster-aware code* is included in the database software. This allows ORAC instances to detect cluster problems without coordinating with the operating system's cluster management software. On detecting a problem within a cluster, the instances communicate among themselves to determine which instances are going to remain active members of the cluster, and reconfigure the database resources accordingly.

Oracle9i real application server HA is achieved by allowing sessions connected to a failed instance to resume work on a surviving instance. The following new features in Oracle9i specific to real application clusters make recovery faster and provide higher levels of availability:

- Faster detection and reconfiguration
- Dynamic resource remastering

Instance Failure Detection

In Oracle8i databases and earlier, any kind of shutdown caused the loss of DLM master resource information residing in the departing instance. During reconfiguration, the information of a locked database had to be completely rebuilt. In Oracle9i real application cluster, an instance shutdown (excluding abort, or any other abnormal instance failure) does not cause any loss of GCS master resource information.

Similar to a hardware vendor's solution, ORAC implements a disk-based heartbeat and a voting procedure. Each member of a cluster gives its vision of the other members' availability. This information is stored in shared disk storage. The arbitrating member of a cluster publishes the final configuration. All members then examine the published configuration and, if necessary, terminate their sessions.

ORAC Reconfiguration and Dynamic Resource Remastering

Dynamic Resource Remastering is the ability of the GCS to move the ownership of a resource between instances of the ORAC. Dynamic Resource Remastering is used to implement *resource affinity* for increased performance.

Resource affinity implies that location of the resource masters for a database moves to the instance where block operations are most frequently occurring. This optimizes the system in situations in which update transactions are being executed on one instance. When activity shifts to another instance, the resource affinity will correspondingly move to the new instance. If activity is not localized, then the resource ownership is hashed to the instances.

The GCS and GES can use dynamic remastering to move resources to instances where they are frequently needed. This optimization occurs in the background while users are accessing the system. What is really remarkable is that only the minimum number of resources is remastered while the GRD is frozen. Should an instance leave the group, only the resources mastered by the departing member are remastered. Similarly, when a new instance joins the group, the resources are gradually remastered, adapting to cluster workload.

Instance Leaving a Cluster   Resources are hashed into a constant number of buckets. The number of active instances is not relevant for resource hashing (as it used to be with OPS DML, a time-consuming operation). When an instance leaves the database, only resources with a master hash value mapped to the departing instance have to be remastered, and other resources remain unchanged.

Instance Joining a Cluster   In OPS, a complete redistribution of resources took place whenever a new instance started up. Now, only a portion of the ORAC resources is distributed from each instance to the joining instance.

Instance Shutdown with Normal, Immediate, or Transactional Option   In OPS, the recovery could not begin until DLM and lock database reconfiguration was complete. To reduce recovery time, GCS and instance recovery now proceed in parallel. The GCS closes and remasters all departing instance resources. It notifies *Cluster Group Service (CGS)* about instance departure. On receiving the notification, CGS invokes cluster reconfiguration.

Automatic Resource Remastering   ORAC automatically determines whether a tablespace is being accessed by only one instance. If such a tablespace is identified, the block resource masters for that tablespace are moved to that instance. This reduces the overhead for that instance to open these resources because no messages need be sent to the GCS on another node. The new dynamic performance view, **dba_tablespaces**, indicates which tablespaces have been selected for resource remastering through this algorithm.

Instance and Crash Recovery   The recovery mechanism in OPS relies on forced disk writes. With the ORAC PI concept, recovery can no longer depend on shared disks. Media recovery remains unaffected by Cache Fusion. There is a sequence of events with ORAC recovery:

1. Node fails.

2. Failure detected; failed instance clients Migrated and all database clients suspended.

3. Cluster gets reconfigured; instance recovery began (rolling forward and back).

4. GRD gets rebuilt; users get read access to the data.

5. Recovery data gets identified.

6. Full database access resumed.

7. Roll forward complete.

8. Roll back complete.

Cache fusion recovery relies on two changes in the recovery processing introduced in Oracle9i:

■ SMON, not foreground processes, performs all instance recovery.

■ There is a two-pass, log-read scheme.

First-Pass Log Read

Redo threads of the failed instance are read and merged by SCN. The threads-merging algorithm is similar for media, crash, and instance recovery. SMON creates a hashed-by-DBA DBA table, the *recovery set*. It stores DBAs, first dirty version's SCN, and last dirty version's SCN. The redo can also contain BWRs. When a BWR is read from the merged log stream, the recovering process checks the version. If the BWR version is greater than the last-dirty version in the recovery set, then the block does not need recovery. The block entry is dropped from the recovery set. This avoids unnecessary reads of these data blocks during second-pass redo application. By the end of first pass, the recovery set contains only blocks that were modified by the failed instances.

NOTE
The GCS waits until the recovery process obtains an instance recovery (IR) resource, and then begins cleaning up orphaned blocks. Orphaned blocks are most often created by an instance owning the block but failing before modifying it.

Second-Pass Log Read

The IR process reads the redo threads of the failed instance again and merges them by SCN. Only those records that have entries in the recovery set are considered. IR applies the redo record to the block. If the resulting buffer matches with the latest dirty buffer PI from the recovery set, then recovery is complete. The IR process requests to write this buffer to the disk and then continues trimming more recovery sets by processing its entries step by step. To process redo buffers, IR acquires resources that are similar to the buffer cache block resource model.

If a recovery buffer version is greater than or equal to its last dirty version (stored in the block entry), no redo needs to be applied. An IR resource complete message is issued to the GCS master, and the block is removed from the recovery set. When the last recovery buffer is released, the redo application is complete, even if all the redo information has not been read. This allows the second pass to read fewer log records than the first pass. IR is complete when all dead threads have been checkpointed and closed.

Recovery from Single-Instance Failures

GES must reconstruct states for global enqueues. GCS must reconstruct states for both fusion and nonfusion block resources. At the start of cache recovery, all normal cache resource activity is frozen. The IR process takes a recovery enqueue and rebuilds GRD and buffer cache. If the current version of any given block is in the buffer cache of the crashed instance, the IR process requests the best surviving PI, applies redo from the failed instance logs, and writes the recovered block. If the current copy of the given block was not in the failed instance, the GCS notes this during reconfiguration, and a copy of the current buffer is sent to the recovery instance.

Recovery from Multiple-Instance Failures

In case multiple instances fail or crash, the redo information from the failed instances is merged prior to recovery. Oracle believes that the cost of the merge is proportional to

Number of failed instances × Size of log per instance

This is no worse than the cost in OPS, in which all redo had to be applied from the failed instances. That cost was also proportional to

Number of failed instances × Size of log per instance

Failover and Load Balancing

ORAC uses Oracle Net load balancing and application failover mechanisms to ensure fast failover of clients connecting to the failed nodes/instances. Load balancing distributes client connections to all nodes of the clusters, alleviating the impact of an individual node failure. When using the transparent application failover (TAF) option, Oracle Net will reconnect the failed connections to the failover node in the cluster without the client even being aware of the failure.

Listener Load Balancing and Failover for Dedicated Servers

The Transport Network Services (TNS) listener previously provided load balancing across nodes only in shared servers (formerly called multi-threaded servers). In ORAC, load balancing and failover are also provided for dedicated server configurations. In a dedicated server configuration, a listener selects an instance in the following order:

1. Least loaded node

2. Least loaded instance

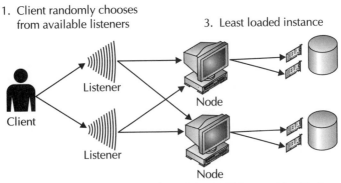

1. Client randomly chooses from available listeners
3. Least loaded instance
Listener
Node
Client
Listener
Node
2. Node with least CPU usage identified

ORAC Guard

In Release 9.0.1, Oracle Parallel Fail Safe (OPFS) was replaced by Oracle Real Application Clusters Guard (ORACG). ORACG also became an integrated feature on UNIX platforms, on which it automatically installs and configures high-availability features.

The parameter files with ACTIVE_INSTANCE_COUNT = 1 are typical for configuration of ORAC guard with two instances. This implies that one instance is identified as a primary, whereas the other one is a secondary. The primary instance masters the entire GRD and is the only instance to allow user connections through Oracle net services. The secondary instance takes over the primary role when the primary instance fails. The following illustration shows a two-node ORACG configuration.

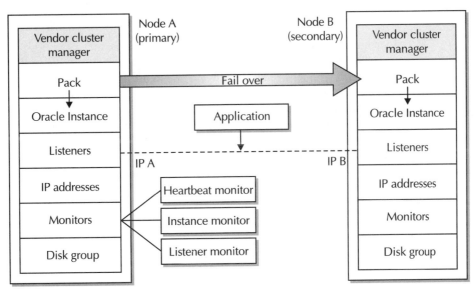

Each node runs the vendor's *Cluster Management Software (CMS)*, which is responsible for running and halting scripts automatically on failover or when you issue the appropriate command. Each node also contains a pack of software. This software controls the startup, shutdown, and restart of Oracle processes. There is one pack for each instance. Packs contain the following components:

- A real application clusters instance. In the previous illustration, node A is running as the primary instance and node B as the secondary one.

- One or more listeners.

- One or more IP addresses, for example, front-end and back-end IP could be used. This ensures transparent application failover to the secondary server, and at the same time, allows the Oracle intelligent agent to provide diagnostics on the failed instance via the separate backend IP.

- A disk group manager (DGM), required only on some platforms, to enable public access to the database disks by the current primary node.

- The following monitors:

    - **Instance**   Detects termination of the local instance and initiates failover to the secondary node or restarts the instance

    - **Listener**   Checks and restarts the listeners. In case a listener fails to restart, the listener monitor exits, initiating a halt script. ORAC guard either begins failover or restarts the primary instance, depending on the state of the secondary node.

    - **Heartbeat**   Checks the availability of the Oracle instance. During normal operation, on each instance, the heartbeat monitor updates its own local heartbeat results and checks the heartbeat results of the other instance. The local Oracle instance is considered unavailable if the heartbeat monitor fails to complete three consecutive attempts and there are no unusual circumstances, such as unusually large numbers of sessions logging on or recovery in progress. If the primary instance is unavailable and the primary instance role has not resumed normal function on its new node, then the heartbeat monitor initiates takeover to itself.

ORACG has the following advantages over the OPFS:

- Simplified pack structure boosts failover performance.

- Improved error and message logging.

- Uptime and downtime logging and reporting capability.

- Improved user interface and commands.

- Improved installation.

- ORACG uses instance role mechanism, which allows resource mastering locally on the primary instance, improving system performance.

- Packs float, minimizing TCP/IP timeouts.

- ORACG uses the **dbms_libcache** package to transfer information from the library cache of the primary instance to the library cache of the secondary instance. Warming the cache improves performance after failover.

Warming the Library Cache   This package can be used via the **compile_from_remote** procedure as a regularly scheduled job and before executing a manual failover or switchover.

After the content of the library cache on the primary instance stabilizes, Oracle recommends that you perform the following steps on the secondary instance:

1. Connect as the user PARSER (precreated user), using SQL*Plus:

   ```
   $ sqlplus parser/password
   ```

2. Turn on server output:

   ```
   SQL> SET SERVEROUTPUT ON;
   ```

3. Execute the **compile_from_remote** procedure. The SQL statement should have the format

   ```
   EXECUTE SYS.DBMS_LIBCACHE.COMPILE_FROM_REMOTE(
   DB_LINK,USERNAME,THRESHOLD_EXECUTIONS,THRESHOLD_SHARABLE_MEM);
   ```

Where **db_link** is the database link pointing to the primary instance; **username** is the user whose information is extracted from the primary instance to be parsed on the secondary instance; **threshhold_executions** is the minimum number of executions of a SQL statement that must have occurred before the SQL statement will be considered for extraction; and **threshold_sharable_ mem** is the minimum size of cursors that will be considered for extraction. Only **db_link** is mandatory. For example, the following command will compile all cursors for all users with default threshold values on the primary instance pointed by database link PRIM:

```
SQL> EXECUTE SYS.DBMS_LIBCACHE.COMPILE_FROM_REMOTE('PRIM');
```

Integration with MSCS

Although, both OPS and OPFS were popular on the Microsoft platform, they used other than MSCS means for cluster management. Oracle9i real application clusters integrated its code with MSCS. This creates the following special benefits:

- MSCS provides ability to change IP addresses dynamically. This eliminates the necessity of complex TNS reconfiguration to failover to a secondary node.

- MSCS facilities provide robust cluster management tools.

- With MSCS, it is getting simpler to Migrate from Oracle fail safe (very popular on Microsoft platforms) to ORAC.

- ORAC's complement to the MSCS is able to execute multiple active instances against a database on a cluster. This provides a scalable solution concurrently with failover options.

Oracle Internet Directory

A built-in application on top of the Oracle9i database, Version 3 of Oracle's Internet Directory uses the lightweight directory access protocol (LDAP). The Oracle Internet Directory is instituted to address the needs of a variety of important applications. Information about changes made to directory data on a server is stored in special tables on the Oracle9i database. These tables are replicated throughout the directory environment by the Oracle9i replication mechanism. The Oracle Internet Directory also takes advantage of all the availability features of Oracle9i. As directory information is stored in the Oracle9i database, it is protected by Oracle's backup capabilities. In addition, the Oracle9i database, running with large data stores and heavy loads, can recover from system failures quickly.

Using the Oracle Internet Directory with ORAC provides more seamless failover from the primary instance to the secondary one, as well as increased system scalability. The directory server instance communicates with the ORAC instance on node 1, which is the primary instance. However, in the event of either a hardware or software failure on node 1, Oracle Net services can redirect database requests to the ORAC instance on node 2, the secondary instance.

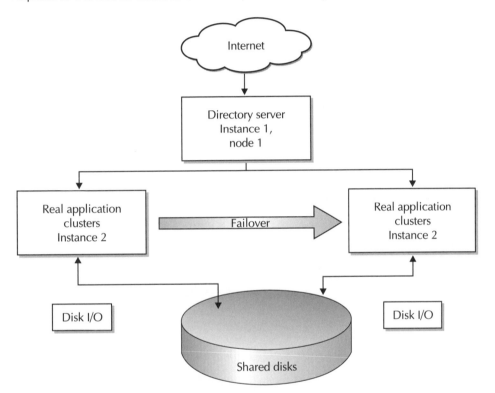

ORAC Management and Diagnostics

ORAC provides a single image of your database over multiple machines in a cluster and offers transparent application scalability by quickly and efficiently sharing cluster-wide caches for data access. Managing such environments efficiently could be a challenging endeavor. Oracle9i introduced substantial enhancements to the OEM and Oracle Configuration Assistant, along with adding additional features to greatly simplify ORAC manageability. In part, it is achieved by offering the same familiar interfaces used for single instance management and extending them with cluster-specific options.

Processes

The following changes have been made for background processes:

- The Block Server Process (BSP) is obsolete. It was responsible for Cache Fusion read consistency. The Lock Manager Server (LMS) process has now taken over this function.

- OPS LMS process no longer exists. As we have discussed earlier, ORAC GCS creates LMS processes.

- OPS Lock Manager Monitor (LMON) no longer exists. ORAC GES monitor spans off the processes with the same name.

- OPS LMD0 process is obsolete. ORAC GES runs as the LMD processes we discussed earlier.

New Instance Control Commands

New instance control commands have been introduced in ORAC to improve cluster maintainability and availability.

Shutdown Transactional Local Command

Sometimes it is necessary to take nodes out of service for maintenance or repair. For example, if you want to apply a patch release to one of the nodes without interrupting service to application clients, use the following command:

 `SHUTDOWN TRANSACTIONAL LOCAL`

This command allows transactional shutdown on a local instance. It prevents new transactions from starting locally, and performs an immediate shutdown after all local transactions have completed. Then all sessions from one instance are moved to another.

Quiescing the Database

Oracle9*i* introduces one more useful command. Oracle Replication used a quiescing concept for a long time, and now it is ORAC's turn to take advantage of this handy functionality.

You might need to perform administrative tasks that require isolation from concurrent user transactions or queries. Quiescing the database prevents you, for example, from having to shut down the database and reopen it in restricted mode to perform such tasks. To do this, you can issue the following statement:

`ALTER SYSTEM QUIESCE RESTRICTED`

The **alter system quiesce restricted** command results in the ORA-25507 error if the Database Resource Manager has not been turned on since all the instances started up, or has been temporarily turned off (even if later turned on again). For example, either issuing the command **alter system set resource _manager_plan = system_plan** or setting the initialization parameter *resource_manager_plan* = **system_ plan** will enable the Database Resource Manager and set up the plan as **system_plan**. The database Resource Manager must be activated for all instances in an ORAC configuration.

Data Dictionary Objects

In Oracle9i, various Data Dictionary objects have been amended to reflect ORAC architectural requirements.

Views and Synonyms

ORAC introduces several new views. These views track the current and previous master instances and the number of remasterings of enqueue (V$HVMASTER_INFO), global cache (V$GCSHVMASTER_INFO), and global cache resources belonging to a file accessed frequently by a single instance (V$GCSPFMASTER_INFO):

- V$HVMASTER_INFO for GES resources

- V$GCSHVMASTER_INFO for GCS resources, except those belonging to files mapped to a particular master

- V$GCSPFMASTER_INFO for GCS resources belonging to files mapped to a particular master

The views and synonyms, shown in Table 7-3, have been replaced in ORAC.

Views, Columns, and Synonyms

A number of OPS views and columns have been replaced to reflect the functionality and features of ORAC:

- View V/GV$LOCK_ELEMENT replaced with V/GV$GC_ELEMENT

- Column LOCK_ELEMENT_ADDR replaced with GC_ELEMENT_ADDR

- Column LOCK_ELEMENT_NAME replaced with GC_ELEMENT_NAME

- View V/GV$BSP replaced with V/GV$CR_BLOCK_SERVER

- Column FREE_LOCK_ELEMENTS replaced with FREE_GC_ELEMENTS

- View V/GV$FILE_PING replaced with V/GV$FILE_CACHE_TRANSFER

Old View	Replaced By
V/GV$DLM_MISC	V/GV$GES_STATISTICS
V/GV$DLM_LATCH	V/GV$GES_LATCH
V/GV$DLM_CONVERT_LOCAL	V/GV$GES_CONVERT_LOCAL
V/GV$DLM_CONVERT_REMOTE	V/GV$GES_CONVERT_REMOTE
V/GV$DLM_ALL_LOCKS	V/GV$GES_ENQUEUE
V/GV$DLM_LOCKS	V/GV$GES_BLOCKING_ENQUEUE
V/GV$DLM_RESS	V/GV$GES_RESOURCE
V/GV$DLM_TRAFFIC_CONTROLLER	V/GV$GES_TRAFFIC_CONTROLLER
V/GV$LOCK_ELEMENT	V/GV$GC_ELEMENT
V/GV$BSP	V/GV$CR_BLOCK_SERVER
V/GV$LOCKS_WITH_COLLISIONS	V/GV$GC_ELEMENTS_WITH_COLLISIONS
V/GV$FILE_PING	V/GV$FILE_CACHE_TRANSFER
V/GV$TEMP_PING	V/GV$TEMP_CACHE_TRANSFER
V/GV$CLASS_PING	V/GV$CLASS_CACHE_TRANSFER
V/GV$PING	V/GV$CACHE_TRANSFER

TABLE 7-3. *Views and Their Replacements*

- Column X_2_SSX_FORCED_WRITE removed from new view
- Column CBR_FORCED_WRITE removed from new view
- View V/GV$TEMP_PING replaced with V/GV$TEMP_CACHE_TRANSFER
- Column X_2_SSX_FORCED_WRITE removed from new view
- Column CBR_FORCED_WRITE removed from new view

Column Names in Views   While the view itself retains the same name as in OPS, column names in the V/GV$BH view have been replaced as follows:

- LOCK_ELEMENT_ADDR replaced with GC_ELEMENT_ADDR
- LOCK_ELEMENT_NAME replaced with GC_ELEMENT_ADDR
- LOCK_ELEMENT_CLASS replaced with GC_ELEMENT_CLASS
- PING replaced with CACHE_TRANSFER

Two new views, V/GV$GES_ENQUEUE and V/GV$GES_BLOCKING_ENQUEUE, mirror the OPS views V/GV$DLM_ALL_LOCKS and V/GV$DLM_LOCKS, respectively. Two of the column names in the new views are replaced as follows:

- LOCKP replaced with HANDLE
- LOCKSTATE replaced with STATE

Events
The following events became obsolete:

- Wait for checking DLM domain
- Wait for influx DLM latch
- Wait for DLM latch

Event names listed in the view V/GV$SYSTEM_EVENT are replaced as follows:

Event	Replaced By
Wait for DLM process allocation	GES process allocation
Lock manager wait for DLM to shut down	GES LMD to shut down
Wait in DLM lock cancel	GES cancel
Wait in DLM enter server mode	GES enter server mode
DLM generic wait event	GES generic
Wait event I/O clients wait for LMON to join GMS group	GES LMON to join CGS group
Wait for LMD and PMON to attach DLM	GES LMD and PMON to attach
Wait for cached resource cleanup by LMON to resource cleanup	GES cached
Global cache lock open *s*	Global cache open *s*
Global cache lock open *x*	Global cache open *x*
Global cache lock null to *s*	Global cache null to *s*
Global cache lock null to *x*	Global cache null to *x*
Global cache lock *s* to *x*	Global cache *s* to *x*
Global cache lock busy	Global cache busy

Initialization Parameters

Oracle sustains its efforts toward improved maintainability in the Oracle9i release. It approaches closer to the self-tunable database goal by reducing the number of system parameters, and thus simplifying the tuning process.

Gc_files_to_locks Parameter

This parameter was used in the pre-ORAC releases of Oracle cluster software to specify 1:*n* lock granularity. There are two levels of lock granularity:

- **1:1 Locks** One lock (resource in ORAC) per block

- **1:*n* Locks** Lock can manage two or more data blocks as defined by *n*.

Resources can be either *fixed or releasable.* A resource is considered fixed when it is assigned to a specific block. If a lock is acquired from a pool when required, and released back to the pool when it is no longer needed by the instance, then this resource is deemed as releasable.

Releasable resources improve system performance, especially at the instance startup, because there are no fixed resources to open. In addition, there is more flexibility to allocate 1:*n* granularity resources. For similar reasons, ORAC uses only releasable resources for block management. The option R of the parameter is obsolete.

Oracle recommends using 1:*n* locks when instance accesses read-only data. In this scenario, 1:*n* locks can perform faster than 1:1 locks during certain operations, such as parallel execution. Using 1:*n* locks automatically turns off the Cache Fusion mechanism. For example, you can assign 300 locks to file 1, and 100 locks to file 2, by adding the following line to your initialization parameter file:

```
gc_files_to_locks = "1=300:2=100"
```

_gc_defer_time

This parameter defined the number of hundredths of a second that an OPS instance would wait before responding to a request to release or downgrade a lock. It was difficult to take advantage of it while tuning database performance. In ORAC, it is retained as an underscore (hidden) parameter, _gc_defer_time, otherwise it is considered obsolete.

_gc_releasable_locks

In OPS, this parameter allowed specifying values smaller than in the *db_block_buffers* parameter. This could benefit in saving memory when you used 1:*n* locks across the whole database. With ORAC, you are less likely to use 1:*n* locks. ORAC also uses releasable resources. For these reasons, this parameter is obsolete in Oracle9i and is retained as an underscore (hidden) parameter, *_gc_releasable_locks.*

Gc_rollback_locks

This parameter was used to specify the lock mapping for rollback segments in OPS. This parameter is obsolete in Oracle9i. The undo segments in an ORAC database are protected by resources with a grouping of 16. Oracle believes that, because the undo blocks are created and processed sequentially, this large grouping factor should provide the best performance.

New Initialization Parameters

ORAC introduces two new initialization parameters:

- The *trace_enabled* parameter is a dynamic parameter that provides low overhead memory tracing. It is enabled by default.

- The *cluster_database* parameter replaces *parallel_server*. This Boolean parameter must be set to TRUE for all instances if you want to start more than one instance in an ORAC database.

- The *cluster_database_instances* parameter replaces *parallel_server_ instances*. This parameter must be set to the highest number of instances you want to start at one time for an ORAC database.

NOTE
Before using an initialization parameter from an OPS database, you will have to change these parameters for your ORAC database.

Shared Initialization Parameter Files

In Oracle9i parameters for multiple instances can be mixed in a single initialization parameter file. This creates the following maintenance benefits:

- Only one file to maintain

- Less chance of error when modifying parameters that need to be propagated to multiple instances

Dot notation with the instance name allows you to set instance-specific parameter values. For example, you can specify the *db_block_buffers* parameter for ORCL1 and ORCL2 instances:

```
orcl1.db_block_buffers=103000
orcl2.db_block_buffers=100000
```

The shared initialization parameter file must be allocated at the shared disk raw partition. The following example depicts two instances, ORCL1 and ORCL2, with

Oracle homes at /local1 and /local2 correspondingly. ORCL1 has parameter file /local1/dbs/initORCL1.ora and ORCL2 has parameter file /local/dbs/initORCL2.ora. Both parameters files contain only one line, which references a Shared Initialization Parameter File.

SPFILE=/DEV/RDISK/SPFILE

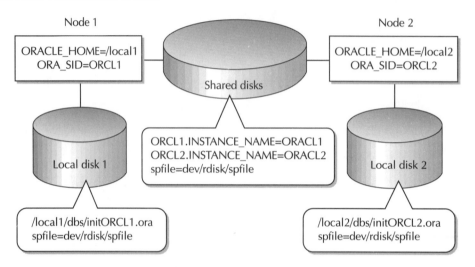

Instance Names and Numbers

On some platforms, earlier releases of Oracle clustering software allowed the same SID for multiple instances of the same database. ORAC requires SID uniqueness to provide maintainability consistency.

OPS did not require the *instance_number* parameter to be set explicitly. By default, it assigned instance numbers in the order instance was started.

ORAC requires that you specify *instance_number* for each instance explicitly. This ensures that tools can correctly and consistently identify an instance. It is also necessary for internal algorithms to manage space and GRD access.

The following rules must be used while creating instance identification:

■ Two databases sharing a node can have the same names for their instances if they use separate Oracle homes.

■ The SID must be unique on the same node. For Windows platforms, this restriction relates to the requirement of having only one process with the name OracleServise<SID>. Although on UNIX platforms, from the database standpoint, you can have multiple SIDs on the same node, it is impossible to ensure consistency while using maintenance tools because there can be only one **/etc/oratab** entry for a particular name.

The combination of unique instance names and associated instance numbers enables database administrators to identify instances reliably when using database-management tools, and ensures that redo threads and extents are mapped to the same instances.

OEM and Oracle Configuration Assistant

ORAC is a robust clustering software that realizes Oracle's key technology to provide database HA and scalability. Managing such an environment efficiently could be a challenging endeavor. OEM and Oracle Configuration Assistant greatly simplify its management by offering interfaces with the same look and feel used for single instance management, and extending them with cluster-specific options.

OEM

Oracle9i OEM provides the following enhancements for ORAC:

- OEM simplifies the process of creating and setting a new UNDO tablespace for each cluster instance. The new Undo tab displays the name of the active UNDO tablespace and the current undo retention time. You can modify the retention time based on the largest transaction time, and a graphical display of space requirements per minute of retention time can help deciding on an optimal value for it

- You can assign redo log groups for specific threads.

- OEM improves reporting capabilities. You can generate reports in the context of an object, such as a database instance or a tablespace.

- OEM extends tools (database wizards, application management, change management, database applications, diagnostic pack, and tuning pack) for cluster databases.

- Jobs can be scheduled on a single node or multiple nodes where intelligent agents are running. OEM tasks related to various activities such as data management (export, import, and load), backup management, analyzing tasks, and SQL scripts can be scheduled against cluster database and cluster database instance targets.

- Instance management capabilities:

  - You can conveniently maintain via the graphical interface server side SPFILE.

  - You can create, edit, and store multiple startup configurations for each cluster database instance.

- You can view sessions of individual instances in a cluster and inspect a session in detail to determine which SQL statement a user is running.

- You can kill an unwanted session.

- You can view a list of details for currently held user and system locks for each cluster database instance.

- Diagnostics and monitoring:

  - ORAC employs the diagnosability daemon. It is a real-application-clusters background process that captures diagnostic data on instance process failures.

  - You can create and modify resource consumer groups, and define, modify, and activate resource plans for each cluster database instance. You can monitor performance statistics of active resource plans. OEM's Performance Manager and Capacity Planner have 23 new OEM statistics charts that are specific to real application clusters.

Oracle Configuration Assistant

In OPS, OPSM stored configuration information in a Registry for Windows platforms and in a text file on each node for UNIX platforms. Maintaining consistency of the configuration files on multiple instances required substantial efforts.

Oracle9i provides a portable mechanism for storing across all nodes an ORAC configuration that no longer requires manual configuration files synchronization. The node-to-instance mapping is stored on a raw device so that it can be shared among the nodes. At any time, a configuration file in a binary format contains the currently configured list of instances and which nodes they should run on. In addition, you can use API to retrieve information on cluster configuration or use the SRVCTL utility command-line interface, as well as GUI tools such as DBCA, to alter this file.

SRVCTL Utility

The SRVCTL utility is a tool that provides you with capabilities to manage your ORAC environment from the command line. It replaces and extends the capabilities of the OPS managing tool, called OPSCTL, which supported only the **start** and **stop** subcommands.

start Command

This command allows you to start database instances and listeners. For example, to start instance ORCL of database PROD on NODE1 and all instance listeners, you can issue the following command:

```
srvctl start -p prod -i ORCL -n node1
```

Stop Command

This command allows you to stop database instance and/or listeners. For example, to stop instance ORCL of database PROD with an option transactional, you can issue the following command:

```
srvctl stop -p prod -i ORCL -s inst -o transactional
```

Status Command

You can obtain database status using the **status** command. For example, to get status of all listeners for database PROD, you can use the following command:

```
srvctl status -p prod -s lsnr
```

Config Command

The **config** command allows you to obtain information on database cluster components.

To obtain configuration of NODE1, use the following command:

```
srvctl config -n node1
```

Another example: if you need configuration of NODE1 for database PROD, you can run the following command:

```
srvctl config -p prod -n node1
```

Add, delete, and rename Commands

These commands help you to add, delete, or rename ORAC components. For example:

- To add an instance ORCL1 to a database PROD on NODE1, use the following command:

  ```
  srvctl add instance -p prod -i ORCL1 -n node1
  ```

- To delete database PROD, you can issue the following command:

  ```
  srvctl delete db -p prod
  ```

- To rename instance ORCL1 to ORCL2, you can issue the following command:

  ```
  srvctl rename instance -p prod -i ORCL1 -e ORCL2
  ```

Move, set, unset, and get Commands

In the following example, we moved the instance ORCL1 of the database PROD from NODE1 to NODE2:

```
srvctl move instance -p prod -i ORCL1 -n node2
```

- To set environment variables, use the **set** command. For example, to change NLS_LANGUAGE instance variable for instance ORCL1, use the following command:

```
srvctl set env -p prod -i ORCL1 -t NLS_LANGUAGE=american
```

- To unset ORAC environment for database PROD, use this command:

```
srvctl unset env -p prod -t NLS_LANGUAGE
```

- To obtain ORAC environment settings for database PROD, use the **get** command:

```
srvctl get env -p prod
```

New SQL Scripts

A number of SQL scripts were replaced in ORAC:

- The *utlopslt.sql* script was replaced with *utlclust.sql*.
- The *catparr.sql* script was replaced with *catclust.sql*.
- The *ops.sql* script was replaced with *clustdb.sql*.

Supported Platforms

Oracle-certified platforms are additional guarantees for better performance and robustness. Although the Oracle9i real application clusters product was recently announced, it has been certified on multiple platforms.

Linux, Windows, and Veritas Cluster Server

Real application clusters for Linux, Windows, and Veritas cluster server certification is underway, and Oracle will be providing information on it in the near future.

UNIX

ORAC was certified for the following UNIX configurations:

- Compaq Tru64 on DEC platform (Certification Matrix—ORAC for UNIX on Compaq Tru64 UNIX [Digital UNIX]):

OS	ORAC Version	Status
5.1a	9.0.1 (9i) 64-bit	Certified
5.1	9.0.1 (9i) 64-bit	Certified

- Fujitsu PRIMEPOWER platform (Certification Matrix—ORAC for UNIX on Fujitsu PRIMEPOWER):

OS	ORAC Release	Status
Solaris 8	9.0.1 (9i) 64-bit	Projected
Solaris 8	9.0.1 (9i)	Certified
Solaris 2.6	9.0.1 (9i)	Not planned

- HP 9000 Series HP-UX platform (Certification Matrix—ORAC for UNIX on HP 9000 Series HP-UX):

OS	ORAC Release	Status
11i	9.0.1 (9i) 64-bit	Certified
11.0	9.0.1 (9i) 64-bit	Certified

- IBM RS/6000 AIX platform (Certification Matrix—ORAC for UNIX on IBM RS/6000 AIX):

OS	ORAC Release	Status
4.3.3	9.0.1 (9i) 64-bit	Certified

- IBM SP AIX platform (Certification Matrix—ORAC for UNIX on IBM SP AIX):

OS	ORAC Release	Status
4.3.3	9.0.1 (9i) 64-bit	Certified

■ Sun SPARC Solaris platform (Certification Matrix—ORAC for UNIX on Sun SPARC Solaris):

OS	ORAC Release	Status
8	9.0.1 (9i)	Certified

CHAPTER
8

New Oracle9i XML
and iFS Features

- New XML features in Oracle9i
- Brief introduction to XPath
- New iFS features

his chapter introduces the new XML and iFS (Internet file system) features in Oracle9i. XML has become the standard for exchanging documents and information on the Web. Today's applications require strong XML support and the ability to read and write XML data to and from a database. Here is a list of the important new features that we will cover in this chapter:

- XML database type

- DBMS_XMLGEN

- SYS_XMLGEN

- SYS_XMLAGG

- URI types

- XML development kits (XDKs)

New XML Features in Oracle9i

One of the new advances made by Oracle was delivering the ability to store and speak XML natively within the Oracle9i database. Typically, you had to convert XML documents into strings and then store them into a database, or read from a database and convert the data into an XML document. Anyone who has done this knows it can be difficult. Oracle has simplified this process by delivering native XML in the database.

This is accomplished by introducing a new database type called the XMLType. It is a unique SQL data type that is stored as a CLOB within the database. This data type is understood by all the standard interfaces into Oracle that recognize SQL, such as OCI, JDBC, and PL/SQL. For example, to create a simple table composed of a single XMLType column, you could use the following SQL:

```
CREATE TABLE test(
    name     SYS.XMLTYPE
);
```

A big advantage of the XMLType is that variables of its type can be used in PL/SQL applications, stored procedures, and SQL queries. These variables can be used as parameters or return values, or you can use one of the XMLType's built-in functions for manipulating XML content. Let's start digging into how to use this new feature.

The first step to using XMLType is to create an instance of it. For those of you familiar with Java, it is similar to creating an instance of a Java class using a factory method. The following is a simple example of creating an XMLType variable:

```
DECLARE
  myxml  SYS.XMLType;
BEGIN
  -- NOTE: The input is an XML document identified by the <?xml ?> tag
  myxml := sys.xmltype.createxml('<?xml version="1.0" ?>
       <name>
          <fname>John</fname>
          <lname>Doe</lname>
       </name>');
END;
```

It isn't enough just to declare an instance of the XMLType since it is an object data type. The createXML method is used to create it. Think of it as the factory method for the XMLType. The createXML method can be invoked with either a VARCHAR2 or CLOB as input.

XMLType Static Methods	Description
createXML(varchar2)	Static method to create an XML document from a string. Returns an instance of type XMLType.
createXML(clob)	Static method to create an XML document from a CLOB. Returns an instance of type XMLType.

Once an XMLType instance has been instantiated with the createXML method, there are a number of member methods available to use on it. The following table lists the methods available:

XMLType Member Method	Description
getClobVal	Returns the contents of the XMLType as a CLOB
isFragment	Tests to see if the document is actually an XML fragment
getStringVal	Gets a string value from an XML node. If the value is greater than 4,000 bytes, an error is thrown.
getNumVal	Gets a numeric value from an XML node
extract(varchar2)	Extracts a portion of the document based on an XPath expression
existsNode(varchar2)	Checks whether there are any resultant nodes in the XPath expression

Before we delve into examples of using XMLType, we need to understand XPath, which is used as input to the extract and existNode methods. This will be covered in the next section.

Brief Introduction to XPath

To make full use of the XMLType methods, it is critical to understand XPath. XPath is a search language defined by the W3C organization that describes a way to locate and process items in XML documents. In XPath, a document is modeled as a tree in which all the nodes are considered objects. These include root nodes, element nodes, text nodes, attribute nodes, namespace nodes, processing instruction nodes, and comment nodes. There are five constructs that are used to navigate and search these nodes:

- **■** / Child traversals

- **■** // Descendant searches

- **■** - Wildcard tests

- **■** [ ] Index searches

- **■** @ Attribute traversals

To describe how to use these constructs, let's start with a simple XML example:

```
<?xml version="1.0" ?>
   <inventory>
      <item id="101">widget</item>
      <area>
         <location>New York</location>
         <number>95</number>
      </area>
      <area>
         <location>Chicago</location>
         <number>101</number>
      </area>
   </inventory>
```

The first construct in our list is the slash (/). It is used as the path separator to identify the children in a node. If the path starts with the slash, then it represents an absolute path to the element, for example:

```
/inventory
```

This directive points to the top element, or root, of our XML example. If we wish to delve deeper into and return the ITEM element, all we need to do is specify the path to it:

```
/inventory/item
```

This will return the ITEM element found within the inventory root element. The return value would be

```
<item id="101">widget</item>
```

The double slash (//) is used as a match construct to find all the elements in the document that match the element name given after the double slash, for example:

```
//area
```

This would return both AREA elements from the example:

```
<area>
   <location>New York</location>
   <number>95</number>
</area>
<area>
   <location>Chicago</location>
   <number>101</number>
</area>
```

The asterisk (*) construct can be thought of as the wildcard operator. It selects all elements located by the preceding path to it, for example,

```
/inventory/area/*
```

retrieves all the elements located underneath the area element:

```
<location>New York</location>
<number>95</number>
<location>Chicago</location>
<number>101</number>
```

The bracket [ ] construct is used to specify an element. A number in the brackets gives the position of the element in the selected set. For example, if I wanted to specify the first AREA element in the example XML, the following would work:

```
/inventory/area[1]
```

The @ construct is used to retrieve attributes. For example, if I wanted to extract my widget ID from the ITEM node, I would use the following syntax:

```
/inventory/item@id
```

The final part of the XPath introduction is about using XPath functions. Oracle currently supports using the **text** node test function. It is used to retrieve values from XML elements so they can be converted to SQL data. For example,

```
/inventory/item/text()
```

will retrieve the data from the element. The result from this query would be

```
widget
```

This functionality is limited. Only non-order-dependant searches, such as child (/) and descendant (//), work with the **text** function.

In summary, by supporting XPath, Oracle9*i* is providing a standards-based way to search XML documents stored within the database. One more thing to note is that there are other utilities and data types in addition to the XMLType that leverage the XPath syntax, such as the DBUriType, which will be covered later in this chapter.

XMLType Examples

Now that we've covered the basics of the XPath syntax, let's dig into some examples. The method that XML developers use the most is the EXTRACT method. It is the method used for searching for data within XML. This data can be anything from XML elements to the XML attributes or the character data contained within an element.

Earlier we extracted the item ID from the ITEM element in the XML example. At some point, you will want to access the data from these queries. For example, to retrieve the string value of the item ID from our previous query, just append the getStringVal method to the EXTRACT method:

```
dbms_output.put_line(myxml.extract('/inventory/item@id').getStringVal());
```

This will return the ID value 101. If you are interested in the numeric value, then simply use the getNumVal method:

```
DECLARE
   myid   number;
   myxml  SYS.XMLType;
BEGIN
```

```
    .
    .
myid := myxml.extract('/inventory/item@id').getNumVal();
```

At this point, it's easy to extrapolate from the examples in the XPath section and use them as arguments in the extract method. There is one thing to remember when using the XMLType extract method. If the size of the results being returned is going to be greater than 4,000 bytes, then use getClobVal instead of getStringVal.

DBMS_XMLGEN

DBMS_XMLGEN is a PL/SQL package that supports creating XML from SQL queries. It then stores the results either in a CLOB or as a XMLType. This package has many features that make it very flexible. You can

- Create XML documents from any SQL query.

- Specify a maximum amount of rows to fetch, or set an amount of rows to be skipped.

- Convert characters that are considered special by XML into their XML equivalents—for example, < would be &lt, and & would be &amp.

  The above &lt and &amp could be wrapped in double quotes, but the information itself is correct. It is describing the mapping of characters < and & to &lt and &amp.

- Set the name of the root element of the XML to be generated; otherwise, it is ROWSET by default.

- Set the element name of each row returned from a SQL query; the default element name is ROW.

The DBMS_XMLGEN package has many functions and procedures. Table 8-1 is a list of the functions available in this package.

The first step in using the DBMS_XMLGEN package is to create a context handle. This handle is a number that is used to define whether an XML, DTD, or XML schema document is going to be generated. The following is a list of possible context values.

- **Neither DTD nor XML schema**   Context handle = 0

- **DTD**   Context handle = 1

- **XML schema**   Context handle = 2

DBMS_XMLGEN Function	Description
newContext(varchar2)	Creates a new DBMS_XMLGEN context. The input is a SQL query string. It returns a DBMS_XMLGEN context handle.
setRowTag(ctxHandle,varchar2)	Sets the name of the element tag used for describing each row returned from a query. The inputs are the context handle and the new name of the row element.
setRowSetTag(ctxHandle,varchar2)	Sets the name of the root element tag. The inputs are a context handle and the new name of the root element.
getXML(ctxHandle)	Returns the XML results from a SQL query as a CLOB. The input is a context handle.
getNumRowsProcessed(ctxHandle)	Returns the number of rows processed, excluding the number of rows skipped. The input is a context handle. Returns the number of rows processed.
setSkipRows(ctxHandle,number)	Sets the number of rows to skip before fetching a row. The inputs are a context handle and the number of rows to be skipped.
getXMLType(ctxHandle)	Returns the XML results from the SQL query as a XMLType. The input is a context handle.
setMaxRows(ctxHandle,number)	Sets the maximum number of rows returned from the SQL query. The inputs are a context handle and a number that represents the maximal rows returned.

TABLE 8-1. *Package Functions*

For the initial release of Oracle9i, both XML schema and DTD options are not enabled. If the default DMBS_XMLGEN.ctx handle declaration is used, then XML is generated by default. To see how this package works, let's start with an example of using DBMS_XMLGEN:

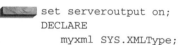

```
set serveroutput on;
DECLARE
    myxml SYS.XMLType;
```

```
   -- default value is 0 for ctxhandle
   ctx DBMS_XMLGEN.ctxhandle;
BEGIN
   -- create an initial context
   ctx := dbms_xmlgen.newContext('SELECT * FROM EMP');
   -- Set the max rows to be fetched to be 1.
   dbms_xmlgen.setMaxRows(ctx,1);
   -- extract the xml
   myxml := dbms_xmlgen.getXMLType(ctx);
   -- Now print it out using an XPath wildcard that grabs everything
   dbms_output.put_line(myxml.extract('/*').getStringVal());
END;
/
```

The first step is to declare a context handle variable. This will be used in all our calls to the package:

```
ctx DBMS_XMLGEN.ctxhandle;
```

The second step is to get a context from the package by inputting a SQL query and executing the newContext procedure call. In the following example, we do a full table select from the SCOTT schema's EMP table:

```
ctx := DBMS_XMLGEN.newContext('SELECT * FROM EMP');
```

At this point, we can start using any of the DBMS_XMLGEN functions. In our example, we use the setMaxRows such that we return only the first row in the EMP table. We then extract the XML and place it into an instance of XMLType:

```
dbms_xmlgen.setMaxRows(ctx,1);
myxml := dbms_xmlgen.getXMLType(ctx);
```

The final step is to print the results using what we learned from the XMLType section. Make note that the root element's default name is ROWSET and the row element's default name is ROW.

```
<ROWSET>
   <ROW>
      <EMPNO>7369</EMPNO>
      <ENAME>SMITH</ENAME>
      <JOB>CLERK</JOB>
      <MGR>7902</MGR>
      <HIREDATE>17-DEC-80</HIREDATE>
      <SAL>800</SAL>
      <DEPTNO>20</DEPTNO>
   </ROW>
</ROWSET>
```

The goal of the DBMS_XMLGEN package is to make generating XML from SQL queries a simple task. It also adds the flexibility to manipulate the results of these queries.

SYS_XMLGEN

The **SYS_XMLGEN** function is a new Oracle9i SQL function with functionality similar to **DBMS_XMLGEN**. It can take a result from a SQL query and return the result as XML, where the DBMS_XMLGEN package created XML from a SQL query result set.

The **SYS_XMLGEN** function takes a scalar value, object type, or XMLType instance as an argument, and returns an XML document as a XMLType. The following example shows a simple use of the **SYS_XMLGEN** SQL function:

```
DECLARE
   myxml SYS.XMLTYPE;
BEGIN
   select SYS_XMLGEN(ENAME) into myxml from EMP where SAL = 950;
```

If we examined the contents of the MYXML XMLType, we would see the following:

```
<?xml version='1.0' ?>
   <ENAME>JAMES</ENAME>
```

SYS_XMLGEN will soon be a standard piece in any Oracle developer's arsenal. It is simple to use, and it provides the unique functionality of being able to produce XML from a SQL select query.

SYS_XMLAGG

SYS_XMLAGG is a function that combines multiple XML documents or XML fragments to produce a single XML document. It does this by concatenating these pieces together and then adding a surrounding root element.

Let's use the GROUP BY operation to aggregate data from the SCOTT schema EMP table. In this example, we will ask for employees whose salary is less than $1,300, and have the results grouped by department number:

```
select SYS_XMLAGG(SYS_XMLGEN(ENAME)).getClobVal() XML_VAL from EMP
   where SAL < 1300 GROUP BY DEPTNO;
```

The resulting query will return the following data:

```
XML_VAL
-------------------------------------------------------------
<?xml version="1.0"?>
```

```
<ROWSET>
<ENAME>SMITH</ENAME>
<ENAME>ADAMS</ENAME>
</ROWSET>
<?xml version="1.0"?>
<ROWSET>
<ENAME>WARD</ENAME>
<ENAME>JAMES</ENAME>
<ENAME>MARTIN</ENAME>
</ROWSET>
```

SYS_XMLAGG is a versatile tool. It can create XML from OLAP aggregation operations such as ROLLUP and CUBE. It also works with Oracle OLAP windowing functions that are used to compute cumulative, moving, and centered aggregates.

URI Reference Types

The URI (uniform reference indicator) reference type is a new object type that has been added to Oracle9i. The URI type is actually a family of types that can store and query URI references in the database. For those of you who are not familiar with URIs, they are similar to URLs and consist of two parts.

- **URL**   A location reference to a document or data:

  ```
  http://www.oracle.com/document
  ```

- **Fragment**   Identifies a location within a document or data:

  ```
  chapter1/intro
  ```

This family of types is currently composed of two URI subtypes, the DBUriType and the HTTPUriType.

DBUriType

The DBUriType is known as the intradatabase URI. It specifies a URI for database rows or columns inside a database. It uses the XPath syntax introduced earlier in this chapter for locating these objects within a database. For example, if you wanted to point to the DEPT table in the SCOTT schema, you would use the following XPath notation:

```
/SCOTT/DEPT
```

HTTPUriType

The HTTPUriType is used to reference remote data by means of HTTP. This makes it easier to point to data that resides outside of the database. By using these URI types, you can create columns based on UriType that can point to data either inside or outside the database.

Examples of URI Reference Types

These types can be stored as text within the database, and then converted to a UriType with the URIFACTORY.getUri function call. The following example creates a table with a single column of VARCHAR2 text, writes two references to the table, and then retrieves these text items as URIs using the getUri PL/SQL function:

```
create table URI_TABLE(uri_ref  VARCHAR2(80));
-- create a DBUri reference
insert into URI_TABLE values ('/SCOTT/EMPLOYEE/ROW[ENAME="ADAM"]');
--create a HTTPUri reference
insert into URI_TABLE values ('http://www.yahoo.com/index.html');
-- select the text URIs from the table and convert them to URIs
select URIFactory.getUri(uri_ref) from URI_TABLE;
```

The results from the SQL select would look like the following:

```
URIFACTORY.GETURI(URLCOL)(URL)
------------------------------------------------------
HTTPURITYPE('www.yahoo.com/index.html')
DBURITYPE('/SCOTT/EMPLOYEE/ROW[ENAME="ADAMS"]', NULL)
```

Note that the getUri will automatically detect what type of URI to generate based on the input argument. If the argument has an HTTP:// in it, then it creates an HTTPUriType; otherwise, it will create a DBUriType.

If you are not comfortable creating the necessary XPath syntax to describe your DBURIs, then there is another solution for you. It is the new SYS_DBURIGEN() SQL function. This function can dynamically create XPath from a SQL query:

```
select SYS_DBURIGEN(ENAME) MYURI from EMP where ENAME='MILLER';
```

The results from the SQL select would look like the following:

```
MYURI(URL, SPARE)
------------------------------------------------------
DBURITYPE('/PUBLIC/EMP/ROW[ENAME=''MILLER'']/ENAME', NULL)
```

These URIs are not necessarily useful in themselves; there needs to be a way to use them. To do this, Oracle has provided a servlet called OraDBUriServlet, which is a Java class that runs within Oracle's servlet engine (OSE). Please note that OSE needs to be configured, a web service port enabled, and the OraDBServlet servlet published before this functionality is available.

XML Development Kits

Oracle has consolidated all its previous XML components and utilities into a series of development kits known as XDKs. These XDKs were then packaged based on their languages: Java, PL/SQL, C++, and C. Oracle9i has also added support for the following new features:

- XML schema 1.0

- DOM 2.0 and SAX 2.0

- DBAccess and DBView Java Beans

XML Schema Support

A new area in XML is the idea of XML schemas (XSDs). Schemas were invented to fix the limitations of document type definitions (DTDs). A DTD is a document that is used for checking the structure of an XML document. For example, you can make sure that the <name> element contains the <fname> and <lname> elements within it:

```
<?xml version="1.0" ?>
<name>
  <fname>Joe</fname>
  <lname>Smith</lname>
</name>
```

If it doesn't contain both of these elements, then the document isn't acceptable. You can use a DTD to describe the elements and attributes allowed within an XML document and how they can be used. The following is a DTD of the NAME example XML:

```
<!ELEMENT fname ( #PCDATA ) >
<!ELEMENT lname ( #PCDATA ) >
<!ELEMENT name ( fname, lname ) >
```

The limitations of DTDs are numerous, the most noticeable being DTDs are not written in XML, and therefore it isn't easy to transform an XML document into an appropriately matching DTD document. DTDs also support only 10 data types, whereas XML schema supports more than 44 data types.

One major feature of XML schemas is that you can also create your own data type. For example, if you wanted to create a data type called NAME, it would look like the following:

```
<datatype name="name">
   <element name="fname" type="string" />
   <element name="lname" type="string" />
</datatype>
```

For a DBA, this is very powerful! Now you can make XML schema data types that match the data in their databases. It would take several chapters to explain XML schemas in detail, but their function is the same as DTDs: to check the structure and content of the underlying data.

Oracle9i also supports the use of XML Schema using the Java XDK. It is located in the xschema.jar Java archive, and it can be found in the $ORACLE_HOME/lib directory.

New Support for DOM 2.0 and SAX 2.0

In Oracle8i, Oracle added XML support by including an XML parser. This parser supported version 1.0 of the Document Object Model (DOM) and the simple API for XML (SAX) APIs. In Oracle9i, these parsers have been updated to support the new DOM 2.0 and SAX 2.0 specifications.

These parsers are available in Oracle XDKs. This means the same APIs are available in Java, C, C++, and PL/SQL. Also of note, the PL/SQL parser is now built on the C parser instead of the Java parser, to improve performance.

DBAccess and DBView Java Beans

The XDK kit has two new beans that are used to support reading, writing, and viewing XML in a CLOB within an Oracle database. This bean support includes documentation and descriptors that can be accessed directly from Java IDEs such as JDeveloper.

The DBView bean is a visual bean that extends the Java JPanel swing class. It is used to visualize database information using XML and XLST transformations. The DBAccess bean is used to read and write XML data into an Oracle database CLOB. The DBView bean uses the DBAccess bean for reading and writing.

New iFS Features

Oracle iFS is a database-based file system that provides quick-and-easy access to content stored on an Oracle database. By using standard interfaces such as a web browser, FTP, and e-mail, users can see documents and media stored in a database as files and folders. iFS also allows valuable content to be safely managed and searchable from a single location. Collaboration is simplified through iFS by providing checkin/checkout facilities, event notification, and version control to your team of users. The iFS Developer's Kit allows you to customize files for different application purposes. The Developer's Kit is based on Java, and it simplifies development while allowing for strong data integration.

9iFS has a number of new features. This section will illustrate these features based on the type of user each feature will affect. The three types of 9iFS users who will be covered are iFS administrators, the collaboration team, and the development team.

Administrative Features

OEM Integration

The 9iFS Manager is now integrated with Oracle Enterprise Manager (OEM), with new system monitoring capabilities, administrator options, and a dashboard interface. To help understand OEM integration, a few terms should be defined. 9iFS now uses the concept of domains, nodes, and domain controllers.

The domain is a basic administrative unit of 9iFS. It is a single 9iFS instance and can consist of several elements running on the same computer or running across a network of computers. A domain's configuration is changeable over time in response to ever-changing requirements. The repository, nodes, and domain controller are all elements of a domain.

- The repository is all the data managed by 9iFS. It resides inside an Oracle9i database schema.

- 9iFS software runs on an Oracle9i database machine and also as a set of middle-tier processes. These processes are called *nodes.* Each node can run on a particular computer (host). A single host can have more than one 9iFS node, or the nodes can be split across multiple hosts. Each node has a unique name that is used for identification in a 9iFS domain. A clearer distinction is that nodes managed by OEM are different from these types of nodes. OEM nodes are servers connected by a network, and 9iFS nodes are processes of 9iFS that manage one or more services (agents) and servers (protocols).

- A domain controller manages the nodes that compose a domain. It can track node status, control which nodes to run, and allow nodes to be monitored and administered. There can be only one domain controller in a domain.

Once OEM has been properly configured to support 9iFS, you will be able to see an Internet File Systems folder in the Navigator tree of the OEM console. OEM integration has made it possible to administer iFS with the same application you use to administer your database and HTTP servers. With this additional feature, you can use OEM's job scheduling and event system to auto-manage and auto-recover parts of a failed iFS domain.

With the OEM integration, you are now able to start and stop domains, and start your 9iFS nodes in the domain from the OEM console. This integration also allows DBAs to monitor and dynamically tune all elements of a domain. If OEM detects a domain that has a problem, it can identify what the problem is, and try to fix whatever part of the domain is having issues. This involves creating an OEM event and the corresponding fix-it job.

To support these new administrative features, 9iFS has significantly modified its protocol server and agent infrastructure. When installing and configuring 9iFS, it will be a requirement to define a domain controller and the nodes residing within that domain, all of which you can then jointly administer from OEM.

You can still launch Oracle 9iFS Manager as a stand-alone application and it will provide the same repository management functionality, but you will not be able to administer the Oracle 9iFS domain or its nodes from Oracle 9iFS Manager.

Dashboard Interface

The Dashboard provides an overall view of a domain's performance and also allows you to monitor the domain. It does so using a dashboard-type GUI. The Dashboard displays general information such as number of users, users owning documents, quota allocated to users, and quota used. The Dashboard in other sections shows information pertaining to document storage, including total number of documents and total consumed space, and sorts and displays document information by MIME type. Connected session information is displayed in chart or table format. This shows the number of online sessions by the server type (or what protocol is used to access iFS). Another section of the Dashboard displays overall usage information, including sessions and threads used, and memory usage.

Import/Export Utility

Another important new feature for administrators is the Import/Export utility. This tool allows you to export content, its structure, and its associated metadata from one 9iFS instance and import them into any other 9iFS instance. The utility allows you to do this without losing versioning information and custom subclassing information.

The Import/Export utility can also be used to move users in 9iFS instances. You will also need to move their passwords.

Another key advantage to the Import/Export utility is that it can be used to back up a smaller portion of the 9iFS repository, rather than the entire database. Again, all the data, metadata, versioning, and so on, is retained.

Lower Memory Usage

During installation, 9iFS gives the administrator the option to install to run with lower memory usage. The iFS development team have worked to reduce memory usage for larger numbers of concurrent users. iFS also permits the ability to run multiple protocol servers in a single JVM. This reduces memory overhead when you have a smaller amount of concurrent users.

Java Web Server No Longer Supported
Oracle HTTP server powered by Apache has replaced JWS as the web server.

Collaboration Features

Network File System Protocol Server
The collaboration team can now access Oracle 9iFS content through the network file system (NFS) protocol server. NFS protocol is a standard protocol that is used for file sharing across UNIX platforms.

FileSync Utility
The FileSync utility is used to synchronize files edited locally on computers (running Windows) and stored in 9iFS. It provides users with a client to 9iFS that can be thought of as running disconnected from 9iFS mode, and it synchronizes changes between the local version of a file and that stored in 9iFS.

Arbitrary Metadata (Categories) for Any File or Folder
Prior to 9iFS, attributes were based on the type of file the attribute was defined for. With arbitrary metadata, or categories, attributes can be lumped into a set of attributes. Attributes can now be applied singly to a file, or be part of a category that is then applied to any files or folders in 9iFS.

There are a couple of default categories that 9iFS provides: Mountpoint and Intermedia Source. Mountpoint is used to add another entry point to a folder hierarchy. Intermedia Source contains a subset of categories for multimedia files. As these types of files are inserted into the repository, the associated attribute information accompanying them is pulled and used to populate the categories for these files and other interMedia categories. The subset of Intermedia Source categories are InterMediaMovie, InterMediaAudio, InterMediaAudioCdTrack (a subset of InterMediaAudio), InterMediaVideo, and InterMediaImage.

Multimedia Metadata Extracted Automatically
With the use of the new category feature just described, metadata encoded in multimedia files can be extracted automatically and stored in these categories. 9iFS can now automatically extract the number of colors in an image, sound quality in an audio file, play length, closed-caption text, and other types of information encoded in audio, video, and image files. You can then use these attributes to search or perform other custom processing to certain types of files with minimal user intervention through the 9iFS API.

With the majority of multimedia files, you can use the built-in metadata extraction; however, to pull metadata from uncommon multimedia formats, a custom parser will need to be written.

Oracle9iFS Portlet
9iFS now comes with a portlet that you can register within Oracle Portal. The portlet provides shortcuts to commonly used 9iFS features, such as folders, files, and simple searches.

Improvements to Oracle9iFS Windows Utilities
There have been many significant improvements made to 9iFS Windows utilities. This is primarily through the Find engine and multi-select support. A couple of other improvements have been made in basic operations.

With multi-select operations, your users can now apply an access control list to a group of files or to a folder and all its subfolders and files. You can also check in/out, cancel checkout, lock, unlock, and create link on multiple items.

The Find engine in 9iFS has been greatly improved. You can now search custom attributes, subclasses, and categories (and a category's subclasses) that are defined for a document, the language of a document, and on all versions of a document. The performance of the Find engine in 9iFS has improved due to faster server-side searches confined within folders and incremental retrieval of results. A find can also be interrupted after a subset of the results has been returned.

Development Features

SQL Ability in Oracle 9iFS Database Transactions
One new feature is the ability to write applications that use the database transaction that 9iFS makes when it commits changes to the database. This provides the flexibility to call PL/SQL procedures in the database concurrently with a 9iFS operation.

New Options for Arbitrary Metadata (Categories)
With the introduction of categories, a new API has been developed to access metadata. This API is called the 9iFS Software Development Kit (SDK), and it provides the functionality to programmatically edit, apply, create, and search categories.

New E-Mail Object and API
In the past, an e-mail object consisted of several different objects that needed to be accessed and manipulated for any type of e-mail processing. In the 9iFS SDK, e-mail consists of a single object. This allows a programmer to use the Java mail API instead of the 9iFS specific interfaces.

XML Namespace Support

The XML parser installed with Oracle9i has been updated to recognize the 9iFS namespace. Previously, document definitions and attribute names located in XML files, and those that were used to configure 9iFS, could create conflicts. This was due to tags used in the XML files having the exact same name as 9iFS content objects. An example of this is the <CONTENT> tag. Now these conflicts are resolved by using XML namespaces.

Roundtrip XML

Previously, comments and unrecognized elements in an XML file were discarded as they were parsed. With roundtrip XML, 9iFS can be configured to save these unparsed fields. This provides the capability to re-create an XML file by putting it back to its original form, thereby preserving comments and unrecognized elements. It also gives the ability to remove elements, such as 9iFS attributes, that appear in the rendered XML but not in the original file.

Custom XML Rendering

With custom XML rendering, you have greater control over which elements are rendered. The default behavior renders only the extended elements specific to a 9iFS class. You can select a subset of elements, choose to add other elements from its superclasses, or omit these extended elements for rendering.

Index

INTERNATIONAL CONTACT INFORMATION

AUSTRALIA
McGraw-Hill Book Company Australia Pty. Ltd.
TEL +61-2-9417-9899
FAX +61-2-9417-5687
http://www.mcgraw-hill.com.au
books-it_sydney@mcgraw-hill.com

CANADA
McGraw-Hill Ryerson Ltd.
TEL +905-430-5000
FAX +905-430-5020
http://www.mcgrawhill.ca

GREECE, MIDDLE EAST,
NORTHERN AFRICA
McGraw-Hill Hellas
TEL +30-1-656-0990-3-4
FAX +30-1-654-5525

MEXICO (Also serving Latin America)
McGraw-Hill Interamericana Editores S.A. de C.V.
TEL +525-117-1583
FAX +525-117-1589
http://www.mcgraw-hill.com.mx
fernando_castellanos@mcgraw-hill.com

SINGAPORE (Serving Asia)
McGraw-Hill Book Company
TEL +65-863-1580
FAX +65-862-3354
http://www.mcgraw-hill.com.sg
mghasia@mcgraw-hill.com

SOUTH AFRICA
McGraw-Hill South Africa
TEL +27-11-622-7512
FAX +27-11-622-9045
robyn_swanepoel@mcgraw-hill.com

UNITED KINGDOM & EUROPE
(Excluding Southern Europe)
McGraw-Hill Education Europe
TEL +44-1-628-502500
FAX +44-1-628-770224
http://www.mcgraw-hill.co.uk
computing_neurope@mcgraw-hill.com

ALL OTHER INQUIRIES Contact:
Osborne/McGraw-Hill
TEL +1-510-549-6600
FAX +1-510-883-7600
http://www.osborne.com
omg_international@mcgraw-hill.com

GET YOUR FREE SUBSCRIPTION
TO ORACLE MAGAZINE

Oracle Magazine is essential gear for today's information technology professionals. Stay informed and increase your productivity with every issue of *Oracle Magazine*. Inside each free bimonthly issue you'll get:

- Up-to-date information on Oracle Database, E-Business Suite applications, Web development, and database technology and business trends
- Third-party news and announcements
- Technical articles on Oracle Products and operating environments
- Development and administration tips
- Real-world customer stories

IF THERE ARE OTHER ORACLE USERS AT YOUR LOCATION WHO WOULD LIKE TO RECEIVE THEIR OWN SUBSCRIPTION TO ORACLE MAGAZINE, PLEASE PHOTOCOPY THIS FORM AND PASS IT ALONG.

Three easy ways to subscribe:

① Web

Visit our Web site at www.oracle.com/oraclemagazine. You'll find a subscription form there, plus much more!

② Fax

Complete the questionnaire on the back of this card and fax the questionnaire side only to +1.847.647.9735.

③ Mail

Complete the questionnaire on the back of this card and mail it to P.O. Box 1263, Skokie, IL 60076-8263

Oracle Publishing

ORACLE®

FREE SUBSCRIPTION

○ Yes, please send me a FREE subscription to *Oracle Magazine*   ○ NO

To receive a free subscription to *Oracle Magazine*, you must fill out the entire card, sign it, and date it (incomplete cards cannot be processed or acknowledged). You can also fax your application to +1.847.647.9735.
Or subscribe at our Web site at www.oracle.com/oraclemagazine/

○ From time to time, Oracle Publishing allows our partners exclusive access to our e-mail addresses for special promotions and announcements. To be included in this program, please check this box.

○ Oracle Publishing allows sharing of our mailing list with selected third parties. If you prefer your mailing address not to be included in this program, please check here. If at any time you would like to be removed from this mailing list, please contact Customer Service at +1.847.647.9630 or send an e-mail to oracle@halldata.com.

signature (required)   date

X

name   title

company   e-mail address

street/p.o. box

city/state/zip or postal code   telephone

country   fax

YOU MUST ANSWER ALL NINE QUESTIONS BELOW.

❶ WHAT IS THE PRIMARY BUSINESS ACTIVITY OF YOUR FIRM AT THIS LOCATION? (check one only)

- ☐ 01 Application Service Provider
- ☐ 02 Communications
- ☐ 03 Consulting, Training
- ☐ 04 Data Processing
- ☐ 05 Education
- ☐ 06 Engineering
- ☐ 07 Financial Services
- ☐ 08 Government (federal, local, state, other)
- ☐ 09 Government (military)
- ☐ 10 Health Care
- ☐ 11 Manufacturing (aerospace, defense)
- ☐ 12 Manufacturing (computer hardware)
- ☐ 13 Manufacturing (noncomputer)
- ☐ 14 Research & Development
- ☐ 15 Retailing, Wholesaling, Distribution
- ☐ 16 Software Development
- ☐ 17 Systems Integration, VAR, VAD, OEM
- ☐ 18 Transportation
- ☐ 19 Utilities (electric, gas, sanitation)
- ☐ 98 Other Business and Services

❷ WHICH OF THE FOLLOWING BEST DESCRIBES YOUR PRIMARY JOB FUNCTION? (check one only)

Corporate Management/Staff
- ☐ 01 Executive Management (President, Chair, CEO, CFO, Owner, Partner, Principal)
- ☐ 02 Finance/Administrative Management (VP/Director/ Manager/Controller, Purchasing, Administration)
- ☐ 03 Sales/Marketing Management (VP/Director/Manager)
- ☐ 04 Computer Systems/Operations Management (CIO/VP/Director/ Manager MIS, Operations)

IS/IT Staff
- ☐ 05 Systems Development/ Programming Management
- ☐ 06 Systems Development/ Programming Staff
- ☐ 07 Consulting
- ☐ 08 DBA/Systems Administrator
- ☐ 09 Education/Training
- ☐ 10 Technical Support Director/Manager
- ☐ 11 Other Technical Management/Staff
- ☐ 98 Other

❸ WHAT IS YOUR CURRENT PRIMARY OPERATING PLATFORM? (select all that apply)

- ☐ 01 Digital Equipment UNIX
- ☐ 02 Digital Equipment VAX VMS
- ☐ 03 HP UNIX
- ☐ 04 IBM AIX

- ☐ 05 IBM UNIX
- ☐ 06 Java
- ☐ 07 Linux
- ☐ 08 Macintosh
- ☐ 09 MS-DOS
- ☐ 10 MVS
- ☐ 11 NetWare
- ☐ 12 Network Computing
- ☐ 13 OpenVMS
- ☐ 14 SCO UNIX
- ☐ 15 Sequent DYNIX/ptx
- ☐ 16 Sun Solaris/SunOS
- ☐ 17 SVR4
- ☐ 18 UnixWare
- ☐ 19 Windows
- ☐ 20 Windows NT
- ☐ 21 Other UNIX
- ☐ 98 Other
- ☐ 99 None of the above

❹ DO YOU EVALUATE, SPECIFY, RECOMMEND, OR AUTHORIZE THE PURCHASE OF ANY OF THE FOLLOWING? (check all that apply)

- ☐ 01 Hardware
- ☐ 02 Software
- ☐ 03 Application Development Tools
- ☐ 04 Database Products
- ☐ 05 Internet or Intranet Products
- ☐ 99 None of the above

❺ IN YOUR JOB, DO YOU USE OR PLAN TO PURCHASE ANY OF THE FOLLOWING PRODUCTS? (check all that apply)

Software
- ☐ 01 Business Graphics
- ☐ 02 CAD/CAE/CAM
- ☐ 03 CASE
- ☐ 04 Communications
- ☐ 05 Database Management
- ☐ 06 File Management
- ☐ 07 Finance
- ☐ 08 Java
- ☐ 09 Materials Resource Planning
- ☐ 10 Multimedia Authoring
- ☐ 11 Networking
- ☐ 12 Office Automation
- ☐ 13 Order Entry/Inventory Control
- ☐ 14 Programming
- ☐ 15 Project Management
- ☐ 16 Scientific and Engineering
- ☐ 17 Spreadsheets
- ☐ 18 Systems Management
- ☐ 19 Workflow

Hardware
- ☐ 20 Macintosh
- ☐ 21 Mainframe
- ☐ 22 Massively Parallel Processing

- ☐ 23 Minicomputer
- ☐ 24 PC
- ☐ 25 Network Computer
- ☐ 26 Symmetric Multiprocessing
- ☐ 27 Workstation

Peripherals
- ☐ 28 Bridges/Routers/Hubs/Gateways
- ☐ 29 CD-ROM Drives
- ☐ 30 Disk Drives/Subsystems
- ☐ 31 Modems
- ☐ 32 Tape Drives/Subsystems
- ☐ 33 Video Boards/Multimedia

Services
- ☐ 34 Application Service Provider
- ☐ 35 Consulting
- ☐ 36 Education/Training
- ☐ 37 Maintenance
- ☐ 38 Online Database Services
- ☐ 39 Support
- ☐ 40 Technology-Based Training
- ☐ 98 Other
- ☐ 99 None of the above

❻ WHAT ORACLE PRODUCTS ARE IN USE AT YOUR SITE? (check all that apply)

Software
- ☐ 01 Oracle9i
- ☐ 02 Oracle9i Lite
- ☐ 03 Oracle8
- ☐ 04 Oracle8i
- ☐ 05 Oracle8i Lite
- ☐ 06 Oracle7
- ☐ 07 Oracle9i Application Server
- ☐ 08 Oracle9i Application Server Wireless
- ☐ 09 Oracle Data Mart Suites
- ☐ 10 Oracle Internet Commerce Server
- ☐ 11 Oracle interMedia
- ☐ 12 Oracle Lite
- ☐ 13 Oracle Payment Server
- ☐ 14 Oracle Video Server
- ☐ 15 Oracle Rdb

Tools
- ☐ 16 Oracle Darwin
- ☐ 17 Oracle Designer
- ☐ 18 Oracle Developer
- ☐ 19 Oracle Discoverer
- ☐ 20 Oracle Express
- ☐ 21 Oracle JDeveloper
- ☐ 22 Oracle Reports
- ☐ 23 Oracle Portal
- ☐ 24 Oracle Warehouse Builder
- ☐ 25 Oracle Workflow

Oracle E-Business Suite
- ☐ 26 Oracle Advanced Planning/Scheduling
- ☐ 27 Oracle Business Intelligence
- ☐ 28 Oracle E-Commerce
- ☐ 29 Oracle Exchange
- ☐ 30 Oracle Financials

- ☐ 31 Oracle Human Resources
- ☐ 32 Oracle Interaction Center
- ☐ 33 Oracle Internet Procurement
- ☐ 34 Oracle Manufacturing
- ☐ 35 Oracle Marketing
- ☐ 36 Oracle Order Management
- ☐ 37 Oracle Professional Services Automation
- ☐ 38 Oracle Projects
- ☐ 39 Oracle Sales
- ☐ 40 Oracle Service
- ☐ 41 Oracle Small Business Suite
- ☐ 42 Oracle Supply Chain Management
- ☐ 43 Oracle Travel Management
- ☐ 44 Oracle Treasury

Oracle Services
- ☐ 45 Oracle.com Online Services
- ☐ 46 Oracle Consulting
- ☐ 47 Oracle Education
- ☐ 48 Oracle Support
- ☐ 98 ther
- ☐ 99 None of the above

❼ WHAT OTHER DATABASE PRODUCTS ARE IN USE AT YOUR SITE? (check all that apply)

- ☐ 01 Access
- ☐ 02 Baan
- ☐ 03 dbase
- ☐ 04 Gupta
- ☐ 05 BM DB2
- ☐ 06 Informix
- ☐ 07 Ingres
- ☐ 08 Microsoft Access
- ☐ 09 Microsoft SQL Server
- ☐ 10 PeopleSoft
- ☐ 11 Progress
- ☐ 12 SAP
- ☐ 13 Sybase
- ☐ 14 VSAM
- ☐ 98 Other
- ☐ 99 None of the above

❽ DURING THE NEXT 12 MONTHS, HOW MUCH DO YOU ANTICIPATE YOUR ORGANIZATION WILL SPEND ON COMPUTER HARDWARE, SOFTWARE, PERIPHERALS, AND SERVICES FOR YOUR LOCATION? (check only one)

- ☐ 01 Less than $10,000
- ☐ 02 $10,000 to $49,999
- ☐ 03 $50,000 to $99,999
- ☐ 04 $100,000 to $499,999
- ☐ 05 $500,000 to $999,999
- ☐ 06 $1,000,000 and over

❾ WHAT IS YOUR COMPANY'S YEARLY SALES REVENUE? (please choose one)

- ☐ 01 $500, 000, 000 and above
- ☐ 02 $100, 000, 000 to $500, 000, 000
- ☐ 03 $50, 000, 000 to $100, 000, 000
- ☐ 04 $5, 000, 000 to $50, 000, 000
- ☐ 05 $1, 000, 000 to $5, 000, 000

123101